Studies in German Literature, Linguistics, and Culture

Translations from Medieval Literature
Edited by Evelyn S. Firchow
(University of Minnesota)

The Lament of the Nibelungen

sider da geschach· vvan riter
vnd vrovven weinen man da
sach· daz zv di edeln knehte ir
lieben friunde tot· di hat daz
mære ein ende diz ist der
Nibelunge liet· ·

Diu Chlage·

ie hebt sich ein mære· daz
vvære nu redebære· vnd
wære gut ze sagene·
hivven daz ez ze chlagene· den
livten allen gezimt· swer iz
rehte vernimt· der muz iz
vnerliche chlagen· vnd iamer
in dem herzen tragen·

Hete ich nv bi sinne daz siz gar
ze minne· heten di ez erfunden·
ez ist von alten stunden· her
vil wærlich gesagt· ob ez
iemen misbehagt· der sol iz lazen
ane haz· vnd hore di rede
fvrbaz·

Diz alte mære hat ein tihtare·
an ein buch schriben· besen
chunder niht beliben· ez en si
ovch noch da von bechant· wi
di von Burgonden lant· di
ir ziten vnd di ir tagen· mit
eren heten sich betragen·

Danchrat ein chvnech hiez· ver
in div wirin lant liez· den
stolzen helden gvten· vnd ovch
der edelen Vten· div di chrone
mit im trvch· si heten alles
des genvch· daz riche kvnege
solden· haben ober wolden·

Si heten ovch ane vvan ane
zwester wolgetan· div nam
sider einen man· da von sich
prvven began· vil maneges
gvten recken not· vnt daz er
selbe den tot· gewan von
siner vbermut·

Sit namse aber einen helt
gvt· vz Hivnisschem riche· mit
dem si herliche· nach ir zimer
sit gesaz· der rede meister hiez
daz· ihten an dem mate· wi
sich der kvnech wære·

Div rede ist genvch wizenlich·
er het aller tægelich· zwelf
ander chvnege vnder im· von
der warheit ich daz nim· er

pflach vil grozer eren· man
gevrisch nieman so heren· vnder
heiden vnde christen· genvge di
daz wisten· di riten zv zim
in daz lant· er vvas Ecel genant·

Botelvnch sin vater hiez· der im
vil gewalres liez· nach sinem
rode vnz an di stvnt· daz mære
tvt vns von im chunt· daz er
het ze wibe ein wip· daz tvgent
licher vrovven lip· bi ir iaren
niemen vant· Helche so vvas si
genant· von der schier er sit
mit not ver vil gewaltige tot·
der nam im sine wnne· so riet
im sin chvnne· an vrovn Crien
hilden· der edeln vnt der milden·

Nv ist iv vvol geseit daz·
wie si cen hivnen gesaz· also
div edele Helche e· doch tet
ir zallen ziten we· daz si da
ellende hiez· vvand si der iamer
niht enliez· geruven setten
ein tach· wand ir an dem
herzen lach· wi si verlos ir
wnne· ir aller næhestez chvnne·
er ir lieben man benomen· do
vvas ez an di rede chomen·
daz vrovn Vten chinde· allez
daz gesinde· viente vz hivnen
riche· vnd also vorhtliche·
sam si vrovn Helchen tæten e·
si het ovch da vrovven me·
danne in ir vater lande· der
gvten vvigande· her si vil
groze chrapft· tægeliche riter
schapht· di ir ovgen sahen·
daz enchvnde niht ver vahen·
ir weinten ane lovgen· alle
zit ir ovgen·

Sit do brahte siz dar an·
do si den gewalt gar gevvan·
daz si ane vnder sprieche ge
halt ir einer riche· vmbe
Ezsibe ir lieben man· dem vil
vbel an gewan· ir brvder
Gvnther den lip· vnd Hagen
vnt des chvneges vvip· von
dem er doch deiz tot genam·
dem helde sterben niht gezam·
von deheines recken hant· wand
er het vvol ellu lant· mit siner
chraft ver cherer· da von vvas
ir geseret· beidiv herce vnd ovch

The Lament of the Nibelungen

(Div Chlage)

Translated and with an Introduction

by

Winder McConnell

CAMDEN HOUSE

Published by Camden House, Inc.
Drawer 2025
Columbia, SC 29202 USA

Printed on acid-free paper.
Binding materials are chosen for strength and
durability.

ISBN 1-879751-73-9

Library of Congress Cataloging-in-Publication Data

Klage. English & German (Middle High German)
    The lament of the Nibelungen = (Div Chlage) / translated and with
an introduction by Winder McConnell. -- 1st ed.
        p.   cm.   -- (Studies in German literature, linguistics, and culture.
        Medieval texts and translations)
    Includes bibliographical references and index.
    ISBN 1-879751-73-9 (alk. paper)
    1. Epic poetry, German--Translations into English. 2. Nibelungen--Poetry.
I. McConnell, Winder. II. Title. III. Title: Chlage.
IV. Series: Studies in German literature, linguistics, and culture
(Unnumbered). Medieval texts and translations.
PT1624.A25   1994
831'.22--dc20   94-28718
                                                                          CIP

Acknowledgments

I owe a profound debt of gratitude to Werner Hoffmann at the University of Mannheim and Brian Murdoch at the University of Stirling for having given selflessly of their time to read through the manuscript in its entirety and offer some much needed constructive criticism. Their suggestions pertaining to both style and semantics were, virtually without exception, adopted by me in the course of undertaking revisions and throughout the "polishing" process. They bear no responsibility, of course, for any inconsistencies or incongruities which may have slipped into the final version. If the translation merits a positive reception among scholars, it will be in large part owing to their role in its preparation.

To Professor Evelyn S. Firchow of the University of Minnesota and the editor of this series, my sincere thanks for having offered encouragement along the way, and for having provided me with the benefit of her insights, particularly in the final stages of manuscript preparation.

This is the second volume that I have had the pleasure of publishing with Camden House. I am especially grateful to Professor James Hardin of the University of South Carolina for his technical advice and support of what might justifiably be considered a most esoteric undertaking.

Publication of this book was made possible by a generous grant from the College of Letters and Science as well as the Office of Research of the University of California at Davis. Thanks are extended to Dean Robert O. Crummey, Robert N. Shelton, Vice Chancellor for Research, and, in particular, to Albert A. Harrison, Executive Associate Dean in the College of Letters and Science, for their support of the project. The preparation of a camera-ready copy of the manuscript was greatly facilitated by the assistance and cooperation of the Principal Staff Assistant in the Department of German and Russian, Judith F. Brooks.

I thank the Stiftsbibliothek, St. Gall, Switzerland, for permission to publish the first page of the *Chlage*-manuscript B (Cod. Sangall 857).

As ever, I am grateful to Kathy, Karen, and Kerry for their patience.

W.McC.
June 1994

This book is dedicated to the memory of a gentleman whom I met in 1973 in the beautiful medieval town of Hannoversch Münden, Lower Saxony. He was a man of remarkable vision and erudition; the many hours spent at his home in the company of his family are among my fondest memories of the year I had the good fortune to spend in that town.

In memoriam

Ernst Hahn (1908-1982)

Gentleman, Teacher, Friend

Contents

The Lament of the Nibelungen

(Div Chlage)

Introduction

ez ist div grôzeste geshiht.
div cer vverld ie geschach.
(*Div Chlage*, vv. 3480-3481)

A FEW YEARS AGO, I began to jot down translations of individual sections of the *Chlage*[1] (*Lament*) so that I might use them in undergraduate courses on the *Nibelungenlied* that were taught in English. With time, the file containing these excerpts grew until it became clear to me that it represented the core of a project which, if completed, might prove of some benefit to medievalists concerned with the genre of heroic epic in general and with the *Nibelungenlied* in particular.

There were compelling reasons to produce this volume. No complete English translation had ever been printed, and the last modern German language translations date from the mid-nineteenth century. The *Nibelungenlied*, in contrast, is readily accessible to English-speaking readers, above all in the translation which A. T. Hatto produced for the Penguin series in 1965 and which has seen numerous reprints since it first appeared. Undoubtedly because it has been judged aesthetically "inferior" to the *Nibelungenlied*, a claim that is difficult to refute, the *Chlage* has not been accorded the same attention as its predecessor. Yet, as Werner Hoffmann has stated: " ... die beiden Werke gehören in der mittelalterlichen Rezeption so eng, ja offenbar notwendig zusammen, daß ein Referat über das Nibelungenlied ohne Einbeziehung der »Klage«, zumindest unter historischer Perspektive, nicht vertretbar wäre."[2]

A similar sentiment has been expressed by Lutz Mackensen: "Die »Klage« war für das »Lied« so notwendig, daß keine Abschrift auf sie ver-

---

[1] *Div Chlage*, which is given as the name of the poem in verse 4322 and added by Ildefons von Arx at the beginning (page 416 of the manuscript) is usually normalized to *Diu Klage*. I have adhered throughout my text to the original spelling, except, of course, for occurrences of *Klage* in quotations.

[2] Werner Hoffmann, *Das Nibelungenlied*, 6th revised and expanded ed. of *Das Nibelungenlied* by Gottfried Weber and Werner Hoffmann, Sammlung Metzer No. 7 (Stuttgart and Weimar: J. B. Metzler Verlag, 1992) 126. The sixth edition of this indispensable reference work is the first to contain a separate chapter on the *Nibelungenklage*.

zichten konnte. Die Überzeugung, daß das »Lied« ohne die »Klage« nicht
bestehen konnte, ist nicht u n s e r e Ansicht; es ist die Meinung der
Zeitgenossen von damals."[3] The *Nibelungenlied* and the *Chlage* were tradi-
tionally linked to one another by medieval scribes. The major purpose of
the *Chlage* appears to have been to offer a response to the *Nibelungenlied*.
While scholars may be of varying opinions as to the aesthetic value of this
initial commentary to one of the world's greatest epics, it has served to
provide us with a better idea of the latter's place in the literary milieu of
the first quarter of the thirteenth century.

The primary purpose of this translation is, then, to make the *Chlage*
accessible to English-speaking readers. So that those familiar with Middle
High German can make comparisons between the original and my rendering, I have included a parallel transcription of Manuscript B, to be found
in the Stiftsbibliothek St. Gall, Switzerland.

Appended to most of the complete manuscripts of the *Nibelungenlied*,[4]
the *Chlage* was composed by an anonymous Bavarian or Austrian poet[5] in
2180 rhyming couplets. Dating from approximately the beginning of the
third decade of the thirteenth century,[6] it represents the first "commentary" on, although some might say "interpretation"[7] of, the epic. In contrast to the *Nibelungenlied*, the *Chlage* was intended from the outset to be

---

[3] Lutz Mackensen, *Die Nibelungen. Sage, Geschichte, ihr Lied und sein Dichter* (Stuttgart: Dr. Ernst Hauswedell & Co., 1984) 181.

[4] It is not included with Manuscript k, the Viennese Piarist Manuscript, which dates from the middle of the fifteenth century and which also contains extensive changes to the text of the *Nibelungenlied*.

[5] There has been much speculation as to the origins of the *Chlage* and the *Nibelungenlied* as well as to the role played by Bishop Pilgrim of Passau (Bishop between the years 971 and 999) who appears in the *Chlage* and gives directions to his clerk, Master Conrad, to write down in Latin ("in latinisschen bϴchstaben," v. 4299) all the events which have tran-spired. Is this the bϴch referred to in verses 19 and 569 of the *Chlage*, as Adolf Holtzmann conjectured (*Untersuchungen über das Nibelungenlied* [Stuttgart: A. Krabbe, 1854])? Or is it more likely that the poet of the *Chlage* is referring to a later rendition that had already been translated into German, to which he himself refers in verses 4316-4317?

[6] See Helmut de Boor, *Die höfische Literatur. Vorbereitung, Blüte, Ausklang 1170-1250*, 8th ed., *Geschichte der deutschen Literatur von den Anfängen bis zur Gegenwart* by Helmut de Boor and Richard Newald (Munich: C. H. Beck'sche Verlagsbuchhandlung, 1969) 2: 167; Werner Hoffmann, *Mittelhochdeutsche Heldendichtung*, Grundlagen der Germanistik No. 14 (Berlin: Erich Schmidt Verlag, 1974) 92, with a succinct overview of the various perspectives. An important contribution to the dating question is Werner Schröder, *Wolfram von Eschen-bach, das Nibelungenlied und 'Die Klage.'* Akademie der Wissenschaften und der Literatur. Abhandlungen der Geistes- und Sozialwissenschaftlichen Klasse 5 (Mainz: Akademie der Wissenschaften und der Literatur; Stuttgart: Franz Steiner Verlag Wiesbaden Gmbh., 1989, particularly 13-21: "Die Datierung der 'Klage'").

[7] See Hoffmann, *Mittelhochdeutsche Heldendichtung* 94: "die erste zeitgenössische Interpretation des Nibelungenliedes, was bereits Josef Körner gesehen hat."

read rather than performed. The elegiac quality of the *Chlage* underscores its very different spirit and, one might add, its function. Gustav Ehrismann maintained that the *Chlage* was to be understood as having its roots in "der germanischen Totenfeier, bei welcher Kultus und Sitte geboten, dem Dahingeschiedenen Klageworte oder einen Klagegesang zu widmen ...,"[8] a theory that has been viewed more critically in recent years.[9]

The *Chlage* poet appears to have been deeply disturbed by both the events and the outcome of the *Nibelungenlied*. His attention is devoted to three things in particular: 1) underscoring through a graphic depiction of immoderate grief and lamentation by Attila and others the extent of the carnage at the court of the Hunnish king (with particular attention being paid to Rüedeger and the significance of his death); 2) vindicating Kriemhild (while simultaneously identifying Hagen as the source of the catastrophe; 3) insuring that the Armageddon-like conclusion of the *Nibelungenlied* is countered by a sense of continuity through the crowning of young Siegfried, son of Gunther and Brünhild, in Worms.

Although the *Chlage* picks up where the *Nibelungenlied* has left off, i.e., following the decimation of Burgundian, Hunnish, and Amelung forces, the extent to which the despair of Attila, in particular, is portrayed in the *Chlage* may well strike the modern reader as overdone pathos. He will find here little of the stoicism so characteristic of Hagen, Volker, and others among the Burgundians destined to die in the land of the Huns. The repeated calls for moderation in expressing one's grief that are heard from figures such as Hildebrand,[10] Bishop Pilgrim, or Sindolt, do little to erase the image of a *world* in mourning. There is also considerable emphasis on the plight of Dietrich who, having lost all of his Amelungs, must lament not only their demise but also any chance he may have had of re-establishing himself as a powerful monarch.

Particularly noteworthy, however, is the *Chlage*-poet's alternative perspective on the character of Kriemhild. While most of the manuscripts of the *Nibelungenlied*, with the exception of Manuscript C, portray the queen as a she-devil out of control, the poet attempts to reassure his readers that Kriemhild has earned her place in heaven, as a consequence of the supreme loyalty demonstrated towards her murdered husband, Siegfried.

---

[8] Gustav Ehrismann, *Geschichte der deutschen Literatur bis zum Ausgang des Mittelalters*, 2. Teil: *Die mittelhochdeutsche Literatur*, Schlußband (1935; Munich: C. H. Beck'sche Verlagsbuchhandlung, 1966) 143-144.

[9] See Hoffmann, *Das Nibelungenlied* 126-127.

[10] Hildebrand's urging of Dietrich that he depart the Hunnish realm and leave this sorrow behind reminds one of Hyperion's allusion to the "wise men" in Hölderlin's work who pass on this advice to the "leidend Gemüt": "klage nicht, handle!" See Friedrich Hölderlin, *Werke und Briefe*, vol. 1: *Gedichte. Hyperion*, ed. Friedrich Beißner and Jochen Schmidt (Frankfurt am Main: Insel Verlag, 1969) 296.

Inasmuch as her revenge was an expression of that loyalty, it was not to be condemned. Hagen, after all, was, in the opinion of the poet, the source of the misery and suffering, and the Burgundian kings brought disaster upon themselves through their *übermuot* ('haughtiness, arrogance').[11] That so many had to die before Hagen could be slain, the *Chlage*-poet attributes to Kriemhild's "krankem sin," her 'weak mind,' a reflection of the widely held view at the time that woman's mind (spirit) was intrinsically weak.[12] It may be assumed that the poet was reacting against a negative judgment of Kriemhild on the part of a considerable number of those contemporaries who had become familiar with the epic.[13] What is remarkable, however, is the manner in which the poet combines a relatively "weighty" layer of Christianity (when compared to the rather non-substantive allusions to the latter in the *Nibelungenlied*) with the more archaic Germanic code of ethics. Is it not a terrible irony that adherence to a core element of that code, namely *triuwe* ('loyalty, faithfulness'), which, in the case of Kriemhild, ultimately leads to the butchery at Attila's court, is regarded as the catalyst for insuring a place in heaven for Siegfried's widow?

There is much more emphasis placed on Christianity in the *Chlage* than is the case in the *Nibelungenlied*: "Die viel berufenen christlich-moralischen

[11] Friedrich Panzer has suggested that both the *Nibelungenlied*-poet and the author of the *Chlage* were concerned with presenting a moral judgment with respect to the actions of the leading characters. In the former, there was a noticeable attempt to be objective, while the *Chlage*-poet preferred decisive, one-sided verdicts. See Friedrich Panzer, *Das Nibelungenlied. Entstehung und Gestalt* (Stuttgart and Cologne: W. Kohlhammer, 1955) 81.

[12] Note Friedrich Panzer's allusion to the "physiologische[n] Schwachsinn des Weibes" (83), clearly a reference to Paul Julius Möbius's *Über den physiologischen Schwachsinn des Weibes*, 3rd ed. (Munich: Matthes & Seitz, 1901). The book enjoyed numerous subsequent editions, the 12th appearing in 1922. Michael Curschmann has referred to Attila's later allusion to the "weiblichem Unverstand" of his wife (Michael Curschmann, "'Nibelungen-lied' und 'Klage,'" *Die deutsche Literatur des Mittelalters. Verfasserlexikon*, 2nd revised ed., ed. Kurt Ruh, vol. 6, Lieferung 3/4 [Berlin and New York: Walter de Gruyter, 1987] col. 953). This could be understood as 'female thoughtlessness, senselessness, stupidity, igno-rance.' "Daz kränker gesleht" has been recorded by Matthias Lexer (*Mittelhochdeutsches Handwörterbuch*, 3 vols. [1872-1878; Stuttgart: S. Hirzel Verlag, 1974] 1: col. 1707) as a general term in Middle High German for the female sex, but most likely here with the accent on 'weak.' Perhaps the poet is using 'krank' in another sense, namely, to underscore the terribly distorted state of Kriemhild's mind at the time the slaughter takes place, i.e., to provide a 'psychological' (rather than 'physiological') explanation for her behavior.

[13] Ironically, however, Curschmann sees the *Chlage*-poet as being responsible for insuring that the image of Kriemhild would continue in the future to remain a negative one: "... selbst der 'Kl.'-Dichter hat Kriemhild das alte Odium der Verräterin nicht nehmen können; vielmehr hat gerade sein Einschwenken in die Dietrichsage paradoxerweise nicht nur die Hauptlinie der mal. Rezeptionsgeschichte vorgezeichnet, sondern auch das Fortbestehen des negativen Kriemhild-Bildes gesichert" (col. 960).

Obertöne sind ebenso vorhanden wie das christliche Ritual."[14] Werner Hoffmann has suggested that the *Chlage* represents, in fact, "eher eine christlich-moralische Lehrdichtung als eine Heldendichtung."[15] Attila himself attributes his misfortune to having turned his back on the Christian God he had embraced for five years! If one contrasts the "spirit" of the *Nibelungenlied* with that of the *Chlage*, the veracity of Hoffmann's statement becomes immediately apparent. The actions of the characters and the events of the former lead with an irrevocable and unnerving certainty to the cataclysmic conclusion with no indication of any consolation to follow in either the physical or spiritual world. As a devout Christian,[16] the *Chlage*-poet, on the other hand, was concerned with the matter of continuity also in this world and, more specifically, in the now leaderless realm of the Burgundians, as the emphasis on the crowning of the young Siegfried (only son of Gunther and Brünhild) underscores (note verses 4004-4005 and 4009-4010, in particular). The *Nibelungenlied* had left a gaping vacuum in the political structure of the Burgundian ruling class. Despite the devastating events at the court of Attila, the world goes on. It may be somewhat ironic that, despite the hyperbolic manner in which the lamentations of the survivors are depicted, there is no statement in the *Chlage* about joy ultimately turning to sorrow such as the one we encounter in the second-to-last strophe of the *Nibelungenlied* and which may well mirror the philosophy of its creator. While the poet is not in a position to effect a complete turnaround in the mood left by the conclusion of the *Nibelungenlied*, he is able to hold out the promise of a new future:

Allenthalben ist sie [*Div Chlage*] bestrebt, die Ordnung der Feudalwelt wiederherzustellen, sie verstärkt das kirchliche Fundament und überzieht die Gestalten, nämlich Hagen und Kriemhild, mit einem einfachen schlichten Bewertungsraster, sie denkt streng in den Gegensätzen von Gut und Böse. So wird es möglich, die Trauer des Nibelungenschlusses zu verdrängen und Perspektiven auf Freude zu öffnen.[17]

---

[14] Curschmann col. 953.

[15] Hoffmann, *Mittelhochdeutsche Heldendichtung* 94.

[16] See Mackensen 188–189: "Der Klagedichter war ein Geistlicher nach Überzeugung und Temperament, ein Seelsorger, dessen Gedanken durch Himmel und Hölle begrenzt waren und der gern ein Wegweiser zum Himmel gewesen wäre." See also Panzer 96: "Vom Verfasser der Klage darf man wohl mit Bestimmtheit annehmen, daß er Geistlicher gewesen ist."

[17] Otfrid Ehrismann, *Nibelungenlied: Epoche–Werk–Wirkung*, Arbeitsbücher zur Literaturgeschichte, ed. Wilfried Barner and Gunter E. Grimm (Munich: Verlag C. H. Beck, 1987) 245.

My translation follows the text of Manuscript B of the *Chlage* found in the Stiftsbibliothek St. Gall, Switzerland (Cod. Sangall. 857) and published in 1962 in a facsimile edition by K. Bischoff, H. M. Heinrichs, and W. Schröder.[18] *Div Chlage* is to be found on pp. 416-451 of the manuscript between the *Nibelungenlied* and *Karl der Große* by the Stricker. The work is preceded by six lines containing vv. 2379,1b-4 of Manuscript B of the *Nibelungenlied*, and is introduced by the title "Div Chlage" which was inserted about 1800 by Ildefons von Arx, librarian in the Stiftsbibliothek St. Gall. I have also consulted the edition published by Karl Bartsch which occasionally, but not radically, deviates from the original Manuscript B.[19]

Manuscripts of the *Chlage* are appended to the following versions of the *Nibelungenlied*:

A: Hohenems-Munich, Bayerische Staatsbibliothek (Munich), Cod. germ. 34, parchment, dating from the last quarter of the thirteenth century. The *Chlage* is found on pp. 94ᵛ-116ʳ.

B: St. Gall, Stiftsbibliothek, Cod. Sangall. 857, parchment, dating from the middle of the thirteenth century. Hoffmann suggests that it may already date from the first half of that century. The *Chlage* is found on pp. 416-451.

C: Donaueschingen, Fürstliche Fürstenbergische Hofbibliothek (earlier: Hohenems-Laßberg), Ms. 63, parchment, dating from the first half of the thirteenth century. The *Chlage* is found on pp. 89-114.

D: Second Munich Ms., Cod. germ. 31, parchment, dating from the first third of the fourteenth century. Krogmann/Pretzel suggest a dating from the last third of the fourteenth century. The *Chlage* is found on pp. 144-168, but breaks off after verse 3140 in the incomplete column 168ᵈ.

G: A damaged parchment in Donaueschingen, dating from ca. 1300 which contains only portions of the *Chlage*.

[18] K. Bischoff, H. M. Heinrichs, W. Schröder, eds., *Das Nibelungenlied und die Klage. Handschrift B (Cod. Sangall. 857)*, with an introduction by Johannes Duft, Deutsche Texte in Handschriften 1 (Cologne and Graz: Böhlau Verlag, 1962).

[19] *Diu Klage mit den Lesarten sämtlicher Handschriften*, ed. Karl Bartsch (1875; Darmstadt: Wissenschaftliche Buchgesellschaft, 1964).

I (J): Berlin parchment manuscript, SB Preußischer Kultur-besitz, Ms. germ. fol 474, dating from the fourteenth century, contains an excerpt from the *Chlage* encompassing 944 lines.

N: Parchment manuscript from the fourteenth century in the Germanisches Nationalmuseum in Nuremberg (No. 4365), which contains just over 400 verses of the *Chlage*.

a: The Wallenstein Manuscript, paper, dating from the late fifteenth century. The *Chlage* is contained on pp. 191^v-260^r under the title: "abentewer von der klag." Now found in the Bibliotheca Bodmeriana in Geneva-Coligny.

b: Berlin, SB Preußischer Kulturbesitz. Ms. germ. fol. 855. The Hundeshagen Manuscript, paper, named after the former owner, Bernd Hundeshagen. Fifteenth century. The *Chlage* is found on pp. 159^a-188^b.

d: The Ambras Manuscript in the Österreichische National-bibliothek, Vienna, Ser. n. 2663, parchment, beginning of the sixteenth century. The *Chlage* is found on pp. 131-139. Fragment, breaking off at verse 4206.

h: The Meusebach Manuscript, a copy of J (formerly known as the Berlin Paper Manuscript), first half of the fifteenth century.[20]

The text of the *Chlage* in the St. Gall manuscript is presented throughout in two columns on each page on ruled lines to insure evenness. The end of each line does not correspond to the end of a particular verse. Periods are used to indicate the latter. The number of lines per column ranges from a low of forty-five (all four columns on pp. 427-428) to a high of fifty-four (right-hand column on p. 416) and in virtually all cases, columns on pages facing one another contain the same number of lines. The final page contains two columns, each with fifty-three lines, followed by thirteen complete run-on lines. The change in format is clearly conditioned by considerations of space which would also account for the relatively high number of *er*-ligatures on p. 451.

---

[20] For a more complete description of the individual parchment and paper manuscripts, see the bibliography edited by Willy Krogmann and Ulrich Pretzel (1966) as well as Peter Jörg Becker's work on medieval manuscripts and early prints (1977).

In numerous instances, place and personal names have been underlined
by a previous owner of the manuscript, most likely the Swiss historian and
humanist, Aegidius Tschudi (1505-1572), who also made copious marginal
notations (usually simply a repetition of the name or the place) next to
underlined sections. We can only speculate as to why this was undertaken;
as a chronicler and historian, Tschudi may have been particularly intrigued
by places and people(s) whom he immediately recognized and hoped to
determine more specifically the locations in which the action of the *Nibelungen* tale took place. The notations to be found next to verses 395ff. may
be indicative of an attempt to link the poetical figures with actual historical
personalities, but it is impossible to state with complete assurance that this
was the case.

In his New High German translation of the *Chlage*, August Zeune
divided the work into five sections: 1) "Etzels Hofhalt" (verses 1–586); 2)
"Wegschaffung der Toden" (verses 587–1450); 3) "Etzels Klage über die
Verwandten" (verses 1451–2278); 4) "Begräbniss" (verses 2279–2708); 5)
"Heimsendung der Waffen" (verses 2709–4322).[21] Gustav Ehrismann
identified four separate sections of the *Chlage*: 1) verses 1–568: introduction with summary of *Nibelungenlied*; beginning of lament at Attila's court;
2) verses 569–2584: lamentation of Attila, Dietrich, Hildebrand for Kriemhild and the heroes who have been killed, burial of the dead; 3) verses
2585–4322: lament in Burgundy; 4) verses 4323–4360: conclusion, confusion
over Attila's end.[22] Werner Hoffmann also suggests a four-part structure
to the work:

Der erste [Teil] gibt eine Zusammenfassung der Ereignisse im zweiten
Teil des Nibelungenliedes, die in eine Erörterung über Kriemhilts
Schicksal nach ihrem Tode einmündet (v. 552ff.); der zweite erzählt
von der Auffindung der gefallenen Helden, die jedesmal den Anlaß zu
maßlosen Klagen bietet, ihrer Aufbahrung und Bestattung; der dritte
berichtet von der Übermittlung der Nachricht von den Geschehnissen
am Hunnenhof nach Bechelaren, Wien und Worms; der vierte, kür-
zeste, schließlich von dem Aufbruch Dietrichs, der zusammen mit
seiner *gemahele* Herrat und Hildebrant, trotz Etzels Bitten, ihn nicht
allein zu lassen, in sein eigenes Land zurückkehren will.[23]

---

[21] August Zeune, trans., *Nibelungennoth und Klage nach ältester Gestalt in ungebundener
Rede übersetzt*, 2nd rev. ed. (Berlin: Nicolai'sche Buchhandlung, 1836). Zeune based his
translation on Lachmann's 1826 edition of the *Nibelungenlied* and the *Chlage* (Hohenems-
Munich, Manuscript A) and did not include the final verses (4323–4360), but rather stated
in a footnote that the Laßberg manuscript contained "noch 37 Zeilen über Etzels unbekann-
tes Ende" (408).

[22] Ehrismann 144.

[23] Hoffmann, *Mittelhochdeutsche Heldendichtung* 92.

Michael Curschmann has described a tripartite division of *the Chlage*: 1) vv. 17–586: Introduction; 2) vv. 587–2489: the actual Lament, which Curschmann further divides into two sections: a) vv. 587-2174: lament for various family members and heroes; b) vv. 2175-2489: the removal and burial of the dead, including 1700 noble warriors on both sides and 9000 Burgundian squires; 3) vv. 2490–4360: dissemination of the news concerning the catastrophe, whereby Curschmann identifies three major sections: a) vv. 2661-3286: the carrying of the news to Pöchlarn; b) vv. 3287–4113: sojourn of the envoys at Passau (Bishop Pilgrim), imparting of news to Earl Else, and arrival in Worms; c) vv. 4114-4294, Dietrich's departure from Attila and arrival in Pöchlarn + vv. 4323–4360 (the thirty-eight verses that are mistakenly placed at the end of Manuscript B).[24]

Most recently, Angelika Günzburger has also divided the *Chlage* into three major parts, but with very different content for parts 2 and 3 when compared to Curschmann's structure: 1) verses 1–586 (prolog); 2) vv. 587–4294 (*narratio*, with location, lament, burial of the dead, and dissemination of information); 3) vv. 4295–4322 (epilog).[25]

I concur with Ehrismann and Hoffmann with respect to the four-part structure of the *Chlage*. The final thirty-eight verses dealing with Attila's fate after the departure of Dietrich, which appear in Manuscript B after the formal conclusion of the lay, could be either a later addition to the work or have been misplaced by the scribe of this manuscript.

The importance of the *Chlage* does not lie in the poet's style, for if one word had to be chosen to describe the latter, it would be monotonous. Lutz Mackensen has less than flattering words for the overall impression left by the work:

> Der Dichter gehört nicht zu den Großen der Zunft. Sein Plan legt ihm die unablässige Wiederholung des gleichen Themas auf: die Namen wechseln, die Klage bleibt. Aber er kann nicht variieren. So rieseln seine Reimpaare, ohnehin nur wechselnden Handlungen oder lebhaften Gesprächen zweckdienlich, in zäher Einförmigkeit. Sein Wortschatz ist nicht groß; seine Reime wiederholen sich. Das Ganze würde ermüden, hätte er es nicht in geschickter Steigerung aufgebaut.[26]

---

[24] Curschmann, cols. 940-941.

[25] Angelika Günzburger, *Studien zur Nibelungenklage. Forschungsbericht – Bauform der Klage – Personendarstellung*, Europäische Hochschulschriften 685 (Frankfurt am Main, Bern, New York: Peter Lang, 1983) 86. Günzburger agrees with the earlier view (advanced by Josef Körner) that verses 4323–4360, which speculate on the end of Attila, constitute a later "Interpolation" into the text and does not include them in her structural analysis.

[26] Mackensen 180.

The diction of *Div Chlage* contrasts starkly with that of the *Nibelungen-lied*. Variation in the former is at a premium and monotonous repetition[27] is more the order of the day. As de Boor has pointed out, *guilt*, not *fate*, is preeminent in the poet's mind. In contrast to the author of the *Nibelungen-lied*, who could indulge in condemnation without becoming absolute (as in the case of the narrator's judgment of Hagen following the murder of Siegfried and the relatively positive portrayal of the same figure throughout the second half of the work), the *Chlage*-poet clearly leans to unequivocal judgments in his treatment of the two chief protagonists. Here, as elsewhere, dualistic thinking characterizes his view of the world.

Individual sections within the manuscript are normally introduced by bold, and occasionally ornate, capital letters. (See, for example, the elaborate "I" at the beginning of verse 2267.) The work is introduced by a large capital "H," the first letter of the poem, which extends to the top of page 416 perpendicular to the last six lines of the *Nibelungenlied* immediately preceding *Div Chlage*. Capitals occur usually, but not always (see the new section introduced in verse 2197, "Ein teil...", on p. 434, col. 2, line 11 of the ms.) at the beginning of a new line, and are often immediately preceded by the corresponding lower case letter in small script, perhaps as a reminder to the scribe that the letter following was, in fact, to be in bold form. Divisions in my translation are normally based on these individual sections in the original and not on the blocks to be found in the edition by Bartsch, which do not necessarily coincide with the divisions of the manuscript. (Note, however, the sections of the translation beginning with verses 176 and 206 instead of 175 and 207 respectively. Such deviations from the original divisions were occasionally necessary for obvious semantic reasons.)

There is considerable variation with respect to capitalization. Apart from the beginnings of individual sections referred to above, the poet generally capitalizes personal and place names, but also frequently uses lower-case forms for the latter, taking particular liberty with names beginning with "H." The reader will also note the use of the small capital "R" in "Rin" which appears consistently throughout the work, as well as the small "N" which often is used at the beginning of personal names (for example, vv. 1542, 1543). In several instances, capital letters introducing new sections have been placed deliberately in the left margins. While this may have been done to save space, it is not a practice which is followed consistently throughout the manuscript as it occurs for the last time in verse 638. Those capital letters that do appear in the margins differ from the others in that they are often not in bold script and also evince variant forms. (Contrast,

---

[27] See de Boor 168.

for example, the solid, bold "**D**" at the beginning of verse 198 with the
character introducing verses 138 and 207.)

I have attempted as much as possible to keep the length of the translation
on the right-hand side in conformity with the transcription on the left-hand
pages. This has necessitated a compromise with respect to aesthetics, or,
in computer jargon, the retention of unsightly "widows" and "orphans"
(which Brian Murdoch has wryly suggested might be quite appropriate,
given the nature of *Div Chlage*). I have assumed, I hope with some justification, that my readers would prefer that the transcription and the translation
on parallel pages correspond with one another as much as possible, although, in some instances, there are run-overs in the English rendering
which are unavoidable if the sense of the original is to be preserved.

For the most part, I have adhered in the transcription to the orthography
of the original manuscript so that the reader may gain an accurate impression of what is actually there. For technical reasons, I have used "s"
throughout, although the latter is usually to be found in lower case, with
very few exceptions, only in final position, the most common form of "s"
in the manuscript being " ſ." The character "v" is used by the scribe to
represent both "w" (as in "vvigande") and "u" (as in "vnde"), or "fu" as
in "vvnde," and in those instances when it denotes "w" and is not followed
by a "v" with the quality of a "u," it is doubled: "vvaz" = 'was.' I have
used "W" in those cases where a bold, capital "**W**" appears at the beginning of a new section of the text (see, for example, verses 1681, 2455,
2515). The character "u" may also be used to denote "u" as in "stunde,"
but while it is tempting to suggest that this occurs prior to nasals, there is
no consistency: note "chvnde" in verse 132. Occasionally, "u" may also
appear with the quality of "v" as in verse 184: "uon" = 'von.'

The critical editions of the *Chlage* provide the usual diacritics to indicate
long vowels. These are normally not to be found in the manuscript. Exceptions in Manuscript B include, however, the (relatively) regular occurrence
of the adverb "ê" and the long "î" in the adverb "sît." There are also a few
isolated instances of other diacritics, as in the case of "mâge"/"lâge" in
verses 839–840. I have followed the original when providing them in the
transcription. The reader may also wish to note erasures in the original
manuscript in verses 1000, 1001, 1167, 3673, 4174, and 4230.

I have used square brackets, pointed brackets, and parentheses to indicate
the following: square brackets to contain the verse numbers (corresponding
to the edition by Bartsch which should be readily acceptable to most
readers), the rendering of the *er*-ligature, and, within the text of the transcription itself, page numbers indicating the *beginning* of a new page (and,
simultaneously, the top of the left-hand column on that page) in the
Bischoff/Heinrichs/Schröder facsimile edition as well as in the original
manuscript respectively; pointed brackets to indicate errors in the text,
ranging from omitted periods, letters, and words, to doubling of letters and

words, as well as for two sections lifted from Bartsch: vv. 1171-1174 which
the manuscript is lacking, and vv. 4354-4360 of the original manuscript
which fell victim to a bookbinder's cut; parentheses to indicate sections of
the text obscured by blotching and reconstructed using the Bartsch edition.
I have also indicated the end of each left-hand column on a particular page
of the manuscript by a single slash (/). The transcription itself is arranged
in rhyming couplets; I have refrained from marking the end of individual
lines in the columns of the original manuscript primarily because the
insertion of thousands of slashes could quite likely prove more of a distrac-
tion than an advantage in an edition of this sort. The major reason for the
scribe's decision to adhere to lines rather than verses when structuring his
columns was clearly the matter of space conservation. Indicating the end
of such lines would be of little significance to most readers; there are no
great revelations to be made regarding syllabification.

The reader will also note numerous occasions in the transcription on
which inseparable prefixes have, in fact, been separated from the stem of
the verb. I cannot state with assurance that I have always been correct in
my judgment of what was intended here by the poet, although I have made
every effort to be consistent.

In general, my emendations to the original have been held to a minimum.
The letter "Ꝑ" (= "Per") in verses 4227 and 4271 has been retained, but
the "er-ligature" has, for technical reasons, been transcribed as [er]. The
caron has been retained in instances such as "n̄" and "m̄". For technical
reasons, I have transcribed the superscript "o" above the first letter of
Ute's name when it is capitalized (V) so that it appears next to the latter:
"Vote."

At first glance, the *Chlage* may not appear to offer great problems to the
translator. Once involved in the process, however, it becomes quickly
apparent that this is not the case. There are nuances of the language which
do not lend themselves readily to rendering into either New High German
or English, and what of those expressions which we no longer recognize as
nuances? While I have not attempted to provide a word-by-word rendering
of this often quite formulaic poem into English, I have made every effort
to remain close to the original text. A compromise is always involved in
such a process; where it became a choice between a smoother reading in
English and adherence to the original text, I have usually opted for the
latter. In many instances the author makes use of the "man sah/man
hörte" ('One saw/one heard') construction which I have frequently rendered into English without reference to the impersonal pronoun. The same
applies to the use of "beginnen" which has often been dropped in the
translation for stylistic reasons, for example, verse 400: "daz volch do raten
began." I have also not found it necessary to translate the adverb "do"
('there'/'then') in every instance.

With its immoderate use of the *flagellum Dei* tradition, the *Chlage* is hardly a work that will impress the modern reader. It is impossible to gauge with any certainty how it might have been received by a medieval audience which was also familiar with the *Nibelungenlied*. If Mackensen and Panzer are correct in their assumption that the scribe was a man of the church, then it is quite likely that he wrote to edify, but simultaneously with the intention of offering an alternative to the bleak, nihilistic outlook conveyed by the poet of the *Nibelungenlied*. Yet he does not "overdo" the Christian element in a one-sided fashion, but rather finds (sometimes quite remarkable) ways in which to combine the ethos of Christianity with the ideals (loyalty, moderation, continuity) of early thirteenth-century knighthood as well as the older Germanic idea of revenge. However it may be judged from an aesthetic point of view, the *Chlage* represents the first known reaction to the *Nibelungenlied*, or, to put it another way, the genesis of the *Rezeptionsgeschichte* surrounding the great epic.

Davis, June, 1994   Winder McConnell

The Lament of the Nibelungen

(Div Chlage)

[Div Chlage]

Hie hebt sich ein mære.
daz vvære uil redebære.
vnd vvære gut ce sagene.
nivvan daz ez ce chlagene.
[5]   den livten allen gezimt.
svver iz rehte vernimt.
der mvz iz iamerliche chlagen.
vnd iamer in dem hercen tragen.

Hete ich nv̊ di sinne<.>
[10]   daz siz gar ce minne.
heten di ez erfvnden.
ez ist von alten stunden.
her vil vværlich gesagt.
ob ez iemen missehagt.
[15]   der sol iz lazen ane haz.
vnd hôre di rede fv̊rbaz.

Diz alte mære<.>
bat ein tihtære.
an ein bvch schriben.
[20]   desen chvndez niht beliben.
ezen si ovch noch da von bechant.
vvi di von Bvrgonden lant.
bi ir zîten vnd bi ir tagen.
mit eren heten sich betragen.

[25]   **D**anchrat ein chv̊nech hiez.
der en div vviten lant liez.
den stolzen helden gvten.
vnd ovch der edelen v̊ten.
div di chrone mit im trvch.
[30]   si heten alles des genvch.
daz riche kv̊nege solden.
haben oder vvolden.

Si heten ovch ane vvan.
eine svvester vvolgetan.
[35]   div nam sider einen man.
da von sich prv̊uen began.
vil maneges gvten recken not.

THE STORY THAT FOLLOWS would certainly be worth recounting and would also make good telling were it not for the fact that it is quite fitting for everyone to lament over it. Whoever truly comprehends the tale will undoubtedly be moved to tears by it and will surely feel sorrow in his heart.

[9] If only I had [sufficient] artistic ability that those who hear it might receive it kindly. The story has been passed down faithfully to us from long ago. Should it prove displeasing to anyone, he ought to put aside his rancor and listen further to it.

[17] A poet had this old tale written down in a book.[1] It could not remain in this form for it is still known today how the Burgundians in their time conducted themselves with honor.

[25] There was a king by the name of Dancrat who left his extensive land holdings to these proud, brave warriors[2] as well as to noble Ute, who had been his queen. Everything that mighty kings should have or might want to have was at their disposal.

[33] These knights also had, to be sure, a sister who was very beautiful. She later married a man and from this [marriage] many a brave warrior encountered misfortune;

---

[1] In Manuscript C (Hohenems–Laßberg) and D (second Munich manuscript), the word "latine" appears at the beginning of verse 20. In his edition of the work, Anton Edzardi remarks: "Latine ist wol sicher eine (vielleicht dem schluße entnommene) randglosse, die in den text geraten ist" (*Diu Klage mit vollständigem kritischen Apparat und ausführlicher Einleitung* [Hannover: Carl Rümpler, 1875] 91, fn.). Considering the verse that follows, however ("desen chvndez niht beliben"), it may well be that the reference to "Latin" was intended in the text, with the sense being that, given the wide dissemination of the story and the reputation of the Burgundians that had been passed down, the tale could hardly have remained only in Latin. Note verses 4295–4299 of Manuscript B in which reference is made to the direction given by Bishop Pilgrim of Passau to have the work written down "in latinisschen b❢chstaben" (4299). It is also possible that the *Chlage*-poet is referring in verse 20 to the written form per se, implying that widespread knowledge of the Burgundians' fame had to have been passed along orally.

[2] The poet is clearly referring here to the sons of Dancrat, namely, Gunther, Gernot, and Giselher.

vnt daz er selbe den tot.
gevvan von siner ỽbermvt.

[40]   Sît namse aber einen helt gvt.
vz Hivnisschem riche.
mit dem si herliche.
nach ir iamer sit gesaz.
der rede meister hiez daz.
[45]   tihten an dem mære.
vvi rich der kỽnech vvære.

Div rede ist genvch vvizenlich.
er het aller tægelich.
zvvelf ander chỽnege vnder im.
[50]   von der vvarheit ich daz nim.
er / pflach vil grozer eren.
man gevrish nieman so heren.
vnder heiden vnd(e) christen.
genvge di daz vvisten.
[55]   di ritten zv zim in daz lant.
er vvas Ecel genant.

Botelvnch sin vater hiez.
der im vil gevvaltes liez.
nach sinem tode vnz an di stvnt.
[60]   daz mære tvt vns von im chunt.
daz er het ze vvibe ein vvip.
daz tvgentlicher vrovven lip.
bi ir iaren niemen vant.
Helche so vvas si genant.
[65]   von der schiet er sît mit not.
der vil gevvaltige tot.
der nam im sine vỽnne.
sît riet im sin chỽnne.
an vrovn Criemhilden.
[70]   der edeln vnt der milden.

Nv ist iv vvol geseit.daz.
vvie si cen hivnen gesaz.
also div edele Helche ê.
doch tet ir zallen ziten vve.
[75]   daz si da ellende hiez.
vvand si der iamer niht enliez.
gervven selten cheinen tach.

he himself [Siegfried] met his death as a consequence of his arrogance.

[40] After that she wed a magnificent warrior from the kingdom of the Huns, with whom she lived in splendor[3] following her earlier misery. The original teller of this tale had his story tell just how wealthy this king happened to be.

[47] The facts are quite well known. He had twelve kings constantly at his disposal. I know that from the source. This man enjoyed great honor and there was no one among either the Christians or the heathens who was considered more distinguished. Many knights who were aware of that rode into his kingdom to join him. His name was Attila.

[57] His father's name was Botelung and the latter had bequeathed great power to his son, which Attila inherited after his father's death and retained until quite recently. The story goes that his wife was a woman whose fine appearance, for her years, could scarcely have found a match in anyone else. Helche was her name and it was with great sorrow that he took his leave of her. All-powerful death deprived him of his joy. Somewhat later, his kinfolk advised him to marry Queen Kriemhild, a noble and generous woman.

[71] You have certainly been told how it came to pass that she [Kriemhild] reigned over the Huns, just as noble Helche had done before her. But it always bothered her that she was a foreigner in this land.[4] The misery she felt would allow her no peace, not even for as much as a single day,

---

[3] Zeune translates "herliche" in verse 42 as 'fröhlich' (337). This can scarcely be appropriate, however, as it is clear from the *Nibelungenlied* manuscripts that Kriemhild led a miserable existence as Attila's wife because she was neither willing nor capable of forgiving and forgetting. Moreover, the *Chlage*-poet later praises Kriemhild for having remained loyal to Siegfried, a characteristic that could hardly have accorded with her being 'happy' at the court of the Huns.

[4] A reference to Kriemhild's distress at being uprooted is appropriate in this context, as this would tie in with the information imparted to us in the *Nibelungenlied* that, even after Siegfried's murder, she preferred to stay in Worms with her kin rather than journey back to the (familiar) environs of Xanten in the company of her father-in-law.

vvand ir an dem hercen lach.
vvi si verlos ir vͮnne.
[80]   ir aller næhestez chͮnne.

Het ir lieben man benomen.
do vvas ez an di rede chomen.
daz vrovn vten chinde.
allez daz gesinde.
[85]   diente vz hivnen richen.
vnd also vorhtlichen.
sam si vrovn Helchen taten ê.
si het ovch da vrovven me.
danne in ir vater lande.
[90]   der gvten vvigande.
het si vil groze chrapft.
tægeliche ritterschapft.
di ir ovgen sahen.
daz enchvnde niht ver vahen.
[95]   ir vveinten ane lovgen.
alle zit ir ovgen.

Sît do brahte siz dar an.
do si den gevvalt gar gevvan.
daz si ane vnder sprache <.>
[100]   gedaht ir einer rache.
vmbe Sifride ir lieben man.
dem vil vͮbel an gevvan.
ir brvder Gͮnther den lip.
vnd Hagen vnt des chͮneges vvip.
[105]   von dem er doch den tot genam.
dem helde sterben niht gezam.
von deheines recken hant.
vvand er het vvol elliv lant.
mit siner chraft ver cheret.
[110]   da von vvas ir geseret.
beidiv herce vnd ovch [128/417] der mut.
ez duhte si vil selten gut.
svvaz iemen vrevde chvnde pflegen.
si hetes alles sich bevvegen.

[115]   Svvi diche zietvvederr ir hant.
gechrônte kͮnege bi ir vant.
Criemhilt div here.
zehene vnd mære.

for it pained her to the heart how she had been deprived of her life's joy. Her immediate kin had robbed her of her beloved husband. Now the word had spread that all of the warriors in the lands of the Huns owed homage to Lady Ute's daughter and that they were serving her with the same reverence they had previously accorded Helche. Moreover, she had quite a few more ladies-in-waiting than she had had in her father's land. She also had at her disposal many good knights, so that she was able to watch them engage in their knightly sport every day. Yet it was all to no avail, for, quite frankly, her eyes were always filled with tears.

[97] As time passed she managed to acquire enough power to contemplate without anyone gainsaying her the prospect of avenging her dear husband, Siegfried. He had lost his life at the hands of her brother, Gunther, Hagen, as well as Gunther's wife. It was not appropriate for the knight to die by the hand of any [fellow-]warrior, for by virtue of his strength, he had conquered all the lands.[5] Because of this, both her heart and her mind had been wounded. Regardless of whatever happiness one might have enjoyed, she turned her back on all of it.

[115] No matter how often noble Kriemhild found crowned heads of state by her side — whether ten or more —

[5] A very astute comment by the *Chlage*-poet who may condemn Hagen, in particular, for the murder of Siegfried, but who is also very much aware of the problematic nature of the hero of Xanten! This may explain the use of the extremely ambiguous verb "vercheret" in verse 109. While Zeune has rendered this into New High German as 'erobert' (338), the entries in Lexer's *Mittelhochdeutsches Handwörterbuch* (3: 140) do not include a definition that is so unambiguous. Some of those listed include 'umkehren, -wenden, ändern, verwandeln, verdrehen, ins entgegengesetzte (gute oder böse) verändern.'

daz vvas ir allez ein vvint.

[120]   daz Sigemundes chint.
                 het si mit dienst braht dar zv.
                 daz si spat vnd frv.
                 daht an Sigelinde.
                 vvi sie mit ir chinde.

[125]   het vrevde vnd vŷnne.
                 ezen chvnde ir beider chŷnne.
                 den vvillen ni ervvenden.
                 sine hete mit ir henden.
                 ob si mohte sin ein man.

[130]   ir schaden als ich mich verstan.
                 errochen manege stunde.
                 geschehen ez nine chvnde.
                 vvande si hete vrovven lip.

Ez hete daz iamerhafte vvip.

[135]   den vvillen in ir mvte.
                 daz en chom in niht ce gvte.
                 von den si den schaden nam.
                 vvand ez ir rechen gezam.

Des ensol si niemen schelten.

[140]   sold er des engelten.
                 der trivve chvnde pflegen.
                 der hete schiere sich bevvegen.
                 daz er mit rehten dingen.
                 mŏhte niht vvol bringen.

[145]   deheinen getrivlichen mvt.
                 trivve div ist dar zv gut.
                 div machet vverden mannes lip.
                 vnd eret ovh also schoniv vvip.
                 daz ir zvht noch ir mvt.

[150]   nach schanden nimmer niht getvt.

Also vrovn Criemhilde geschach.
                 der von schulden nie gesprach.
                 misseliche dechein man.
                 svver diz mære merchen chan.

[155]   der sagt vnschuldich gar ir lip.
                 vvan daz diz uil edel vverde vvip.
                 tæte nach trivve<.>
                 ir rache in grozzer rivve.

it was of no consequence whatsoever to her. Through the [loyal] service he had shown her, Siegmund's son had brought her to a point where day and night she could only think of Sieglinde and the joy and pleasure she had had with her child [i.e., Siegfried]. None of her relatives on either side could make her waver in her resolve to avenge with her own hands the injury done her, as she would have done on many an occasion, as I understand it, had she been a man. But this could never occur because she was, after all, a woman.

[134] The wretched lady was nonetheless determined to do it and this did not turn out well for those who had inflicted the injury upon her; for it was fitting that she should seek revenge.

[139] No one should reproach her on this account. Were one to be punished for having demonstrated true loyalty, one would soon desist from exhibiting a sense of loyalty through honorable actions. Loyalty is important because it constitutes the essence of a worthy man. It also does honor to a beautiful woman so that neither her bearing nor her intentions will ever give her cause to be ashamed.

[151] This was the case with Lady Kriemhild, and no man was ever justified in speaking badly of her. Anyone capable of understanding this tale will proclaim her completely free of any guilt, for this most noble woman acted out of loyalty when, in a state of terrible grief, she exacted her revenge.

                  Iv ist daz diche vvol gesagt.

[160]   vvi Ecel hete beiagt.

                  fŭrsten lobliche <.>

                  heim in siniv riche.

                  dvrch eine grozze vvirtschapft.

                  daz er mit siner helde chrapft.

[165]   vvolde zeigen sinen pris.

                  do vvas vrov Criemhilt so vvis.

                  daz siz also vie.

                  daz si der deheinen beliben lie.

                  di si da gerne sæhe.

[170]   vvenne daz geschæhe.

                  oder vvi uil der vvile vvære.

                  iane vveiz ich niht der mære.

                  oder vvi si chomen in daz lant. /

                  di da hete besant.

[175]   Ecel der vil riche.

                  so rehte herliche.

                  chomen di herren ŭber Rin.

                  daz mŭst in grozer schaden sin.

                  an mannen vnd an magen.

[180]   des endorfte niht betragen.

                  Criemhilt di richen.

                  daz si so loblichen.

                  zen hivnen chomen vvaren.

                  da uon do gebaren.

[185]   nach vrevden sold ir der mvt.

                  So vvol gezogen helt gvt.

                  man so manegen nie bevant.

                  als vz Bvrgonden lant.

                  her gefŭret Gŭnther.

[190]   vnd ovch sin brvder Giselher.

                  vnd ovch der herre Gernot.

                  daz Criemhilde golt rot.

                  heten si ce Rine lazen.

                  div vvile si ver vvazen.

[195]   daz sis ie gevvunnen chŭnde.

                  ich vvæne si ir alten sŭnde.

                  engvlten vnd niht mere.

[159] You have often been told how Attila, by means of a marvelous festival, had been able to persuade praiseworthy nobles[6] to join him in his kingdom. He had wished to demonstrate how great his reputation was through the large number of warriors [who served him]. Now, Lady Kriemhild was clever enough to make sure that no one was left at home whom she wished to see. I have no idea when this was supposed to have happened or how many were there at the time. Nor do I know how those whom mighty Attila had summoned[7] journeyed into the country.

[176] With much pomp and circumstance, these lords crossed the Rhine, but this culminated in great injury to both their men and their kinfolk. Mighty Kriemhild could not have been anything but happy over the fact that they had ridden in such a stately manner to the Huns. It was reason enough for her to feel great joy.

[186] One could never have found a group of more refined knights than those whom Gunther, together with his brother, Giselher, and Lord Gernot, brought along from the land of the Burgundians. They had given up to the Rhine Kriemhild's gold. Cursed be the day that they ever laid eyes upon it! I believe they simply paid for their old sin, nothing more.[8]

---

[6] On a first reading, this section (verses 159-175) might be understood to contain references to the fine noblemen whom Attila, through his great generosity, had succeeded in gathering about him (for example, Rüedeger) and that Kriemhild had also been instrumental in making sure that anyone of stature within the Hunnish territories was invited to Attila's court so that his allegiance might be secured. From other versions of the manuscript it is clear, however, that the invitation to the Burgundian warriors is what is intended.

[7] Panzer has maintained that this passage cannot refer to the Burgundians but rather to the envoys sent out by Attila (79). Lexer (1: 213) clearly indicates, however, that one of the meanings of "besenden" is 'holen lassen,' which would certainly accord with the invitation sent to the Burgundians by the Huns in the *Nibelungenlied*.

[8] There is an intriguing difference to be noted between manuscripts B (St. Gall, on which this translation is based), C (Hohenems-Laßberg or Donaueschingen), D (second Munich ms.) and Manuscript A (Hohenems-Munich) with respect to the text of verses 196-197:

B, C, D:	ich wæn si ir alten sünde engulten, und niht mêre.
A:	ich wæn si alter sünde engulten, und niht mêre.

(Karl Lachmann, ed., *Der Nibelunge Noth und Die Klage* [Berlin: G. Reimer, 1878] 308)

With the inclusion of the possessive pronoun "ir" in the first group of manuscripts, the Burgundians are associated directly with the 'old sin,' whatever it may have been (the killing of Siegfried, the theft of the Nibelung treasure from Kriemhild). Manuscript A leaves that

Der vvolgelobte here.
chom vrôliche zv zin gegangen.
[200]   von dem si vvol enpfangen.
vvrden in sinem riche.
der in vil frivntliche.
sinen dienest gehiez.
den in leisten niht vol liez.
[205]   Criemhilt div edel chvnegin.
daz mｖze got gechlagt sin.

Daz si di helde ie gesach.
da von uil leide geschach.
maneger mｖter chinde.
[210]   daz Eceln ingesinde.
sich vreﬂten gegen in sere.
si vvanden daz ir ere.
nv hohe vvære erstanden.
div sider in den landen.
[215]   vil harte iæmerliche lach.
in vvas ir vrteillich tach.
chomen nv ze nahen.
di si da gerne sahen.
daz vvas iedoch ein groziv not.
[220]   daz si von den gelagen tot.

Svvi gerne in gedienet hæte.
vnd ez vil gerne tæte.
Ecel der kｖnech riche.
dem ovch si pilliche.
[225]   dienest solden bringen.
do mｖs in misselingen.
von einen alten shvlden.
ez het vvider ir hvlden.
gevvorben also sere.
[230]   hagen der vbermｖte here.
daz siz lazen niht enchvnde.
sine mｖste bi der stvnde.
rêchen allez daz ir getan vvas.
da von vil vvenich der genas.
[235]   di da vvaffen mohten tragen.
ê hagen eine vvrde erslagen.
ê stvrben vvol vierzech[129/418]tusent man.
svvi gerne in gesheiden het her dan.
Criemhilt div chｖnegin.

[198] The most illustrious Lord [Attila] approached them with a happy demeanor and they were given a hearty welcome to his country. He offered them his service in a most friendly manner, the promise of which, however, noble Queen Kriemhild did not allow him to fulfill.

[206] It should be lamented to God that she ever laid eyes on these warriors then, for many a mother's son was to suffer as a consequence. Attila's followers were extremely happy to see them, for they believed that the visit greatly augmented the esteem in which they were held — an esteem which since that time has greatly diminished throughout all the lands. Their day of judgment was now at hand. It was a terrible thing that they were to be killed by those whom they had rejoiced to see.

[221] No matter how much or how willingly mighty King Attila would have served them — they, too, should rightfully have offered him their services — they were destined to fail because of their former guilt. Hagen, that arrogant fellow,[9] had compromised any chance of friendly relations with her[10] to a point that she could not just let it pass. She had to avenge herself then and there for everything that had happened to her. As a consequence, very few men who bore weapons there survived. Before Hagen himself was finally slain, about forty thousand men had met their deaths. No matter how much Queen Kriemhild might have liked to single him out,

possibility open, of course, but through the omission of "ir" it is also worth considering whether the poet had in mind a more archaic 'sin' associated with the Nordic tradition: the blood of Otter that has stained Fafnir's treasure. See also Zeune's translation, footnote on p. 340. Compare, however, verse 227: "von einen alten shvlden," where the context makes it abundantly clear that the *Burgundians'* earlier transgression is what the poet had in mind.

[9] I have taken some liberty here in translating "hagen der vbermûte here" (verse 230) as 'Hagen, that arrogant fellow.' "Here" is certainly used as a sign of rank, delineating someone who, even if a vassal, was of distinguished stature within the medieval community. Given the *Chlage*-poet's less than affectionate attitude towards Hagen, however, I feel that in this case the appellative "fellow" is not entirely inappropriate.

[10] The reader may be inclined to inquire whether "ir" refers to Kriemhild or to the Huns in general. In a footnote to this verse, Edzardi remarks: "ir *fällt auf, da unmittelbar vorher nicht von Kriemhilt die rede war*" (100). I have interpreted it as a reference to Kriemhild rather than collectively to the Huns, since it is more likely that the *Chlage*-poet will have been impressed by the unrelenting animosity which prevailed in the *Nibelungenlied* between Hagen and Kriemhild than the (albeit undeniable) hostility which evolves between the former and his Hunnish hosts. This reading is supported grammatically by the occurrence of the third person singular in verses 231-233.

[240]   des enchvnd et niht gesin.

                 Do lie siz gen als iz mohte.
                 vvan ir niht anders tohte.
                 daz chom von chranchem sinne.
                 der tot het[er] minne.
[245]   di da sterben solden.
                 di doch vrevde haben vvolden.
                 ob siz geleben chvnden.
                 do het ovch in den stunden.
                 den sich so verre genomen.
[250]   der rat der da vvas bechomen.
                 von Criemhilde mvnde.
                 daz si sich zv der stunde.
                 niht chunde scheiden her dan.
                 da von do Ecel gevvan.
[255]   di aller grôzesten not.
                 di ein kv̂nech ane tot.
                 ie gevvan an sinem libe.
                 daz chom von sinem vvibe.

                 Div enhetes niht also gedaht.
[260]   si het iz gerne dar zv braht.
                 do siz prv̂uen began.
                 daz nivvan der eine man.
                 den lip hete verlorn.
                 so vvære ir svvære vnd ir zorn.
[265]   da mit gar ver svvnden.
                 son vvære ovch zv den stvnden.
                 da niemen arges niht getan.
                 done vvolden in slahen lan.
                 sine herren mit den er dar vvas chomen.
[270]   des vvart in allen samt benomen.
                 daz leben in den ziten.
                 do si begonden striten.
                 den chvnden mit den gesten.
                 den bôsen sam den besten.
[275]   den christen zv den heiden.
                 di lieben von den leiden.
                 den herren sam den knehten.
                 si begonden alle vehten.
                 di verren vnt di nahen.
[280]   do si vor in ligen sahen.
                 ieslicher sinen frivnt tot.

it was simply not possible.

[241] So she just let things take their course because there was nothing else she could do. It all came about because she lacked good sense.[11] Death held dominion there over those doomed to die,[12] men who would have rejoiced had they managed to survive. For this time the plan which Kriemhild had forged had achieved such success that it was impossible for them [the Burgundians] to take their leave.[13] As a consequence, Attila found himself faced with the worst plight that a king had ever personally experienced, short of death. His wife had caused all of this to come about.

[259] But it was not at all what she had intended. When she initially considered the matter, Kriemhild would have preferred to have arranged it so that one man alone would have lost his life. Had that occurred, the sorrow and anger she felt would have disappeared and then no one else would have had to suffer. However, his lords, with whom he had ridden to this place, did not want to turn him over to be slaughtered. As a result, all of them eventually lost their lives when they began to fight: the hosts and their guests, the common along with the best, Christians and heathens, friends and enemies, the lords and the squires. They all engaged in combat, those from near and far away, as each man saw his friend lying dead before him.

[11] This may be an understatement. We are possibly dealing with a medieval equivalent of 'out of her mind' [i.e., with grief, hatred, frustration]. It is intriguing to compare here the text of verse 243 in Manuscript B ("daz chom von chranchem sinne") with that of the same verse in Manuscript A: "daz kom von Krimhilt sinne" (after Lachmann). I suspect that the original *Chlage*-manuscript had "krankem" and that other scribes could not do anything with this *interpretation* of Kriemhild's motivations for allowing the mass slaughter to occur. See my article, "Animus Possession in Kriemhild: A Medieval Insanity Plea?" in the *Journal of Evolutionary Psychology* 11 (1990) (Nos. 1/2): 22-33.

[12] Or perhaps in the sense of a 'toast to the dead' as offered by Hagen in the *Nibelungenlied* (1960,3) immediately prior to his decapitating of Ortlieb. If that is, in fact, the case, verses 244-245 might be translated as: 'Death offered a final toast to those who were to die....' My thanks to Werner Hoffmann for this suggestion.

[13] Verses 248-253 pose something of a challenge for the translator. They appear to offer an explanation for the inability, or unwillingness, of the Burgundians to leave the Hunnish court. Kriemhild's "rat" could refer on the surface to the words of advice she has given in the *Nibelungenlied* to Attila (namely, to invite the Burgundians to Hungary) and/or possibly to the challenge she has posed for her kinsmen through her taunts. In any event, the "rat" has been so successful that it has made it impossible for the Burgundians to leave Attila's camp and the verses that follow make it abundantly clear what dire consequences this fact has for the Hunnish leader. "Sich scheiden" might also be interpreted in the sense that the Burgundians and Huns could not be kept apart.

diz vvas doch allez an not.
man moht ez liht ervvendet han.
der Eceln hete chvnt getan.
[285] von erste div rehten mære.
so het er di starchen svvære.
harte lihtechlich er vvant.
di von Bvrgonden lant.
liezenz dvrch ir ꝸbermvt.
[290] do het ovch Criemhilt behut.
mit listechlichem sinne.
daz ers niht vvart inne.
des vvart im do der schade bechant.
den er sit nimmer mer ꝸbervvant.

[295] Diz hiez man allez schriben.
vnd vvaz ir von den vviben.
vꝸrde da gescheiden.
vnd vvi in begonde / leiden.
vor iamer daz leben allen.
[300] ia mvsen si der gallen.
vnd ovch ir hercen volgen.
si vurden starch erbolgen.
dē stolzen ʀinfranchen.
als ob si in solde danchen.

[305] Ecel der kꝸnech mære.
ob ez sin vville vvære.
do vvas dem chꝸnge leit.
ez vvas in allen bereit.
vf einen veichlichen tach.
[310] svvi vvol ir der vvirt pflach.
daz enchvnde niht ver vahen.
di in da sazen nahen.
vnd vrꝼliche bi in giengen.
vnd si ê vvol enpfiengen.
[315] di lage<n> sider mit in tot.
daz vvas ein not vor aller not.

Fꝸʀ vvunder sol manz immer sagen.
daz so vil helde vvart erslagen.
von eines vvibes zorne.
[320] di recken vz erchorne.
die ie vvaren vil vverlich.
di der herre Dietrich.

All of this, however, was quite unnecessary and might readily have been avoided. If someone had told Attila from the outset how things really stood, he could very easily have prevented this terrible tragedy. But their haughtiness kept the men of Burgundy from telling him. Moreover, cunning Kriemhild had also taken care that he did not find out. Thus Attila came to suffer the losses from which he never recovered.

[295] Directions were given to have all of this written down, how many died there[14] and how, as a result of their bitter plight, life itself became detestable to them. Necessity dictated that they follow bitter fate and their hearts. They [the Huns] became terribly angry at these proud Franks from the Rhine[15] — as if the renowned Attila, had he been so inclined, were supposed to thank them.

[307] The king himself was sorry about how matters stood.[16] A day of doom awaited them. No matter how well their host treated them, it was all to no avail. Men who had sat next to them and had walked cheerfully among them and who had previously extended to them such a hearty greeting later lay dead alongside them. This was the calamity of all calamities.

[317] It should always be considered a marvel that so many warriors were killed as the result of one woman's anger. Six hundred handpicked men, who had always shown great courage and whom Lord Dietrich,

[14] The Bartsch edition has deviated here from the manuscript which has "vviben" instead of "liben" in verse 296. This emendation certainly fits the context. On the other hand, it is worth considering whether the poet did not, in fact, intend "vviben" in verse 296, the sense being that directions were given to record just how many men were separated there forever (i.e., through death) from their spouses, thus causing all of the latter to experience such misery in their lives.

[15] The manuscript contains a marginal note after verse 303: "Rinfranchen," perhaps for emphasis or clarification. Given the frequency with which place and personal names are underlined in the manuscript, such information was clearly considered of particular importance to a later reader of the text (Aegidius Tschudi?).

[16] Verses 302-307 have been interpreted very differently by Zeune, although the texts in both Manuscript A and Manuscript B are virtually identical. His translation reads as follows: "... und die stolzen Reinfranken wurden sehr erboßt, als ob sie es Etzeln verdankten, und es sein Wille wäre, und doch war es dem König leid" (342). Contextually, this does make good sense, yet the grammar poses something of a problem. "Dē stolzen Rinfranchen" is clearly in the dative case and stands as an indirect object with respect to the pronoun "si" in verse 302. That "si" could only refer to the Huns. "Ecel der kṽnec mære" is the subject of the following sentence and the "in" of verse 304 can only be a reference to the Burgundians. The Huns have, of course, sufficient reason to be furious with the Burgundians after the death of Ortlieb and thousands of their kinsmen.

mit im braht in daz lant.

vn<d> der chŷne Hildebrant.

[325]   der stvrben sehs hundert da.

svvi herliche si andersvva.

in volkes sturmen herten.

sich dicke vvol ervverten.

beide dise vnde die.

[330]   des genuzen si vil lŷcel hie.

da verlos der herre Blôdelin.

der hô<h>sten vnt der besten sin.

drizech hundert siner man.

er viengez boslichen an.

[335]   dvrh eines vvibes sere

sinen lip vnd al sin ere.

in den trivven vvart verlorn.

div im ce vrovven vvas gesvvorn.

der dient er nach ir hulde.

[340]   also daz er der schulde.

alerste mvst vvesen pfant.

vvan di von Bvrgonden lant.

sich vverten also sere.

daz mans in <g>iht fŷr ere.

[345]   Der herzoge herman.

ein fŷrste vzer Pôlan.

vnd Sigeher von Vvalâchen.

uil vvillechliche rachen.

der edeln Criemhilde leit.

[350]   zvvei tvsent ritter gemeit.

si brahten zv der vvirtschapft.

di von der edeln geste chrapft.

sit alle vvurden ver svvant.

der her dvrch Criechisshiv lant.

[355]   braht vz Tŷrkye.

Vvalber der edel vrie.

zvvelf hundert siner man.

di mvsen alle da bestan.

Svvaz ir von Criechen vvas bechomen.

[360]   vnd svvaz di heten ^{da} genomen.

des [130/419] Criemhilde goldes.

vnd Ecelen soldes.

den dienten si vil svvinde.

von ir vil maneges chinde.

together with brave Hildebrand, had led into this country, died there. However magnificent an account the men from the one group or the other had frequently given of themselves elsewhere in tough battles, they enjoyed none of that success here. Lord Blödelin lost three thousand of his most valiant and renowned men. Motivated by the suffering of one woman,[17] he unleashed the hostilities in a most malicious way. He lost both his life and his honor through his allegiance [to Kriemhild]. He served the woman who had been pledged to him in order to gain her favor.[18] Consequently, he was the first one who had to pay the price for the transgression, since the Burgundians put up such a stalwart defense, that one is obliged to accord them all due honor.

[345] Duke Herman, a nobleman from Poland, and Sigeher of Wallachia, were more than willing to avenge the sorrow that had been caused noble Kriemhild. They had brought along with them to the festival two thousand brave knights. All of them were later to die, thanks to the strength of the noble guests. The noble freeman Walber had led twelve hundred of his men from Turkey, passing [on the way] through the land of the Greeks. Not one of them ever left that place [i.e., Attila's camp] alive.

[359] Whoever had joined her from the Greeks and however much of Kriemhild's gold and Attila's pay they had accepted, the service they provided them was fraught with danger. Many of their children

---

[17] The Bartsch edition contains "lêre" instead of the manuscript's "sere" in verse 335. If one concurs with this emendation, the sense is more that Blödelin started the debacle "on the orders of a certain woman." It should be noted, however, that the version contained within manuscript B makes perfectly good sense in the present context: Blödelin was indeed motivated by the suffering of his queen as well as the rewards she promised him for his service.

[18] Although at first glance it might appear that the "vrovven" referred to in verse 338 is Kriemhild, the phrase "ce vvrovven ... gesvvorn" would more likely be an allusion to "Nuodunges wîp" (Nibelungenlied, strophe 1906,3) who, among other things, has been "pledged" to Blödelin by Kriemhild in return for his services in dealing with the Burgundians.

[365]   vvart sît gevveinet sere.
             si vvanden vverben ere.
             vnd vvrben niht vvan den tot.
             div vil shedlichiv not.
             het den sich an in genomen.
[370]   di vf genade vvaren chomen.
             Eceln dem richen.
             di dienten angestlichen.

             Der vvil ich iv nennen dri.
             daz elliv lant des vvaren vri.
[375]   daz iht chv́ners dar inne vvære.
             danne Irnfrit der mære.
             vnd havvart vnd Irinch.
             den recken vvaren iriv dinch.
             von grozen schvlden han ich ver nomen.
[380]   daz si in des riches æhte vvaren chomen.

             Doch vvart des diche sit gedaht.
             daz ^{man} si gerne hete braht.
             von Rome zv des cheisers hulden.
             doch belibens in den schvlden.
[385]   vnz an ir libes ende.
             si het mit gebender hende.
             Ecel vil vvol braht dar zv.
             daz si nv spate vnde frv.
             taten svvaz er vvolde.
[390]   do man nv rechen solde.
             der schônen Criemhilde leit.
             des vvaren si vvillech vnde bereit.

             Man sagt als ich han vernomen.
             von vvannen si dar vvaren chomn.
[395]   Irnfrit der helt vz erchant.
             der het gervmet Dv́rengen lant.
             da er ê lantgrave hiez.
             do in der Cheiser da verstiez.
             Havvart der helt starche.
[400]   vvas vogt in Tenemarche.
             Irinch der degen vzerchorn.
             vvaz von Lvtringe erborn.
             er vvas ein starch chv́ne man.
             mit grozzer gabe im an gevvan.
[405]   havvart daz er vvart sin man.

later on had cause to cry their hearts out. They thought that they were acquiring honor, but in fact they reaped a harvest of death. A great catastrophe was visited upon these men who had come to mighty Attila in the belief that they would prosper, for the service they provided brought them into dire straits.

[373] I would like to tell you the names of three men of whom it may be said that in all of the free lands there were none braver: the renowned Irnfrid, as well as Hawart and Iring. I have heard that the fortunes of these warriors had, as a result of grave transgressions they had committed, taken such a turn that they had been declared outlaws.[19]

[381] But people did think afterwards that it would have been good had they been reconciled with the Roman Emperor.[20] However, they remained outlaws for the rest of their lives. Through his generosity, Attila had easily brought them to a point where they were always ready to do his bidding. When it came time to avenge the sorrow of beautiful Kriemhild, they were willing and ready to do so.

[393] Here is what I heard others say about their origins. The famous warrior Irnfrid had quit the land of Thuringia where he had previously been an earl. Until the Emperor threw him out, mighty Hawart had been ruler of Denmark. The illustrious Iring, a strong, brave fellow, was a native of Lorraine. By offering him fine gifts, Hawart persuaded him to become his liegeman.

[19] It *may* be that the prepositional phrase, "von grozen schvlden," in verse 379 should be interpreted more tangibly as 'on account of their great debts.' I have opted for the more idiomatic sense (the idea being that the warriors in question had on their conscience some severe transgressions against the order of the Reich) because I suspect that the "riches æhte" would more likely have been imposed upon them for defying the Emperor than for having fallen into debt. On the surface, Zeune's translation may appear to be quite neutral: "Die Recken waren durch ihre Schuld in des Reiches Acht gekommen" (343), but I believe that, given his use of the singular form of "Schuld," he, too, was thinking more in terms of acts of defiance on the part of the three heroes than of mercantile indiscretions or tax evasion.

[20] The reference to "von Rome" (verse 383) is to be understood as a prepositional attribute to "cheiser," and does not imply any sense of movement on the part of the heroes mentioned.

Div Chlage

sus ist daz mære vns chomn an.
Si heten vz gesundert <.>
driv vnt drizech hundert.
si brahten mit in in daz lant.
[410]   der vvart von Volkeres hant.
so maneger in dem stvrme erslagen.
daz manz immer vvol mach sagen.

Ovch slvch der helt mære.
der spæhe videlære.
[415]   Irinfride den richen.
in stvrme herlichen.
do slvch von Tronege der helt.
den chv̓nen vnt den vz ervvelt. /
uon Lvthringe Iringen.
[420]   der het des gedingen.
daz iemen chv̓ner. solte leben.
doch het im vollen lon gegeben.
den er da vvolde slahen tot.
Hagene der sit in der not.
[425]   bestvnt vnz hin cem lesten.
bi den vverden gesten.
Havvarten den slvch danchvvart.
des ellen selten vvas gespart.
in deheiner slahte not.
[430]   mich vvndert des daz in der tot.
ie getorste bestan.
vvand er hete da getan.
daz man daz sagt ce mære.
ob ez zvvelven vvære.
[435]   also chv̓nen geschehen.
daz mans fv̓r vvnder mohte iehen.

Von svvannen si dar vvaren chomen.
svva man si het genomen.
mit botsheften in den landen.
[440]   zer Bvrgonden handen.
vvaren si alle geborn.
des livtes vvart so vil verlorn.
von der Gernotes hant.
daz ^{man} dvrh drizech kv̓nege lant.
[445]   gevriesh vvol div mære.
vvelch sin ellen vvære.
der slvch ovch Rv̓degere.

That is the way the story has been passed down to us. They had selected 3,300 men and brought them along to the land of Attila. So many among them were cut down by Volker's hand in the [subsequent] battle that people will be talking about it for a long time to come.

[413] This renowned warrior and marvelous minstrel also struck down powerful Irnfrid in fierce combat. The knight of Troneck killed the courageous and distinguished Iring of Lorraine, who had believed that there was no one alive who could be braver. But the man whom he had wished to strike dead, namely Hagen, paid him in full, and remained there in battle together with the [other] worthy guests to the end. Hawart was slain by Dancwart,[21] whose courage was never found wanting in any sort of peril. I am amazed that death ever got the better of him. For it was said that he gave such an account of himself there that, had twelve brave warriors performed these feats, it would have been nothing short of miraculous.

[437] It did not matter from where they had ridden nor from what lands they had journeyed after having been summoned by messengers, they were all delivered into the hands of the Burgundians. So many of these men were cut down by Gernot's hand that his bravery became known far and wide throughout thirty kingdoms. He also felled the noble Margrave Rüedeger

---

[21] See, however, strophe 2073 of Manuscript B of the *Nibelungenlied*, from which it is quite clear that it is Hagen who kills Hawart.

den margraven here.
da si in stvrme vvaren.
[450] da sach man so gebaren.
Rv̈degere den richen.
daz er vil lobelichen.
den starchen Gernoten slvch.
ir starp da beidenthalp genvch.
[455] ir beider mage vnd man.
fvnfhundert ritter vvol getan.
brahte mit im Rv̈deger.
der lebt deheiner langer mer.
fv̈r daz si in den stvrm gesprvngen.
[460] svvi dicke in vvas gelvngen.
bi Ecele dem Richen.
di slvgen gevvaltechlichen.
di von Bvrgonden lant.
so daz div stæheliniv bant.
[465] dræten von den svverten.
di si da betvvingen gerten.
di vverten sich vil sere.
Giselher der here.
den heizen blvtegen bach.
[470] vngerne er vliezende sach.
in den selben stvnden.
von Rv̈dgeres vvnden.

Svvaz des schaden fvnden vvart.
den si von der hove vart.
[475] cen hivnen genamen.
di ce Eceln qvamen.
daz vvas not vber not.
daz den Giselheres tot.
niemen chonde ervvenden.
[480] der mit rate noch mit henden.
nie [131/420] deheine schult gevvan.
an Sifrid Criemhilde man.
man chlagt ovch Gernoten.
den si da sahen toten.
[485] von der Rv̈dgeres hant.
der helt vz Bvrgonden lant.
da vil iamerliche lach.
der mit eren manegen tach.
het gelebt vnz an di stunde.
[490] got im niht engvnde.

when they met in combat. Brave Rüedeger was also seen to have given a good account of himself, for he, in turn, slew the valiant Gernot. Many men and kinfolk on both sides met their end there. Rüedeger had brought along five hundred splendid knights; not a single one of them is alive today — after having become involved in the fray — however often they may have [previously] enjoyed success in the service of mighty Attila. They dealt the Burgundians powerful blows so that the steel clasps of their swords were loosened. The men whom they wished to subdue defended themselves valiantly. Lord Giselher was distressed to witness at this time the streams of hot blood flowing from Rüedeger's wounds.

[473] Of all the losses sustained as a result of the trip they had made to Attila and the court of the Huns, nothing was worse than the fact that no one was able to prevent the death of Giselher. Neither in word nor deed had he ever been guilty of doing any harm to Siegfried, Kriemhild's husband. Tears were also shed for Gernot, who was seen lying there dead, slain by the hand of Rüedeger. This Burgundian warrior lay there in a pitiful state, a man who, up until then, had lived all of his days in great honor. God did not allow him

beliben in der schulde.
siner svvester hvlde.
chonde Gѷnther niht ervverben.
ia riet er daz ersterben.
[495]   Sifrit mvse ir erster man.
da von er den haz gevvan.
sît von ir deste vaster.
beide schaden vnd laster.
vvrden beidiv da genomen.
[500]   ez vvas ovch leider dar zv chomen.
daz ir chint vvas erslagen.
daz en vvolden niht vertragen.
di ez da rechen solden.
vnd ovch dienen vvolden.
[505]   Eceln dem richen.
daz geschach vil leidechlichen.

Wie mohte man des getrѷven.
daz Criemhilde der vrovven.
selber sterben da geschach.
[510]   daz leit vnd daz vngemach.
het geprѷuet ir selber munt.
nv vvart ir sterben mit in chvnt.
di gerne vværen noch genesen.
des enmoht leider niht vvesen.
[515]   daᶻ si langer leben solden.
di da rachen vnde vvolden.
ir selbes libe vogt vvesen.
der enchunde einer niht genesen.

Svvaz man iamers ê da vant.
[520]   do der alte Hildebrant.
dvrch sins grimmen hercen zorn.
slvch di vrovven vvol geborn.
ê iz Ecel der kѷnech sach.
do hvp sich erst vngemach.
[525]   vnder aller der diete.
dem iamer vvart ce miete.
sin hohester stul gesetzet.
an vrevden vvart gelezet.
da vil maneger vrovven lip.
[530]   ez vvære maget oder vvip.
den mvse ir vѷnne entvvichen.
Eceln den chѷnech richen.

to go on living in guilt. Gunther was unable to regain the favor of his sister. After all, he had plotted the death of Siegfried, her first husband. He subsequently suffered all the more at her hands. Injury and shame were both acquired there. It unfortunately also came about that her child was killed. This was an act which those who were obliged to seek revenge and who also wished to serve mighty Attila were not about to tolerate. All of this transpired in such a miserable fashion.

[507] How could one believe that Lady Kriemhild herself was also to meet her death there? The words from her own mouth had given rise to the sorrow and misery. Now it also became her lot to die along with those who would have gladly survived [the debacle]. Unfortunately, however, it is impossible for those who seek revenge and simultaneously wish to be master of their own fate to go on living. Not one of them was able to survive.

[519] Whatever misery might have previously been witnessed there, real agony was not perceived by the people until King Attila watched[22] old Hildebrand, motivated by the deep rage he felt in his heart, kill the noble lady. Despair then reached its highest point and many a woman was robbed of all her joy. Whether young maidens or women, all of them were bereft of happiness. Mighty King Attila

[22] This version, to be found in Bartsch's edition, accords with the information we have in the *Nibelungenlied* regarding Attila's presence during the final scenes of that epic. From strophes 2373-2374 of Manuscript B we know that he witnessed Kriemhild's decapitation of Hagen and that he was terribly dismayed by it. He must have immediately observed Hildebrand's killing of Kriemhild. Manuscript B of the *Chlage* clearly has "ê iz" in verse 523, however, indicating that Attila was ostensibly not present when his wife was killed. Perhaps the poet intended to put some distance between Attila and the demise of his wife because he could not conceive of a husband observing such a scene and remaining passive, even acquiescing in the actions of Hildebrand. The *Chlage*-poet has, after all, provided a rather enthusiastic defense of Kriemhild in his work.

sah man vil iamerliche stan.
ez vvas nv allez daz getan.
[535]   daz da ce tᵛnne vvas.
sit daz ir einer niht genas.
di da vvaffen torsten tragen.
di lagen alle da erslagen.
vnd tot gevallen in daz plut.
[540]   des vvas besvvært in der mvt.
di mit vrevden vvanden / leben.
di svvære het in got gegeben.
vvande man anders da niht pflach.
beidiv naht vnd tach.
[545]   nivvan vveinens vnd chlagen.
man sol vndanch der vvile sagen.
in der div vvile geschæhe.
vnt daz Criemhilt ie gesæhe.
des edelen Sifrides lip.
[550]   da von vil manech schᵒne vvip.
von liebe vvart gescheiden.
ez vvart den namen beiden.
heiden vnd Christen.
von ir einer listen.
[555]   also leide getan.
daz beidiv vvip vnd man.
gelovben vvil der mære.
daz si der helle svvære.
habe von solhen schulden.
[560]   daz si gein gotes hulden.
gevvorbn habe so verre.
daz got vnser herre.
ir sele niht en vvolde.
der daz bevværn solde.
[565]   der mvse zv der helle varn.
daz hiez aber ich vil vvol bevvarn.
daz ich nach dem mære.
cer helle der bote vvære.

Des bᵛches meister sprach daz ê.
[570]   dem getrivven tut vntrivve vve.
sît si dvrch trivve tot gelach.
in gotes hulden manegen tach.
sol si ce himele noch geleben.
got hat vns allen daz gegeben.
[575]   svves lip mit trivven ende nimt.

could be seen standing there in his grief. Everything had been done that needed to be done, as no one who had been capable of bearing weapons had survived. All of them lay there dead where they had fallen in the blood. That is why those who had fancied themselves living in joy were downcast. God had inflicted upon them this terrible grief, for both night and day they were given to nothing but weeping and lamenting. One should curse the time in which all of this misery came to pass and that Kriemhild ever laid eyes upon noble Siegfried. Many a lovely lady was to be robbed of her happiness as a result. Renowned warriors among both the heathens and the Christians were caused such suffering as a result of the machinations of one woman that men and women alike are inclined to believe the suggestion that she will suffer the pains of hell for her sins. Moreover, [they also believe] that she had fallen so far from God's grace that our Lord God would not want her soul. Anyone wishing to verify this would have to go to hell to do so. For my part, however, I would certainly decline to be the messenger who goes to hell to obtain this information.[23]

[569] It was once said by the master of the book: the loyal person is dismayed by betrayal. Since Kriemhild died on account of her loyalty, she will yet find God's favor forever in heaven. There is one thing which God has promised all of us: whosoever should end his life in loyalty

---

[23] This is a particularly difficult section of the *Chlage* to decipher and I am most grateful to Werner Hoffmann for an explanation which readily fits the context.

daz der cem himelriche zimt.
div vvarheit vns daz chûndet.
vor got er sich versûndet.
svver dem ander dvrch haz.
[580]   verteilet vvi mag er daz.
vvizzen vvaz got mit im getvt.
niemen dvnche sich so gvt.
vnd so gar von svnden vri.
ern bedûrfe daz im got si.
[585]   genædech an der lesten zit.
so man vns allen lon git.

Daz hus daz lach gevallen.
ob den recken allen.
^{di} dvrch striten chomen drin.
[590]   dem vvirte gie si<n> zit hin.
mit leide vnd ovch mit sere.
sin hohez lop vnd ere.
vvarn beide nider chomen.
mit sivften vaste het genomen.
[595]   in des fûrsten hercen.
vil iamerlichen smercen.
an dem ie vil eren lach.
getrûbt vvart sin licht^[er] tach.
vrevde im vvas ce rvnnen.
[600]   ich vvæne in sinem svnnen.
niht mere schinen vvolden.
di vrevden di da solden.
^{im} in sinem hercen vvesen.
[132/421] der mvser ane nv genesen.
[605]   vvand er anders niht ensach.
vvan manegen blûtegen bach.
vliezen vz starchen vvnden.
di im in chvrcen stvnden.
vreude heten benomen.
[610]   vz sinen ovgen vvas im chomen.
vil minnechlichez an sehen.
von des todes schult vvas daz geschehen.
daz er ir lûcel bi im vant.

Er begonde hovbt vnd hant.
[615]   vvinden also sere.
daz ez chûnege nie mere.
vveder sît noch ê geschach.

shall enjoy the kingdom of heaven. The Bible itself has imparted this to us. Any person who damns another out of hatred sins before God. How can he know what God will do with him? No one should consider himself so good and free of sin that he will have no need of God's mercy on the Day of Judgment when we will all receive our just deserts.

[587][24] The Great Hall lay in ruins on top of all the warriors who had entered it to do battle. The host spent his time in sorrow and despair. The high reputation and honor he had enjoyed had vanished. With a deep sigh, terrible pain had taken hold of this nobleman's heart. For a man who had always enjoyed such great honor, he now saw his bright day darken. Happiness had left him, and I believe that the sun was no longer inclined to shine down upon him.[25] He now had to live without the happiness that he should have felt in his heart, for the only thing that he could see were the many rivers of blood flowing from deep wounds which, in a matter of a few hours,[26] had deprived him of all joy. His eyes no longer saw anything that was delightful, for death had left him so few delightful things to observe.

[614] He began to shake his head and wring his hands more than any king before or after him.

---

[24] At this point, Zeune begins the second of five parts of his translation: "II. Wegschaffung der Toden" ('The Removal of the Dead') 347.

[25] The manuscript contains the plural form, "sunnen," in verse 600. This is the one instance of the plural listed by Lexer in his Mittelhochdeutsches Handwörterbuch 2: 1315.

[26] Although the text is essentially the same in Manuscript A, Zeune provides no translation of the prepositional phrase "in chvrcen stvnden" (verse 608).

er hete leit vnd vngemach.
des mohte man vvnder von im sehen.
[620] man mvse Eceln des iehen.
daz also sere gechleit.
vv̊rde mit der vvarheit.
ni me von decheinem man.
vvi lvt er vv̊fen began.
[625] sam man hort eines vvisentes horn.
dem edelen fv̊rsten vvol geborn.
div stimme vz sinem mvnde.
erdoz in der stvnde.
do er so sere chlagte.
[630] daz da von ervvagte.
beide tv̊rne vnd palas.
Svvi lv̊cel vrevden ê da vvas.
ir vvas nv verre deste min.
er hete ver vvandelt den sin.
[635] daz er bi der stunde.
vvizen nine chunde.
ob ez im laster vvære.

Do half im sin svvære.
vil manech richer vveise chlagen.
[640] vvelt ir nv vvnder hôren sagen.
so merchet vmbesheidenheit.
svvaz ie cer vverlt vvart gechleit.
daz vvas allez her ein vvint.
so maneger vverden mvter chint.
[645] chlagen ni begunde.
a(ls)o man da ce stvnde.
bi Ecelen vveinende vant.
maneger ivnchvrovven hant.
mit vvinden vvart ce brochen.
[650] da vvart selten iht gesprochen.
nivvan âch vnd vve.
svvi lvt ie der kv̊nech schre.
di vrovven shrîten allez mite.
ez ist ovh noch der livte site.
[655] svva einem leit ce hercen gat.
daz der ander vrevde bi im lat.
also vvart da vrevde lazen.
daz volch ane mazen.
di chlage ie grôzer macheten.
[660] div lit vil lvte erchrachten.

He felt great sorrow and misery, in fact, he seemed to know nothing else. In all honesty, one would have to say that no one has ever lamented as much as did Attila. How loudly he began to wail! It was as though one were listening to the bellowing of a bison.[27] How the voice of this well-bred nobleman thundered from his mouth! He lamented so loudly that the towers and the palace itself began to shake. If little happiness had previously prevailed there, there was even less [to be enjoyed] now. Attila's frame of mind had changed so much that he could not distinguish at that moment whether he might be bringing dishonor upon himself.

[638] Many a high-bred orphan joined him in his lamentations. If you wish now to hear of some remarkable things, then note this lack of moderation. However much anyone in the world may have previously grieved, it was nothing compared to this. The child of many a worthy mother never mourned in the way men could be found weeping on that occasion in Attila's camp. Many young damsels did injury to their hands by wringing them so much. The only words spoken were "alas, alas." However loudly the king cried out, the women screamed along with him. This is still the custom among people today: whenever a person is pained to the heart, the other abandons his joy. In the same way, happiness was abandoned there. The people intensified their lamentations to the point of excess. The bones of many fine, young ladies' hands cracked loudly

[27] Manuscript B contains a reference to "eines vvisentes horn" in the simile of verse 625. Manuscript A has "ein wisenthorn." Zeune has translated the latter as 'ein Wächterhorn,' that is, 'a watchman's horn.' There are two images here: that of the 'horn' and that of the 'bison.' I believe the poet's use of this particular image was intended to convey the loud, immoderate bellowing that one might associate with such an animal in pain and have consequently retained the allusion to the bison. I have Brian Murdoch to thank for the suggestion that the poet may have been thinking at this point of the shofar, the ram's horn trumpet that brought down the walls of Jericho.

an maneger ivnch vrovven hant.
di man vil sere chlagende vant.

Daz lant volch îlende dů.
lief allez vveinende zů.
[665] do si gehorten / mære.
vvi ez ergangen vvære.
beidiv durch schovven vnd ovch durch chlagen.
sůmeliche chomen dvrch beiagen.
etesliche dvrch frivnde rechen.
[670] slahen vnd stechen.
vvas da deheiner slahte not.
si vvaren ane ir arbeit tot.
di frivnde mit der viende schar.
man gebot dem volche also gar.
[675] daz si sich niht ensůmten.
vnd mit den toten růmten.
eine straze gegen dem sal.
si begonden rvmen ůber al.
von den di man da vze vant.
[680] di div volkers hant.
vnd hagen het ce tode erslagen.
di hiez man von dem hvse tragen.
also verre hin dan.
daz ein ieslicher man.
[685] zv dem sal mohte chomen.
der tot het in da benomen.
also vil ir vůnne.
vvas ir deheines chůnne.
bi dem strite gevvesen.
[690] di noch da vvaren genesen.
di vværn nv gerne mit in tot.
man sach vil manegen rinch rot.
ziehen ab den vvnden.
von in vvart enbvnden.
[695] vil manech důrchel helm vaz.
rot. plůtech. vnd naz.
so vvas allez ir gevvant.
manegen herlichen rant.
sach man bi in vershroten.
[700] di richen vverden toten.
der vvart so vil ᵛᵒⁿ dan getragen.
alle di ez horten sagen.
daz si des michel vvnder nam.

as they stood there in abject grief.

[663] The country folk arrived in haste, all of them weeping as well when they heard what had happened. They had come to see for themselves as well as to lament. Some had come for booty, while others wished to avenge their friends. There was no need, however, for any stabbing or cutting. Their friends, along with the enemy host, were already dead without any help from these people. They were ordered not to tarry, but rather to remove their dead. They began to clear a path toward the Great Hall, removing those whom they found lying outside it, men who had been killed by the hand of Volker or by Hagen. They had them carried far enough away from the Hall so that anyone could approach it. Death had deprived them of so much of their joy. Those of their kinsmen who had been in the battle and who had survived would have preferred to have died with their comrades. They removed many red coats of mail as well as many a pierced helmet visor from those who had been fatally wounded. All of their attire was red, wet with blood. It was also evident that many fine shields had been hacked to pieces. So many mighty and worthy dead warriors were carried out of there that everyone who heard about it wondered

ob iemen vrevden iht gezam.
[705] in allem dem lande.
di gvten vvigande.
vil vvenech mv̊te svvaz man sprach.
vil manech magt von hovbte brach.
mit grozem iamer daz har.
[710] vil maneges trivtinne dar.
vil lvte shriende gie.
div von vvnden enpfie.
daz plv̊t an ir geren.
di armen zv den heren.
[715] vvaren also gelegen.
daz der plv̊tige regen.
si het gemachet alle naz.
svvelch vvip daz versaz.
daz si den vngesvnden.
[720] bevveinten niht ir vvnden.
daz vvas vn vviplicher mvt.
Hildebrant der helt gut.
der horte lvte rv̊ffen.
chrepftechliche vv̊fen.
[725] hort er daz gesinde.
der schônen v̊ten chinde.
lach hi einez vor dem sal.
von des vvnden ce tal.
brach da [133/422] ane lovgen.
[730] vil træhene vz shônen ovgen.
daz vvas div Chv̊neginne.
di mit vnsinne.
het erslagen Hildebrant.
vvand si von Bvrgonden lant.
[735] Hagen ê ze tode slvch.
des man immer genvch.
da von noch ce sagene.
vvi daz chôme daz Hagene.
stv̊rbe von einem vvibe.
[740] vvand er mit sinem libe.
so vil vvnders het getan.
di livte redent sunder vvan.
noch daz ez ein lvge si.
so ist daz der vvarheite bi.
[745] daz in des tvvanch her Dieterich.
daz der helt vil loblich.
in sinen banden gelach.

if it would be appropriate for anyone in the entire country to be happy. These good warriors were not about to be bothered by anything anyone said. In her despair, many a young maiden tore the hair from her head, and the beloved of many a man went about wailing, her clothes stained by the blood of the wounds. Both the low-bred and the high-bred were laid out in such a way that the bloody rain had made them all wet. Any women who neglected to lament the wounds of those who had died there demonstrated unwoman-like behavior. The good warrior Hildebrand could hear the shrill cries of grief and all of the people wailing loudly. The child [daughter] of lovely Ute lay here alone in front of the Hall, and because of her wounds, there gushed forth without a doubt many tears from lovely eyes. It was the queen, whom Hildebrand had senselessly slain[28] because she had earlier killed Hagen of Burgundy. Even today people still have plenty to say as to how it came about that Hagen met his death at the hands of a woman. After all, he had performed such great physical feats. People are still actually suggesting that it is a lie. The truth is that Lord Dietrich subdued him so that this most illustrious hero was placed in fetters by him.

[28] Both Manuscript B and Manuscript A have "mit vnsinne" in verse 732. Zeune interprets this as 'mit Zorn' (349) which certainly fits the context and which may be included within the semantic word field of "vnsinne." (See Lexer, *Mittelhochdeutsches Handwörter-buch* 2: 1937, where one of the definitions of the adjective "unsinnec" is 'rasend.') The more common idea expressed by the noun "vnsinne" (as well as the adjective), however, is that of 'unreasonableness, senselessness, craziness.' One could justifiably argue (as Zeune may well have done) that Hildebrand was 'crazy with anger' (or 'in crazed fury') over the fact that such a marvelous warrior as Hagen had been struck down in his defenseless state by a woman. On the other hand, the *Chlage*-poet is not particularly enthusiastic about Hildebrand's course of action (note verses 750-751), and, given his defense of Kriemhild from the perspective of the loyalty she showed Siegfried, could well have meant that her death was 'senseless.'

da slvch im einen svvertes slach.
mit ir hant des chѵneges vvip.
[750] dvrh daz verlos ovch si den lip.
von Hildebrande ane not.
man chlagt der Chѵneginne tot.
deisvvar von allem rehte.
ritter vnd knehte<.>
[755] di tatenz pilliche.
iamers also riche.
vvrden alle di man vant.
ѵber des kѵnech Eceln lant.

Nu chom der herre Dieterich.
[760] mit einem mvte chlegelich.
da er Criemhilde vant.
er bat di livte ce hant.
daz si dvrch got ir vveinen liezen.
Svvi vil si im des gehiezen.
[765] idoch entaten sis niht.
also groz vvas div geschit.
di si heten gesehen.
vnt div vor in da vvas geshehen.
daz sich da niemen chvnde.
[770] gefrѵn bi der stunde.
Do sprach der her Dietrich.
ia han ich fѵrsten mage rich.
vil gesehen bi minen tagen.
ich gehorte nie gesagen.
[775] von schônerm vvibe.
Ovve daz dinem libe.
der tot so schiere solde chomen.
svvi mir din rat hat benomen.
min aller bestez chѵnne.
[780] Ich mvz mit vn vѵnne.
chlagen dich vnde mich.
deisvvar daz tvn ich.
mit also grozer rivve.
daz ich dich diner trivve.
[785] niht sol lan engelten.
dv hast mir vil selten.
versagt des ich dich ie gebat.
Nv ist ez chomen an di stat.
daz ich ez Vrovve Dienen sol.
[790] da mit vvirt mir nimmer vvol.

Then the king's wife killed him with a swordblow, as a consequence of which she, too, needlessly lost her life at the hands of Hildebrand. The death of the queen is certainly lamented with complete justification by both knights and squires, and throughout all of Attila's land everyone was in a state of great despair.

[759] Then Lord Dietrich, who was completely downcast, approached the spot where Kriemhild's body lay. He immediately asked everyone for God's sake to stop their lamenting. However much they promised him that they would cease, they could not do so. So incredible were the events that they had seen transpire there, which had unfolded before them, that no one could find any joy at that time. Then Lord Dietrich spoke: "In my day I have seen the daughters[29] of many powerful noblemen, and I have never heard tell of a more beautiful woman. Alas, that death should be visited so swiftly upon your person. However true it is that your scheming[30] has robbed me of my best kin, I must, with great sorrow, grieve for you as well as for myself. In truth, it is with deep regret that I cannot properly reward you for your loyalty. You never denied me a thing that I requested of you.[31] Now it has come about that I, dear Lady, should repay the service. I will never be happy,

[29] Verse 772 in both Manuscript B and Manuscript A contains the word "mage" while Manuscript C has "tohter" in its stead. Zeune has translated the expression "fûrsten mage" as 'Fürstentöchter' clearly identifying the 'mage' in A with the female progeny of the noblemen. Within the present context, his rendering does make a good deal of sense and I have followed it.

[30] Under "rat" in verse 778, I understand everything that Kriemhild has said to others in a successful bid to have them take up arms in the struggle against the Burgundians. It might also be rendered into English as 'plotting' in analogy to "riet" with reference to Gunther in verse 494.

[31] The tone of Dietrich's words to the dead Kriemhild stands in marked contrast to the manner in which he had addressed her in the *Nibelungenlied*, specifically in 1748,4a of Manuscript B when he used the appellative "vâlandinne" ('she-devil') to describe her.

svvaz ich es nach dinem tode tꝰ.
do greif der ellenthafte zv.
vnd hiez si schiere / baren.
di livte di da vvaren.

[795] Do man si geleite vf den re.
der fꝟrste het ir hovbt ê.
zv dem libe getragen.
do horte man Hildebrande chlagen.
der si slvch mit siner hant.
[800] do chom vz der hivnen lant.
Ecel der iamersriche.
dem iamer vvol geliche.
vnd als iz im do tohte.
niemen vor iamer mohte.
[805] gelazen ern hvlfe im chlagen.
vndanch begonde er sagen.
sinem grozen vnheile.
vvande im vvas ce teile.
nv vvorden vngelꝟches hort.
[810] diu ie vnvalschiv vvort.
hete bi ir libe.
sinem vverden vvibe.
viel er an di brvste.
ir vvîze hende er chvste.
[815] vil snellechliche er chlagete.
allererst dem chꝟnege sagete.
Dieterich div rehten mære.

Ovve miner svvære.
sprach Ecel der vil vvol geborn.
[820] vvi han ich arman verlorn.
beide min chint vnd min vvip.
darzv manegen vverden lip.
vz minem hohem chꝟnne.
vnde miner ovgen vꝟnne.
[825] an minen chȏn magen.
di grozzer eren pflagen.
di vvile daz si mohten leben.
vvi pin ich mꝟdinch <ge>gegeben.
in alsvs groze rivve.
[830] het ich di ganzen trivve.
an ir vil vverdem libe erchant.
ich het mit ir elliv lant.

whatever I might do after your death." The strong warrior then picked her up and ordered the people who were gathered there to place her body on a bier.

[795] Before Kriemhild was placed upon the bier, the earl [Dietrich] had laid her head down next to her corpse. Hildebrand, the man by whose hand she had been cut down, could be heard lamenting. Then Attila from the land of the Huns arrived, a man filled with misery, the epitome of despair, as one might have expected of him there. There was no one who, in this miserable state, could refrain from joining him in his grieving. He began to curse his terrible misfortune, for he had certainly been plagued by the greatest catastrophe. He fell upon the breast of his worthy spouse, who, throughout her life, had never spoken a false word. He kissed her white hands and grieved terribly.[32] Then Dietrich told the king about the actual course of events.

[818] "Alas for all my troubles," spoke noble Attila. "How is it that, poor man that I am, I have lost both my child and my wife? And, in addition to them, many a worthy man of my noble lineage, and the delightful sight of my in-laws, who enjoyed such high esteem as long as they were alive. Pitiful wretch that I am, how have I ever come to know such great suffering? Had I recognized the extent of my worthy wife's sense of loyalty, I would have forsaken with her all of my lands

---

[32] We note that the manuscript actually has the adverb "snellechliche" in contrast to "seneliche" to be found in the Bartsch edition. The emendation appears to be quite appropriate in the present context. Attila has already been lamenting and it does not make much sense to claim here that he "suddenly" began to grieve.

gervmet ê ich si het verlorn.
getrivver vvip vvart ni geborn.

[835]   von dehein[er] m✴ter mere.
Ovve fvrsten <h>ere.
G✴nther vnt di brvder din.
vnd di hohen recken min.
min br✴der vnd mine mâge.

[840]   di mit des todes lâge.
vvnderliche sint beslagen.
vvi chvnd ich immer verchlagen.
di vil gvten vvigande.
di ich von manegem lande.

[845]   zv miner hohzit her gevvan.
dar zv alle mine man.
der ich niht chan bescheiden.
vnder christen vnd vnder heiden.
von den min ere ie vaste steich.

[850]   nach der chlage er nider seich.
als ob er vvære entslaffen.
dar vmb begonde in straffen.
von Berne her Dieterich.
er sprach ir [134/423] tvt dem vngelich.

[855]   daz ir sît ein vvise man.
daz ivch niht vervahen chan.
daz lat daz ist min lere.

Nv ensvmet ivch niht mere.
sprach der degen gvter.

[860]   tragt zv siner mvter.
ivver vvenigez chindelin.
di boten giengen do dar in.
da si Ortlieben fvnden.
mit einer starchen vvnden.

[865]   in dem blvte ligen hovbtelos.
Ovve vvaz Ecel verlos.
an im der grozzen ere.
ez gevvinnet nimmer mere.
nehein k✴nech sôlhe not.

[870]   an den Blôdelines tot.
der vvirt ovh do gedahte.
er schvf daz man in brahte.
tot zv disen beiden.
svvi si vværen heiden.

[875]   doch vvas ce barmen vmbe sie.

before I would have lost her. Never was a more loyal woman born from a mother's womb. Alas, you noble warriors! Gunther and his[33] brothers, as well as my esteemed warriors, my brother and my kinfolk, have, to our great surprise, been struck down and met their death. How could I ever grieve enough for the many illustrious knights whom I invited from so many lands to come to my festival? To say nothing of my own men, were they Christians or heathens, through whom my honor was steadily increased." Following his lamentation, he sank down as though he had fallen asleep. For this he was admonished by Dietrich von Bern who said: "You are not at all acting like a wise man. My advice is: do not concern yourself with those things that cannot be of any advantage you."

[858] "Do not hesitate any longer," said the mighty warrior. "Carry your[34] little child over to his mother." The messengers went to where they found Ortlieb lying with a terrible wound, headless in his blood. Alas, how much honor was lost by Attila through his death! Never again will a king suffer such agony. The sovereign also thought about Blödelin's death. He ordered that the latter be brought to lie beside these two. Although they were heathens, great pity was shown towards them.

[33] The manuscript clearly contains the second person singular possessive pronoun "din" in verse 837, although Bartsch amends to "sîn" without any indication of the original text in his apparatus. Zeune deviates from his source and translates verse 837 as 'Gunther und deine Brüder' (351), the implication being that the latter stands in apposition to "fvrsten <h>ere" in verse 836, even though Manuscript A contains the possessive pronoun "sîn." This creates the impression that Attila is addressing the dead Gunther and his own slain kinfolk. One might suggest, however, that the reference to "fvrsten <h>ere" in verse 836 is actually to Dietrich and Hildebrand, who are present during Attila's lament. I have translated in accordance with Bartsch's emendation, as it appears that the third person possessive pronoun is the only form that makes sense in this context.

[34] The text of Manuscript B clearly indicates that Dietrich has continued to give advice to Attila and the pronoun to be found in verse 861 is "ivver" ('your'). Bartsch has elected, however, to follow other manuscripts which contain the pronoun "mîn." In such instances, the speaker could only be Attila, giving orders to his men to lay the body of his child next to Kriemhild. Both versions fit the present context. The advantage of the latter is that it allows Attila's men to act directly on his orders which would not be explicitly stated if we adhere to the original version in B.

daz livt dort vnd hie.
vvffens vnd schrîens pflach.
vil manegen grozen brvst slach.
slugen in div vverden vvip.
[880] vil manech minnechlicher lip.
vvas mit grozen leiden.
von liebe gescheiden.

Sins gebotes si vvol gedahten.
do si Blôdelinen brahten.
[885] da in der kŭnech selbe sach.
der svn Botelvnges sprach.
Ovve lieber brŭder min.
div min<i>v lant vnt div din.
geligent nv vil eine.
[890] div herverte seine.
sihet man in den richen.
dv tæte vngŭtlichen.
vil lieber brvder min an mir.
vvi sold ich getrvven dir.
[895] daz dv den minen gesten.
den degenen aller besten.
vvi erzŭrn^destv den mvt.
daz si dich mære helt gvt.
da von ce tode hant erslagen.
[900] di selben helde mvz ich chlagen.
vvand ich in het gesant.
mine boten in ir lant.
daz si mich sehen solden.
di trivve haben vvolden.
[905] vnd getrivve vvolden vvesen.
di solden si han lan genesen.
vnde solden si ver mitten han.
vvie solden si do han getan.
di vil vverlih / vvaren ie.
[910] do man si strîtes niht erlie.
di helde envverten ovch sich.
daz si daz verdagten mich.
daz chom von ir ŭbermvt.
ich hete daz vil vvol behvt.
[915] daz hie iht geschehen vvære.
ovch soldestv helt mære.
si vil pillich han ver born.
vvaz danne ob einen alten zorn.

People everywhere cried and lamented. The worthy women beat terribly upon their breasts and many a lovely girl took leave of love through her sorrow.

[883] They carried out his order. When they brought [the body of] Blödelin over to where the king himself saw him, this is what the son of Botelung said: "Alas, my dear brother. My land and yours are now without heirs. We shall see no more campaigns in these kingdoms. I have not done well by you, my dear brother. Good knight, how could I have believed that you would so incite my guests, the finest warriors to be had, to such a rage that they would strike you down dead? I must also grieve for these very same warriors, because I sent my envoys to their land to invite them to come and visit me. Those men who wished to preserve [their sense of] loyalty and to remain faithful to me should have let them live and refrained from fighting with them. After all, how were these men, who had always been ready to do battle, supposed to act once a confrontation became inevitable? It was their pride that made them keep everything from me. I would certainly have seen to it that all of this was avoided. You as well, brave warrior, should properly have left them in peace. What did it matter

vf si trvch daz edel vvip.
[920] dvne soldest ere vnd lip.
dar vmbe ^{niht} gevvaget han.
daz ir hagen het getan.
des vvest ich vvol div mære.
svvi lieb si mir vvære.
[925] ich het in nimmer doch erslagen.
ob er vor mir ce tvsent tagen.
solde han geslaffen.
sone het ich min vvaffen.
nimmer ѷber in erzogen.
[930] brѷd^[er] nv hat dich betrogen.
din vil tvmplicher mvt.

Waffen sprach der kѷnech gvt.
daz ich ie vvart geborn.
vvaz ich trostes han verlorn.
[935] an in und an den minen.
Gѷnther mit den sinen.
vvære mir gestanden.
mit vvilligen handen.
alles des ich vvolde.
[940] svves ein Chѷnech solde.
an gvte<n> recken han gegert.
des vvær ich vvol an in gevvert.
nv enist des leider niht geschehen.
ovve daz niemen mir ver iehen.
[945] vvolde der reh<t>en mære.
daz in so vient vvære.
Criemhilt ir svvester.
der schade vnde min laster.
div sint beidiv vvol so groz.
[950] svvi mich ce lebene ni verdroz.
nv ver drivzet mich so sere.
daz ich nimmer mere.
gerne lebe deheinen tach.
vvand ez ist der gotes slach.
[955] ѷber mich er gangen.
Nv ligent si gevangen.
di sin gevvalt betvvngen hat.
ie vvold ich des haben rat.
daz ich in niht ensolde.
[960] fѷrhten noch envvolde.

if the noble woman bore them an old grudge? That was hardly grounds for you to have risked both your honor and your life. I know full well what Hagen had done to her. No matter how precious she was to me, I would never have killed him. Even if he had slept here for a thousand nights, I would never have drawn my weapon against him. Dear brother, your youthful zeal has deceived you."

[932] Then the good king said: "A pity that I was ever born! To think of the bright future[35] I have lost through their[36] demise and the death of my own people! Gunther and his kin would have willingly granted to me everything that I wanted. Whatever a king might have desired of good warriors, that he would have accorded me. But unfortunately, that has not come about. Alas, that no one was prepared to tell me how things really stood, and that their sister Kriemhild was so ill-disposed towards them. The injuries and shame I have to bear are both so great that, although I never disdained life previously, it has now become such misery to me that I will never enjoy another day.[37] For God's wrath has been directed against me. Now they lie prisoner, overcome by his power. I always wanted to dispense with any idea that I might wish to or should fear Him.

[35] I have interpreted the word "trostes" in verse 934 perhaps a little freely here as 'bright future.' Lexer includes, as the first of his definitions of the word, the phrase 'freudige zuversicht' (2: 1527) which, I believe, provides us with an excellent description of the state of mind that Attila must have been in following his marriage to Kriemhild, the birth of his son (and only heir), Ortlieb, and the arrival at his court of the most formidable warriors of western Europe. He had emerged from a sense of despair and meaninglessness (for both himself and his people) following the death of his first wife, Helche (who had left him heirless) to assume again a sense of purpose within the framework of assured continuity of his empire. Furthermore, he enjoyed enhanced stature through his marriage to one of the most renowned women of the time and the prospects of a solid alliance with her Burgundian kinfolk. From Attila's perspective, the future must, in fact, have looked particularly bright.

[36] It is interesting to note here that Zeune translates verse 935 as 'an ihm und an den Meinen,' even though Manuscript A also contains the pronoun "in." Zeune has assumed that the poet was referring to the dead Blöedelin, but it becomes quite clear in the following verses that the Burgundians are intended by "in" here, as Attila had hoped to use them to realize his own ambitions.

[37] Zeune tends here to simplify the text found in Manuscript A: "Mein Schaden ist so groß, daß ich keinen Tag mehr leben möchte" (353). Gone is the original reference to "laster" in verse 948 and the reference to happier days when Attila enjoyed life (verse 950).

Nv shilt ich miniv apgot.
sît des gevvaltegen gebot.
gezŏrnet hat so sere.
vva ist nv michel ere.
[965]   [135/424] di mahumet vnd machazen.
<liez> so lange liezen her gesten.
svvaz ich errîten chvnde.
daz vvas bi miner stvnde.
allez gar von mir bediet.
[970]   der mir ce lebene geriet.
dar zv ivden vnd Christen.
mit gotlichen listen.
hiez ershinen den tach.
mit den sinen er min pflach.
[975]   sam ich sin eigen vvære.
nv riete mir min svvære.
ob er min rûchen vvolde.
daz ich mich aber becheren solde.
ob er helffen vvolt dar zv.
[980]   nv fŏrht ich daz ers niht entv.
vvand ich in ovch ê betrâvch.
min Apgot shvffen daz ich lâuch.
siner starchen gotheit.
daz ich lie di Cristenheit.
[985]   daz ist ane zvvifel vvar.
ich vvas Christen vvol fvnf iar.
doch geshŏfen si daz sider.
daz ich mich vernogierte hin vvider.
vnd vvart in als ê vndertan.
[990]   ob ich nv gerne vvolde enpfan.
Christen leben vnt di rehten ê.
daz envvirt mir vvider nimmer me.
vvand ich mich han vnerforht.
so sere vvider in vervvorht.
[995]   daz er min leider niht en vvil.
tvsent Chŏnege heten vil.
an min eines svvære.
Ich vviste vvol daz er vvære.
von dem allerhohesten lvft.
[1000]   vnz in di vndersten grvft.
gevvaldech svves er vvolde.
dem ich da dienen solde.
fŏr den getrŏve ich nimmer chomen.
diz leit hat mir benomen.

[961] Now, however, I curse my false gods, since the commandment of the Almighty has been manifest in such terrible anger. Where is the great honor which Machmet and Machazin allowed to prevail here for so long? Whatever was within my grasp, I was always able to subdue. He who gave life to me, as well as to both Jews and Christians, and who, in His divine wisdom, ordered day to appear, He watched over me along with His own, just as though I were one of them. My sorrow has taught me to turn to Him again, if He still wishes to consider me, and will help me to do so. Yet I fear He may not help me because I earlier betrayed Him. My false gods made me deny His great majesty and turn my back on Christianity. This is without a doubt the truth. For five years I was a Christian, but they saw to it that I denied it and once again became their subject just as before. Even if I now wanted to follow the Christian life and the true law, I will never again have the opportunity to do so, for I have so acted in such a shameful way against Him that, sadly, He no longer wants me. The sorrow I feel would be a burden for a thousand kings. I knew full well that He has power over everything from the highest spheres to the lowest depths[38]. I do not dare appear before the one whom I wished to serve. This sorrow has robbed me

---

[38] Perhaps the sense is best imparted here through the use of the modern idiom: "I know that He has power over everything between heaven and hell."

[1005]   frevde vnd allen hohen mvt.
mich endivhte nv niht so gvt.
so mit den ligenden hi der tot.
der Chŭnech ersŭfte des gie im not.
michels lvter er ershre.
[1010]   daz tet Dietriche vve.
dem fŭrsten von Berne.
er hort iz vil vngerne.

Er vnd meister Hildebrant.
gie da er den Chŭnech vant.
[1015]   als er Eceln gesach.
dem gelich er do sprach.
sam im niht arges vvære. /
Âch vve dirre mære.
gevreishet man div in daz lant.
[1020]   daz ir mit vvintender hant.
stet als ein Blôde vvip.
div ir zvht vnd ir lip.
nach frivnden sere hat gesent.
des sin vvir von iv vngevvent.
[1025]   daz ir vnmanliche tvt.
nv solt ir edel kŭnech gvt.
trosten frivntliche.
mich armen Dieteriche.
Er sprach vvi sold ich geben trost.
[1030]   ia bin ich alles des belost.
daz ich zer vverlde ie gevvan.
nivvan daz ich den lip noh han.
ane gvte sinne.
mich hat mit vnminne.
[1035]   der gotes haz bestanden.
ich vvas in minen landen.
gevvaltech vnd riche.
nv sten ich iamerliche.
reht als ein arman.
[1040]   der ni hŭbe gevvan.

Do sprach der Bernære.
her kŭnech lat ivver svvære.
vnd tŭt dem geliche.
ob ir Dieteriche.
[1045]   vvænet helfen von der not.
si sint mir alle erslagen tot.

of all my joy and my high spirits. Nothing seems as good to me as [to suffer] death as all those who are lying about here." The king let out a great sigh. He was despairing terribly[39] and cried out even more loudly. This pained Dietrich, Lord of Verona, and he was most unhappy to witness it.

[1013] Together with Sir Hildebrand, he approached the king. As soon as he saw Attila he spoke to him as though nothing were troubling him: "Alas the day, if this wretched tale circulates throughout the country, namely, that you are standing here wringing your hands like some silly woman who is moping around pining for her friends. We are not at all accustomed to seeing you act in such an unmanly fashion. My good and noble king, you ought to provide some friendly consolation to me, wretched Dietrich." Attila replied: "How can I provide consolation? I have been robbed of everything that I treasured in this world. The only thing I have left is my life but without any sense or purpose.[40] God's hatred has been directed without mercy against me. In my lands I was a powerful and rich ruler. Now I stand here in despair, just like some poor fellow who never acquired even an acre of land."

[1041] Dietrich of Verona replied: "Your Majesty, put your sorrow aside and act as though you had a mind to help Dietrich out of his plight. All of the men

---

[39] The second half of verse 1008 might also mean that the king had good reason to sigh, or that he was compelled to do so.

[40] Zeune has translated 1032-1033 as 'außer daß ich Leib und Sinne noch habe!' ('except that I still have my life and my senses' 354). Manuscript A also contains "âne guote sinne" [emphasis mine], however, and so Zeune has ignored the preposition in his rendering. I have tried to convey the sense of what I believe Attila is driving at here, namely, that he may have survived the carnage, but that his inner life is in such turmoil as a result of his losses that it no longer makes any sense.

di mir da helfen solden.
vnd mih pringen vvolden.
vvider an mi<n> ere.
[1050]   ia rivvent si mich sere.
di not gestallen mine.
Ia maht dv kůnech di dine.
vil vvol ůbervvinden.
dv maht noch manigen vinden.
[1055]   der dich niht vndervvegen lat.
vmbe mich ez leider anders stat.
als dv maht hi selbe schovven.
ia ligent si verhovven.
gevallen tief in daz plůt.
[1060]   di durch mich lip vnd gut.
satzen vf di vvage.
in ist an einer lage.
der tot vil grivveliche chomen.
vnd hat si alle mir benomen.
[1065]   Der kůnech sprach des vvil ich iehen.
ich han gehort vnt gesehen.
vnd sagen von vil grozer not.
daz der gemeinliche tot.
den gevvalt ni mer gevvan.
[1070]   der kůnech hiez do tragen dan.
beide sin chint vnd sin vvip.
vnd sins veigen brvder lip.
gaparet vf den re.
den livten vvart allen vve.
[1075]   di ez mit im sahen.
[136/425] vor dem hvse nahen.
noch vil maneger veige lach.
ir vveichlicher tach.
daz leben hete da benomen.
[1080]   Nv vvas ovch der kůnech chomen.
da (e)r Iringen vant.
den mit vvillegær hant.
des můtes vnverdrozzen.
Hagen het ershozzen.
[1085]   da er im angestlich entran.
(svv)i der havvartes man.
vvol stritte mit degene.
vnt svvi doch der starche Hagene.
von im vvnt vvære.
[1090]   der chůne Tronegære.

who had intended to help me restore my honor have been killed. I deeply regret the loss of my comrades. Your Majesty, you will be able to replenish your losses. You can still find many who will not abandon you. Unfortunately, I am in a very different situation, as you yourself can see. Those men who risked their lives and everything they had for me are lying here hacked to pieces in a sea of blood. Death has suddenly caught up with them in a terrible way and has robbed me of all of them." The king answered: "Let me say this. I have heard and seen tragedy, and also heard it spoken about, but this coarse fellow death will never again wield such power [as he has here]." The king then had both his wife and his child, as well as the body of his doomed[41] brother carried off and placed on biers. Everyone who witnessed this with him grieved deeply. There were still many corpses lying in front of the Hall, men who had been robbed of their lives on this fateful day. The king had now approached the spot where he found the dead Iring. Hagen had cut him down[42] quite readily and without the slightest regret when he ran away from him in great fear. However well Hawart's man fought against the warrior, and even though mighty Hagen was wounded by him, the brave knight of Troneck

[41] The adjective "veigen" in verse 1072 to describe Attila's brother is best translated as 'doomed' or 'dead,' but it should be pointed out that the spectrum of meaning of the term is much broader in Middle High German. It may convey as well, according to Lexer (3: 46), the sense of 'verwünscht, unselig, verdammt.' Given Blödelin's role in the initiating of hostilities against the Burgundians with all of the ensuing ramifications, it is not unlikely that the word was chosen over "tot" because of the wider connotations with which it was associated. In contrast, the use of "veige" as a noun in verse 1077 to describe the dead men lying in front of Attila's Great Hall is unambiguous and should be understood as "the dead man" or "corpse."

[42] The thirty-fifth âventiure of the Nibelungenlied is entitled "Wie Îrinc erslagen wart" and describes how the Danish warrior is felled by a spear through the head thrown by Hagen (Nibelungenlied 2064-2065).

het den helt ce tode erslagen.
den begonde do chlagen.
mit Ecele dem richen.
also chlagelichen.
[1095] der fŷrste von Berne.
si sahen vil vngerne.
di sine tieffen vvnden.
ovh chlageten ^{in} an den stunden.
der alte Hildebrant.
[1100] also daz man ez vvol ervvant.

Ovch hulfen chlagen in div vvip.
des uil chŷnen Tenen lip.
den chlagete man von schulden.
nah shôner vvibe hulden.
[1105] ellender man ni baz geranch.
ovch mŷs man im des sagen danch.
daz er so herliche vvarp.
vnd also genendechliche ersta<r>p.
vor maneges recken ovgen.
[1110] sine vvoldens niht gelovben.
daz er Hagen torste bestan.
het ez der helt sider lan.
so môhter vvol sin genesen.
do sprach der kŷnech ez solde vvesen.
[1115] ia vvære iz anders mir geseit.
ir not vnd min arbeit.
ich het iz vvol allez vnderstan.
Herre vvaz het ich getan.
Gŷnther vnt dē sinen.
[1120] nv habent si mir der minen.
aller samt en bunnen.
nv ist ovch in cervnnen.
des lebens vnt der ere.
der kŷnech chlagete sere.
[1125] des starchen Iringes ellen.
vnd seiner hergesellen.

In hiez der vvirt ovch tragen dan.
vnd mit im drizech siner man.
di bi im in den stunden.
[1130] ovh tote vvaren funden.
do man si ge- / barot.
dannen trvch als er gebot.

nonetheless killed him. He was also mourned by Dietrich of Verona, who, along with mighty Attila, began to lament [his passing]. They were deeply dismayed to see the deep wounds that Iring had sustained. Old Sir Hildebrand also grieved for him in a manner which was considered to be quite proper.

[1101] The women also joined in the mourning over the death of the brave Dane. They were quite right to lament his passing, for never had an exile better sought the favor of lovely women. He should also be praised for having acted so magnificently and for dying so bravely before the eyes of many warriors. They could hardly believe that he had fought against Hagen.[43] If the warrior had just left well enough alone, he might have gone on living. The king said: "So be it. If only I had been informed differently, I would certainly have been able to prevent their misery and avoid my anguish. My lord, what did I ever do to Gunther and his men? Now they have deprived me of all mine. And they, too, have lost both their lives and their honor." The king lamented greatly the loss of the mighty and courageous Iring and his comrades.

[1127] The sovereign also had the latter's body removed along with the corpses of thirty of his men who were found at the same time lying around him. After they had been placed on biers and carried off, just as he had ordered,

---

[43] My translation of verse 1110 differs considerably from Zeune's, which is based on the presence of "gelougen" ('doubt') in Manuscript A: "sie zweifelten nicht...," 'They had no doubt that he had dared to fight Hagen....'

do vant der kv̓nech here.
noch der recken mere.
[1135]   Gv̓nthern den kv̓nech richen.
ligen iæmerlichen.
da im daz hovbt vvas abgeslagen.
di begonden si do chlagen.
als in Ecel der kv̓nech sach.
[1140]   der fv̓rste senliche sprach.
Ovvi lieber svvager min.
sold ich dich an den Rin.
vvol gesunden senden.
daz ich mit minen henden.
[1145]   hete daz ervohten.
do si selbe nine mohten.
des vvold ich immer vvesen vro.

Her Dietrich der sprach do.
her kvnech von sinen schulden.
[1150]   nach ivvern grozen hulden.
rang ich also sere.
daz ich den helt niht mere.
vvol gesparn mohte.
vvand ez mir niht tohte.
[1155]   do si vns aller vnser man.
heten ane getan.
do schalt mich von dem sal.
hagen der v̓bermv̓te her cetal.
zv allem minem sere.
[1160]   daz ich in niht mere.
leider chvnd vertragen.
do mir min volch lach er slagen.
vnd iv herre ivverr man.
den kv̓nech ich vlegen began.
[1165]   daz erz riete ce einer svne.
hagen der chv̓ne.
des vrides niht en vvo lde.
Er sprach zvviv er in solde.
sît daz di beide lagen tot.
[1170]   Giselher vnd Gernot.
<Bartsch: unde daz mîn Hildebrant
het von Burgonden lant
ze tôde Volkêrn erslagen.
er begunde ez sêre klagen,>
[1175]   vnt daz min alter Hildebrant entran.

the noble king came upon yet more warriors, including mighty Gunther, whose head had been struck off. They also lamented his passing.[44] When King Attila saw him, the monarch sadly commented: "Alas, my dear brother-in-law, if only I could send you back to the Rhine alive! I would be forever happy had I, with my own hands, been able to achieve that, since they themselves were not able to do so."[45]

[1148] Lord Dietrich responded: "Your Majesty, it is his own fault. I was so concerned with acquiring your great favor that I no longer could spare the warrior, for it was not fitting for me to do so. They had, after all, robbed us of all our men. On top of all of my suffering, arrogant Hagen shouted down his taunts at me from the Great Hall, so that I unfortunately could no longer stand back and tolerate what they were doing. Then when my people lay there dead as well your men, my Lord, I begged the king to consider a reconciliation. Brave Hagen, however, did not want peace. He said why should he [be interested in peace] since both Giselher and Gernot were lying there dead, [and my own Sir Hildebrand had killed Volker of Burgundy. He was highly distressed][46] that old Hildebrand had escaped

[44] Verse 1138 has been left untranslated by Zeune.

[45] Verse 1146 is somewhat enigmatic. To what, or whom, does the pronoun "si" refer? In this context, I think it can only be understood as a reference to the Burgundians, the sense being that, since they were not in a position to extricate themselves from the predicament and return to the Rhine, Attila, through the power of his intervention, could have achieved such a goal and thus avoided the ultimate catastrophe.

[46] The bracketed section has been taken from Bartsch. The four verses detailing the killing of Volker by Hildebrand are missing in Manuscript B.

da er di vvnden gevvan.
vvant di slûch im hagene.
hi vze vor dem gademe.
dvrch vlins herte ringe.
[1180]   dem chŷnen getelinge.

Do bat ich Gunthere.
daz er dvrch sin ere.
gedehte an alle mine not.
daz ich vnz an minen tot.
[1185]   sinen vride bære.
daz er din gisel vvære.
vnd ovch kŷnech der mine.
daz ich in zv dem Rine.
gesunden vvolde bringen.
[1190]   do het er des gedingen.
er lieze niemen hi genesen.
daz moht [137/426] ouch vil vvol sin gevvesen.
vvær gerastet im sin hant.
Ia slvch mich der vvigant.
[1195]   daz vvizet drie stvnt nider.
so daz ich vil chvme vvider.
mich erholte mit miner chrapft.
do nerte mich min meisterschapft.
vnd min vvol gerŷvetiv hant.
[1200]   daz ich den fvrsten gebant.
mit einer verchvvnden.
hie bevalch ich in zv den stvnden.
Criemhilde miner vrovven.
vvi moht ich des getrvven.
[1205]   daz si den helt hieze slan.
ich het vngerne daz getan.
daz ich in gæbe in den tot.
ez gemeret im sin not.
von siner svvester zorne.
[1210]   hi lit der vvol geborne.

Der kvnech do vveinende sprach.
ovve daz iz ie geschach.
min grŷzen im vnt sinen man.
vvær ez mir ê chvnt getan.
[1215]   si mŷsen alle sin genesen.
tivverr helde chvnden vvesen.
ninder vf der erde.

after having been wounded. For it had been Hagen who, here in front of the Hall, had dealt this brave fellow these wounds right through his flint-hard ring-mail.

[1181] I asked Gunther, for the sake of his honor, to consider my plight and told him that until I died I would guarantee him peace, were he to agree to becoming your and my hostage, your majesty. I assured him that I wished to bring him back to the Rhine alive. But he had made up his mind not to spare anyone here. That would undoubtedly have come to pass had he had the chance to rest his hand. Let me tell you, the warrior struck me down three times [with such force] that I scarcely succeeded in regaining my senses. The only things that saved me were my skill and the fact that my arm was rested, so that after having inflicted a terrible wound on the nobleman, I was able to take him prisoner. I then immediately turned him over to my Lady Kriemhild. How could I ever have imagined that she would have the warrior killed? I would have been reluctant to have sent him to his death. And so, Gunther's troubles were exacerbated by the anger of his sister. Here lies the well-bred man."

[1211] The king spoke through his tears. "A pity that I ever greeted either him or his men. Had I only been informed ahead of time [what was afoot], all of them would still be alive. Finer warriors were never to have been found on the face of the earth,

ez vvæne ovch immer vverde.

so manech chv́ner vvigant.

[1220]   des ligent elliv miniv lant.

in iamer vnd in vreise.

ia ist vil manech vveise.

da heime in ir richen.

di si nv pillichen.

[1225]   mit frevden solden enpfan.

nvne mach ich vngechlaget lan.

niht den minen viant.

do sprach meister Hildebrant.

herre nv lazet ivver chlagen.

[1230]   vnd heizet den fv́rsten hinnen tragen.

Do sprach aber her Dietrich.

helt also lobelich.

ich vvæne ie vv́rde geborn.

so der edel vz erchorn.

[1235]   vnd envvirt ovch nimmer mere.

des rivvet er mih sere.

Do sprach der Botelvnges svn.

leider ia mvsen si daz tvn.

daz mir ce schaden ist bechomen.

[1240]   ovch hant sis selbe chleinen frv̄m.

do si vvrden bestanden.

von / minen vviganden.

nv rivvent mich di beide.

von schvlden ist mir leide.

[1245]   vmbe mine recken vnd sie.

daz ich so manegen helt hie.

heten di ez verdageten.

daz si mir ez niht ensageten.

Do sprach meister hildebrant.

[1250]   nv seht vva der valant.

lit der ez allez riet.

daz manz mit gv(t) nine schiet.

daz ist von Hagenen schvlden.

ce miner vrovven hvlden.

[1255]   si mốhten vvol sin bechomen.

her kv́nech ia het vvir ver nomen.

harte vvol div mære.

vvir heten ivver svvære.

vil vvol vnderstanden.

[1260]   miner vrovven anden.

nor do I suspect that there will ever again be so many brave knights. For this reason, all of my lands are in a state of despair and wretchedness, as there are many orphans back in their homelands who really ought to be welcoming them back in joy. Now I cannot leave even my enemy unlamented." Sir Hildebrand spoke up: "My Lord, turn aside your grief and have the nobleman carried away." Lord Dietrich added: "I do not believe a greater hero was ever born as this noble, splendid knight, nor will one of his stature ever be born [in the future]. That is why I regret his passing so greatly."

[1237] Botelung's son responded: "It is unfortunate that their actions, when they were attacked by my warriors, have done me such harm (and they themselves have derived little profit from it). I regret [what has happened to] both of them[47] and I am indeed sorry for both my own warriors and for them. For I had so many men here who kept silent and did not inform me [as to what was really going on]." Sir Hildebrand said: "Now observe the devil lying there who was the cause of it all. It was Hagen's fault that we were not able to resolve matters in a satisfactory way. It would have certainly been possible for them to have gained my Lady's favor. My Lord, if only we had known what was really afoot, we would certainly have spared you all this sorrow.

[47] Verse 1243 is ambiguous. "Beide" could refer, as I have understood it, to both Gunther and Hagen, who have been the topic of conversation in the preceding verses, or, perhaps, to the Huns and Burgundians. Zeune has opted for the latter in his translation: "Nun dauern mich Beide, meine Recken und sie" (358). Verses 1244-1245 make it clear that Attila is grieving for the warriors of both camps. Either interpretation appears plausible.

den vvolde rêchen Blôdelin.
des solde niht geschehen sin.
hie ist ꝟbele gebovven.
vver mohte des getrvven.
[1265]   daz also manech chꝟne man.
hi den lip solde lan.
dvrch den Sifrides tot.
vnt daz div vngefꝟgiv not.
in ivverm hove sold ergen.
[1270]   ine chan michs anders niht ver sten.
vvant daz di helde vz erchorn.
den vreislichen gotes zorn.
nv lange her ver dienet han.
done chondez langer niht gestan.
[1275]   ꝟber ir zil einen tach.
do mvsen si den gotes slach.
liden dvrch ir ꝟber mvt.
des lit hi manech helt gvt.
der in manegem stvrm herte.
[1280]   sich diche vvol ervverte.
vnd sint nv hi erstorben.
daz hant si in selbe ervvorben.

Do sprach <der> Chꝟnech riche.
in leide gꝟtliche.
[1285]   nv heizet balde hagen.
zv Gꝟnther sinem herren tragen.
vnd zv den anderen hin.
Ovve deich inder lebendech pin.
daz môhte got erbarmen.
[1290]   vnd lieze mich vil armen.
lebn nv niht mere.
in disem grozen sere.
daz mich næme der tot.
des vvære mir sprach der kꝟnech not.
[1295]   Do di livte hagenen sahen.
si begonden zv zim gahen.
im vvart gevlꝟchet sere.
ir vrevde vnd ovch ir ere.
der [138/427] <der> vvas vil von im verlorn.
[1300]   di livte rieten dvrch ir zorn.
ez vvære von sinen schvlden.
vvider niemens hulden.
het er da niht getan.

Blödelin wished to avenge the insults suffered by my Lady. That should not have happened. A terrible crop has been sown. Who could ever have believed that so many brave men would lose their lives here as a result of Siegfried's death, and that such terrible sorrow should be visited upon your court? I find it hard to believe that these illustrious warriors have not deserved the wrath of God for a long time now. Their day of reckoning could not be put off any longer and they had to bear God's fury on account of their arrogance. As a consequence, many fine warriors are lying here who gave a good account of themselves in many a great battle, and now they have met their end here. They have brought it all upon themselves."

[1283] The mighty king spoke kindly despite his despair: "Have Hagen carried over straightaway to his lord, Gunther, and to the others. A pity that I am still alive. May God have mercy upon me and no longer force me, poor wretch that I am, to go on living in such terrible sorrow. Let death carry me off," said the king, "for that is what I desire." When the people saw Hagen, they walked over to him; Hagen was roundly cursed from all sides for it was because of him that they had been deprived of so much joy and had lost so much honor. In their anger, the people claimed that it was his fault. He would not have fallen out of favor with anyone there

het div Chѷneginne daz eine lan.

[1305] daz si Blôdelinen.

hagene den brvd[er] sinen.

ce tode niht het heizen slan.

sone vværes alles niht getan.

Do vverte sich der vvigant.

[1310] daz di von Bѵrgonden lant.

mûsen chom in den strit.

da von vil manech vvnde vvit.

sider vvart gehovven.

ez vvas also gebrôven.

[1315] von des tivnels schvlden.

nach niemens hulden.

chvnde<n> si gevverben.

des mvsen si ersterben.

Mit der rede giengen dan.

[1320] der Chѷnech vnt di zvvene man.

mit vvffendem lvte.

da her Dietrich sine trvte.

manegen recken ligen vant.

vzen vor des sals vvant.

[1325] sach er einen hi ligen.

sine ringe dvrchsigen.

vvaren von dem plѷte.

do sprach der helt gvte.

hildebrant vver ist daz.

[1330] er antvvrte im an haz.

herre daz ist Volker.

der vns div grôzesten ser.

hat mit sinen handen.

gefrѷmt in disen landen.

[1335] Er hat gedienet so den solt.

daz ich der sele immer holt.

vvol vverden nemach.

er slvch mir einen nit slach.

vf di mine ringe.

[1340] daz der min gedinge.

cem lebne vvas vil chleine.

der helt bestvnt mich eine.

ih het ovch in bestanden.

chѷner helt cen handen.

[1345] videlens ni mer began.

het mich gescheiden niht her dan.

if the queen had only refrained from doing one thing, namely, ordering Blödelin to kill Hagen's brother. For then all of this would not have transpired. The warrior defended himself in such a way that the men of Burgundy were, of necessity, drawn into a battle in the course of which many terrible wounds were inflicted. The brew that was concocted there was of the devil's making. They could not appeal to anyone for help and so they had to die.

[1319] With loud cries of despair, the king and these two men [Dietrich and Hildebrand] walked away from there over to where Lord Dietrich found many of the warriors of his own band lying dead. He discovered another man lying outside the walls of the Great Hall, the iron rings of his mail-coat soaked in blood. The good warrior asked: "Hildebrand, who is that?" The latter answered with no bitterness [in his voice]: "My Lord, that is Volker, whose hand has inflicted upon us the greatest losses that this land has ever seen. He has earned his pay in such a fashion that I personally could never be favorably disposed towards him [his soul].[48] He dealt such an incredible blow to my chain-mail that I hardly expected to survive. The warrior fought alone against me. There was never a braver minstrel-warrior. Had not

---

[48] Zeune also assumes that "der sele" in verse 1336 is a reference to Volker (359). Werner Hoffmann has suggested in correspondence with this writer, however, that it may be an allusion to Hildebrand's own soul and that the sense could be: '... that I personally could never have any peace of mind." I believe that both interpretations are possible. I have been influenced in my choice by the less than generous remarks Hildebrand continues to make about Volker, despite the reference to the lack of bitterness in verse 1330.

helpfrich daz vvil ich iv sagen.
so hete Volker mich erslagen.

Ovve sprach der kᵛnech rich.
[1350]   sin zvht div vvas lobelich.
dar zv vil manlich gemvt.
daz (e)z mir immer vve tvt.
daz er noh solde ersterben.
so gahes verderben.
[1355]   Ecel der vragte mære.
vvann er geborn væere.
Do / sprach meister Hildebrant.
er hete bi Rine daz lant.
mit Gᵛnther besezzen.
[1360]   der helt vil vermezzen.
vvas von Alzey erborn.
sin manheit vz erchorn.
div ist al ce frv gelegen.
do chlagte her Dietrich den degen.
[1365]   dvrch sinen getrivvelichen mvt.
vveinte in der helt gvt.
vvaz chlagt ir sprach do hildebrant.
vns hat div volkers hant.
geshadet hi so sere.
[1370]   daz vvir ez nimmer mere.
chvnnen ᵛber vvinden.
der dinen ingesinden.
er eine hat vvol zvvelve erslagen.
got vvil ich des danch sagen.
[1375]   daz er lang⁽ᵉʳ⁾ niht genas.
do ich pi im <in> in dem stvrme vvas.
so sere vverte sich der degen.
ez doz alsam von dorn slegen.
Idoh ver hiv ich in sit.
[1380]   dise vvnden also vvit.
im slᵛgen mine hende.
daz er in ellende.
vor mir veiger ist gelegen.
des mvz ich sivfen vmben degen.
[1385]   vvand ovh ich ellende bin.
der sin vil hohvertiger sin.
der schadt vns nimmer mere.
er vvarp nach gancer ere.
dvrch daz er videln chvnde.

Helpfrich managed to separate me from him, I can tell you that Volker would certainly have killed me."

[1349] "Alas," the mighty king said, "his manner was so praiseworthy and he was of such manly stature, that I am truly sorry that he also had to die here, that he should have met such an untimely end." Attila asked where he had been born. Sir Hildebrand replied that he had owned land on the Rhine along with Gunther. "This renowned warrior was born in Alzeye. His splendid manliness has met a far too early end."[49] Lord Dietrich also lamented the passing of the warrior and the good knight was motivated through his sense of loyalty to shed tears for him. "Why are you grieving?" Hildebrand asked. "Volker's hand has inflicted such injury upon us here that we can never recover [from the losses suffered as a result]. By himself he killed twelve of your men. For that reason alone, I thank God that he is no longer alive. When I fought against him in the battle, he defended himself with such vigor that it felt as though thunderbolts were striking me. Nevertheless, I was eventually able to cut him down. With my own hands I inflicted these deep wounds upon him, so that this hapless fellow then lay dead before me. I can sigh at his fate, for I, too, am in a wretched state.[50] Never again will we suffer as a result of his arrogance. He was bent on achieving ultimate honor. Because he could play the fiddle,

[49] These words may well have been spoken by Dietrich, rather than by Hildebrand. They seem to imply a more sympathetic tone taken towards the dead Volker than the sentiments expressed a bit later by Hildebrand.

[50] In this particular context, I believe that "ellende" describes more Hildebrand's overall state of mind than the specific attribute of "statelessness."

[1390]   daz volch in zaller stunde.
            hiezen einen spilman.
            als ich iv vvol gesagen chan.
            er vvas von vrien liden chomen.
            vnd het sich daz an genomen.
[1395]   daz er diente schônen vrovven.
            Nv lît von im verhovven.
            so manech edel vvigant.
            daz ni vidlæres hant.
            daz vvnder ni gevvorhte.
[1400]   als der vn ervorhte.
            in disem stvrme hat getan.
            des mvz min herce vrevde lan.

            Der Chѷnech hiez in dannen tragen.
            da der vѷf vnt daz chlagen.
[1405]   dort bi den andern vvas.
            hey vvaz man ir sît las.
            der stolzen helde gѷte.
            dar nah vz dem plѷte.
            di fvnden si dar inne.
[1410]   mit leide in vnsinne.
            Gi do der Bernære.
            vnd schovvete [139/428] sine svvære.
            Der erste den er do vant.
            daz vvas von Bvrgonden lant.
[1415]   hagen bruder danchvvart.
            der vil manegen rinch schart.
            gemacht het dar inne.
            man sagte daz vil grimme.
            von Tronege vvære ѷberal.
[1420]   do slvch ir in dem sal.
            danchvvart der degen ziere.
            mer danne hagen viere.
            Er rivvet mich sprach Dietrich.
            sin mѷt der vvas so tvgentlich.
[1425]   ob ez ein chѷnech vvære.
            son moht der helt mære.
            niht herlicher han getan.
            Ir mѷgt in vngelobt lan.
            vil vvol sprach do Hildebrant.
[1430]   gesæhet ir vvi iv sin hant.
            hat gedienet in sinen lesten tagen.
            so mvz iv deste vvirs behagen.

people always referred to him as a minstrel. I can also tell you that he was born of freemen[51] and had made it his task to serve beautiful women. Now many a noble warrior lies cut to pieces by him so that one can say that no hand of a minstrel ever worked such wonders as this fearless fellow did in battle. For that reason there is no joy in my heart."

[1403] The king had him carried away from there to a place where others were continuing with their wailing and grieving. Ah, what proud, magnificent warriors were subsequently retrieved from the blood in which they were found! Half crazed with sorrow, Dietrich of Verona went over and observed his dilemma. The first whom he found was a Burgundian warrior — Dancwart, Hagen's brother, who had hacked through a great deal of ringmail inside [the Great Hall]. People say that everywhere he appeared, Hagen of Troneck was a grim opponent. Yet that renowned warrior, Dancwart, actually slew in the Hall more than four times the number felled by Hagen.[52] "I am sorry for him," said Dietrich, "for he had a virtuous heart and even if he had been a king, this renowned warrior could not have acted with greater élan." "You could just as soon spare your praise of him," Hildebrand retorted. "If you consider how his hand served you in his last days, then you must regret all the more

---

[51] The same text as in verse 1393 is to be found in Manuscript A, but Zeune has rendered it into New High German as: 'Er war von schlanken Gliedern' = 'He was of slim build' (360).

[52] In terms of his fighting prowess, Dancwart enjoys a much greater reputation than Hagen, his brother, as this statement by the *Chlage*-poet underscores. On the trip to Hungary in the *Nibelungenlied*, the Burgundians are attacked by two Bavarian counts, Else and Gelphrat, who engage Dancwart and Hagen respectively in combat. Hagen fears for his life and finds it necessary to call to his brother for assistance (strophe 1613). It is Dancwart who ultimately deals Gelphrat the death blow.

daz er ellen ie gevvan.
vvand ich des vvizzen nine chan.
[1435]   ob ir decheiner mære<.>
vns habe geschadet so sere.
Der Chΰnech do balde daz bevalch.
von Rine vmb den marschalch.
daz man in ce den andern trvch.
[1440]   do begonde der vveinen der genvch.
di den helt sahen.
si hvben in allen gahen.
ein itenivvez rΰffen.
vil grivvlichez vΰffen.
[1445]   do sprach man vnd vvip.
der <nam> Blΰdeline den lip.

Den schal der kΰnech horte.
sin trΰbez herce in storte.
diz vΰffen vnd chlagen.
[1450]   hi mΰgt ir vvnder hΰrn sagen.
er trat in den palas<.>
da div not gevvesen vvas.
Do vant er ligen einen man.
sine ringe vvol getan.
[1455]   im lvhten vz dem plΰte.
im vvas der helm gΰte.
verhovven dvrh di riemen.
daz enhet ander niemen.
nivvan danchvvart getan.
[1460]   Ez vvas ein Dietriches man.
vnd vvas geheizen Vvolfprant.
do erchande in der vvigant.
der edel Bernære.
aller siner svvære.
[1465]   der gehΰget er da bi.
er vvart ovch aller vrevden vri.
di sin herce ie gevvan.
der helt mit leide began.
vveinen elliv siniv ser. /
[1470]   des half im der kΰnech her.
Ecel fΰr Dietrichen sprach.
Ovve daz ich ie gesach.
geligen disen helt tot.
er ist in maneger stvrmes not.
[1475]   so diche frΰmechlich genesen.

that he ever acquired such courage. For I cannot think of anyone who has ever inflicted worse injury upon us." The king immediately ordered that this marshal from the Rhine be carried over to the others. Quite a number of those who saw the warrior began to weep and once again there arose such terrible wailing and grim lamentation. Men and women alike maintained: "He is the one who took Blödelin's life."

[1447] The king heard all this noise and the crying and lamenting disturbed his joyless heart. Listen now to some of the remarkable things that happened.[53] He entered the palace where the catastrophe had taken place and found a man lying there whose well-fashioned rings of mail were shining through the blood. The straps of his sturdy helmet had been hewn through. It had been no one other than Dancwart who had done this to him. This was one of Dietrich's men, and his name was Wolfbrant. Noble Dietrich of Verona recognized him and was reminded of all his sorrow. He was also deprived of any joy that his heart had ever known. In all of his suffering, the warrior began to weep and the noble king joined in his lamentations. Attila said to Dietrich: "Alas, that I ever had to see this hero lying here dead. He was fortunate enough to survive many battles in the past.

[53] At this point, Zeune begins part III of his translation: "Etzels Klage über die Verwandten," 'Attila's Lament for his Kinsmen' (361).

in svves helffe er solde vvesen.
der môhtes gvten trost han.
sine chvndenz niht ver lan.
sine vveinten harte sere.
[1480]　　ezen vvirt nimmer mere.
ich vvæne gechlagt so grimme.
noch mit so lvter stimme.
so vvart gechlagt vvolfprant.

Bi dem recken man do vant.
[1485]　　Sigestabe den richen.
ligen iamerlichen.
den herzogen von Berne.
lieht also di sterne.
im luhten steine durch di vvat.
[1490]　　vver vvas der dich erslagen hat.
sprach der herre Dietrich.
helt nv rivvest dv mich.
tivver degen vil guter.
min vater vnt din mĝter.
[1495]　　di vvaren eines vater chint.
vvi tief dir dine vvnden sint.
edeler recke here.
vvi vil dv miner ere.
vber rvcke hast getragen.
[1500]　　In hat volker erslagen.
sprach do meister hildebrant.
dar vmbe slvch ovch in min hant.
Ich stvnt da bi in beiden.
ine chvndez niht gescheiden.
[1505]　　nivvan mit dem ende.
Ovve min ellende.
sprach der Bernære.
daz ich erstorben vvære.
so hete got vil vvol getan.
[1510]　　vvaz ich arman verlorn han.
frivnde deiz got er barme.
den schilt er von dem arme.
Sigestabe nemen hiez.
manegen trahen nider liez.
[1515]　　Dietrich vnd Hildebrant.
Eceln vrevde vvas gevvant.
mit in an daz minnist.
sin heten anders deheinen list.

The person who enjoyed his aid was assured of a strong ally."[54] They were not able to control their weeping. I believe that no one has ever been so greatly and grimly lamented as Wolfbrant.

[1484] They also found near that warrior mighty Sigestab, the Duke of Verona, who was lying in a pitiful state. Just like twinkling stars, jewels shone through his ring-mail. "Who killed you?" Lord Dietrich asked. "Brave warrior, splendid knight, how I regret your fate. My father and your mother had the same father. How deep your wounds are, noble warrior. How often you took it upon yourself to see that my honor was upheld." "He was killed by Volker," Sir Hildebrand said. "That is why he [Volker] died by my hand. I was standing near the two of them but I could not keep them apart, except in death." "Alas, what great grief I bear," Dietrich of Verona said. "God would have done well to have let me die. May God have mercy upon me for the kinfolk that I, wretched man, have lost." He ordered that Sigestab's shield should be removed from his arm. Dietrich and Hildebrand shed[55] many a tear. Attila's joy had been reduced along with theirs to nothing. They had no recourse

---

[54] In the *Nibelungenlied*, the word "trôst" was one of the more formidable appellatives used to describe Hagen: "er was den Nibelungen ein helflîcher trôst" (1526,2); "trôst der Nibelungen, dâ vor behüete du dich" (1726,4).

[55] Although it is clear from the context that both Dietrich and Hildebrand are weeping, it should be noted that the verb form 'nider liez' in verse 1514 is decidedly singular (perhaps to preserve the rhyme).

vvand vngefᵛgiv herce ser.
[1520]   dane vvas niht chᵛrzvvile mer.

Do bechand er Vvolfvvine.
von eines helmes schine.
den der helt ᵛfe trvch.
der vvas lvter genvch.
[1525]   nv vvas er naz von plᵛte.
ia vvas [140/429] der degen gᵛte.
tot gevallen an di vvant.
Do sprach meister hildebrant.
herre deist der neve min.
[1530]   vnt der Bvrgrave din.
sûn des chᵛnen Nêren.
ni helt so gar vnheren.
ich geschach bi miner zit.
Nᵛ seht vvi den flvz git.
[1535]   daz plᵛt von sinen vvnden.
der recke vvart ni fvnden.
an deheiner zageheit.
in disem stvrm er hi streit.
vvol einem degene gelich.
[1540]   do slvch in der kᵛnech rich.
Giselher der ivnge.
vogt der Nibelvnge.
der slvch ovh Netgere.
der edel vnt der here.
[1545]   do er si ervalte beide.
er tet vns vil ce leide.
er spranch ce Gerbarten.
di helde nit ensparten.
div sharpfen vvaffen an der hant.
[1550]   do vlvgen in div helm bant.
hohe in rotem fivre.
Giselher der vngehivre.
slᵛch di helde alle dri.
ovch lit in hi benebem bi.
[1555]   der vil chᵛne Vvichnant.
den slvch div Gvntheres hant.
der herre vz Bvrgenden.
daz enchvnde niht ervvenden.
div helfe aller diner man.
[1560]   daz er vvære chomen dan.
Ovh slᵛg er Sigehere.

but to bear the terrible pain in their hearts. There was no longer any happiness for them.

[1521] He [Dietrich] recognized Wolfwin from the reflection of the helmet which the warrior was wearing. It had been very bright and now it was wet with blood. The good warrior had fallen dead against the wall. Sir Hildebrand said: "My Lord, this is my nephew and your burgrave, son of brave Ner. In all my years, I have never seen a tougher warrior. Now look how the blood is flowing from his wounds. This knight was never known to be cowardly and in this last battle he fought like a true warrior. That mighty king, young Giselher, lord of the Nibelungen, struck him down. He also killed Nitger. After that noble and mighty warrior had killed the two of them (thereby inflicting great losses on us), he sprang at Gerbart. These warriors did not spare the sharp weapons they held in their hands and their helmet straps flew off high into the air amid the red sparks. Ferocious Giselher killed all three warriors, and not far away from them lies brave Wignant. He was felled by the hand of Gunther, King of Burgundy. None of your men were in a position to prevent it, so that he might have escaped. He also killed Sigeher,

einen degen mære.
vnt den chvnen Vvicharten.
si beide lͮcel sparten.

[1565] in stvrme di hende.
ir beider ellende.
mͮz vns immer nach gan.
vil diche sivften began.
mit iamer do her Dietrich.

[1570] Ecel der chͮnech rich.
den sͮft mit lͮte erschvfte.
sinen vͮf gegen dem lͮfte.
mit chrapft er schal so sere.
daz ob dem kͮnege here.

[1575] von siner chlage der vesten.
daz hͮs mohte nider bresten.

Do si genvch gechlagten die.
di si fvnden heten hie.
do sahen si daz der palas.

[1580] gemͮret all enthalben vvas.
von den verch vvnden.
svva si vvrden fvnden.
dannen hiez si tragen Dietrich.
ir leit daz vvas so iæmerlich.

[1585] vnd so grôzlich ir chlagen.
daz iv daz niemen chan gesagen.
hi ͮze vveinten div vvip.
vil maneger ivnchvrovven lip.
stvnt mit grozem leide.

[1590] gein / trͮber ovgenvveide.
Ez vvas ein vvnderlich geschih'.
dane vvas so vil der manne niht.
di di toten zͮgen vz der vvat.
di man da veige fvnden hat.

[1595] nv seht vvi er vverte daz ir lip.
daz so shône meide vnd vvip.
entvvaffen mvsen di toten.
vil manegen rinch roten.
sah man von vrovven ab gezogen.

[1600] Der meister sagt daz vngelogen.
sin disiv mære.
in herzenlicher svvære.
vnd mit iamerhaften siten.
di riemen vrovven vf sniten.

a marvelous warrior, as well as brave Wichart. Neither of them held back at all in combat. We shall always be touched by their fate." Lord Dietrich let out deep sighs of despair and mighty King Attila joined in with loud shouts of grief. His desperate cries resounded so powerfully in the air that the noble king's house could have collapsed from the intensity of his lamentations.

[1577] After they had sufficiently lamented the one they had found lying here, they saw that the palace was surrounded by a wall of those who had been fatally wounded. Wherever they were found, Dietrich had them carried away. Their sorrow was so great and so intense their lament that no one can adequately express it to you. The women were weeping outside and many a young lady stood there in great sorrow over the terrible sight. It was a remarkable affair, for the number of men who removed the clothes of those who were found lying doomed [on the field] was not great. But look, how could they have prevented such [a situation from arising that] lovely maidens and ladies were forced to strip the dead of their weapons? Many red rings of armor were pulled off by the women. The master maintains that this report was no lie. In deepest sorrow and terrible distress, the women cut through the straps

[1605]   der si niht enstricken chvnden.
              do der kṽnech daz het erfvnden.
              daz si sie sniten vz der vvat.
              svvaz er her gevveinet hat.
              daz vvas allez noch ein niht.
[1610]   vngemṽte hete pfliht.
              siner vngeteilten spil.

              Er sah gesvnder manne vil.
              di dar chomen dvrh di not.
              da si ir mage fvnden tot.
[1615]   di strafte der kṽnech sere.
              vvelt ir des haben ere.
              daz vvip mit toten vmbe gant.
              vnt daz hi gesvnde manne stant.
              di ez pillicher tæten.
[1620]   er gebot daz si entnæten.
              di recken vz den ringen.
              der vvirt der chvnde bringen.
              daz volch ce grozen sorgen.
              ia mvsen si im porgen.
[1625]   vil herten dienest an ir danch.
              ir vvihze vvaren dar zv chranch.
              vvi sise bræhten vz der vvat.
              der kṽnech het niht zornes rat.
              von in er gie sa cehant.
[1630]   da er aber Dietrichen vant.

              Vnmṽzech vvas her Dietrich.
              ia sah er ligen vmbe sich.
              der livte sam die steine.
              idoch entrvch niht eine.
[1635]   di sorge der von Berne.
              der kṽnech sah vngerne.
              sinen schaden also groz.
              daz plṽt allenthalben vloz.
              dvrh div rigel loch her nider.
[1640]   si giengen her oder vvider.
              sine fvnden niht vvan toten.
              den sal von plṽte roten.
              sah man von den vvnden.
              di [141/430] vil vvol gesunden.
[1645]   vvrden siech von der chlage.
              Ezen vvart ni bi deheinem tage.

which they were unable to undo. When the king learned that they were cutting them out of their armor, the weeping he had done up until now was nothing [compared to what followed] and sorrow overtook him completely.

[1612] He saw many survivors brought by the disaster to the place where they found their kinsmen lying dead. The king cursed them severely: "Do you expect to gain any honor by allowing women to tend to the dead while there are healthy men standing around here who are certainly better suited for such work?" He ordered them to free the dead warriors from their armor. The monarch created considerable anxiety among the people, for they reluctantly had to provide him with a hard service and they really had no idea how to divest the dead of their attire. The king could hardly control his anger and left then and there to seek out Dietrich.

[1631] Lord Dietrich had much to do, for, after all, he saw his men lying around him [motionless] like stones. But the warrior of Verona did not suffer alone. The king was also most unhappy to witness the terrible losses he had sustained. The blood flowed down everywhere through the openings in the wall.[56] Wherever they went, they found nothing but corpses, and the Hall itself was red from the blood of the wounds. Even those who had survived became weak from their lamentations. Never before had there

---

[56] The "rigel loch" referred to in verse 1639 appear to be openings in the palace or castle walls used normally for drainage purposes. Lexer refers to this verse in the *Chlage* and provides the definition: *"maueröffnung zum abflusse vom fussboden"* (2: 430).

gevͦffet also sere.
aht hvndert oder mere.
vvaren ir nv vz getragen.
[1650]   do hup sich svnd[er] niͦvez chlagen.
daz ͦbete me<i>ster Hildebrant.
do er Vvolfharten vant.

Als er sinen neven sach.
zv sime herren er do sprach.
[1655]   nv seht vil edel Dietrich
vvi der tot de sich.
mit chreften hat gebͦven.
vvi solde ich des getrvven.
daz eins so tvmben mannes hant.
[1660]   als Giselher der vvigant.
slͦge disen volch degen.
nv sint beide hi gelegen.
der kͦnech vnt der neve min.
daz mͦze got gechlagt sin.
[1665]   daz si in stvrmes stunden.
ie ein ander funden.
her Dietrich schovvete sinen man.
vvi harte in iamern began.
do sah er vvolfharte.
[1670]   mit rôtelohtem barte.
gevallen nider in daz plͦt.
do mant ez den helt gͦt.
aller siner leide.
do vveintens aber beide.
[1675]   in angestlichen sorgen.
di helfe vn verborgen.
man do an Eceln vant.
da stvnt mit vvintend[er] hant.
hi bi Dietriche.
[1680]   in chlage der kͦnech riche.

Wolfhart der vvigant.
het ver chlvmmen in der hant.
daz svvert in stvrmherter not.
svvi der helt vvære tot.
[1685]   daz Dietrich vnd hildebrant.
im daz svvert vz der hant.
chvnden niht gebrechen.
den zorn mͦtes vrechen.

been such wailing. Eight hundred or more were carried outside. But then a new cry of despair was uttered by Sir Hildebrand when he found [the body of] Wolfhart.

[1653] When he saw his nephew, Hildebrand said to his lord: "Most noble Dietrich, see how death has reaped a rich harvest. How could I ever have imagined that the hand of so young a man as the valiant Giselher could have killed this famous warrior? Now both of them are lying here, the king along with my nephew. God's curse on it, that they ever found each other in the midst of battle." Lord Dietrich looked down at his man; how greatly he began to despair. He saw Wolfhart with his fiery red beard lying there dead in his blood and this reminded the good warrior of all his suffering. In their miserable plight, both of them [Dietrich and Hildebrand] began to weep. Attila openly commiserated with them in this wretched situation, for the mighty king stood there wringing his hands in grief next to Dietrich.

[1681] The warrior Wolfhart had clutched his sword so firmly in battle that, although he was quite dead, Dietrich and Hildebrand could not pry it loose from the hand of this brave man

vnz daz siz mit zangen.
[1690]　vz sinen vingern langen.
mvsen chlôzen dem man.
do man daz vvaffen gevvan.
Ovve sprach her Dietrich.
gvt svvert vver sol dich.
[1695]　nv also herliche tragen.
dv vvirst nimmer mer geslagen.
so vil bi kv̂negen richen.
als dich vil lobelichen.
hat geslagen Vvolfhart.
[1700]　vve deich ie geborn vvart.
vvi mir min helfe ist benomen.
vvar sol ich ellender chomen.
Vvolfhart / vor den vviganden.
mit dvrch pizzen zanden.
[1705]　noch lach in dem plv̂te.
man hiez den helt gvte.
heben vz der asshen.
sin herre bat in vvasshen.
vnd vlevn vz den ringen.
[1710]　vil grozes gedingen.
vvas im an im belegen.
do stvnt er v̂ber den vverden degen.
sin tot im iamer brahte.
hey vvaz er gedahte.
[1715]　des im gedienet het der man.
da von er reden do began.

Ovve sprach her Dietrich.
mich mv̂t daz dv helt mich.
nv bringest nimmer mere.
[1720]　ze stvrme in solher ere.
so dv mich diche hast braht.
got mich v̂bele hat bedaht.
daz er dih leben niht enlie.
svva ez an di herte gie.
[1725]　da vvære dv ie beneben min.
nv getrôst ich mich din.
leider nimmer mere.
Ecel der kv̂nech here.
hat manegen sig von dir genomen.
[1730]　nv ist iz leider also chomen.
din helfe ist vns gesvvîchen.

until they finally managed to free it from his long fingers by using tongs. Once they had obtained the weapon, Lord Dietrich said: "Alas, good sword, who shall now wield you with such fame? Never again will you be used in the service of mighty kings in the praiseworthy way you were wielded by Wolfhart. A pity that I was ever born! What [shall I do] now that my men have been taken from me; where shall I go, homeless wretch that I am?"[57] Wolfhart, his teeth clenched, was still lying there in his blood in front of the warriors. They had the good hero lifted from the ashes and his lord then had him bathed and removed from his armor. Dietrich had placed such great hope in him.[58] He now stood over the worthy warrior whose death caused him much sorrow. His thoughts then turned to how the man had served him and he began to speak of such things.

[1717] "Alas," Lord Dietrich said, "I feel, good warrior, that you will never again bring me such honor in combat as you have so often done before. God could certainly not have been thinking well of me when he decided not to allow you to live. Wherever things became difficult, you were always at my side. Unfortunately, you will never again offer me solace. Noble King Attila owes many a victory to you. Regrettably, it has come about that we have been deprived of your assistance.

[57] It is worth recalling here that the primary meaning of "ellender" in the Middle Ages is 'foreigner, stranger (or exile) living in/from another land,' which is precisely the description that best characterizes Dietrich.

[58] Zeune has opted for a different understanding of "grozes gedingen" in verse 1710: "Er hatte große Sehnsucht nach ihm," 'He missed him greatly.' (365). I believe, however, that Wolfhart, with his spirited youthfulness and the uncompromising loyalty he had demonstrated towards Dietrich, was the type of individual in whom the Lord of Verona placed all of his hope for a bright future for himself and his Amelungs. "Gedingen," as a neuter noun, conveys the sense of 'das zuversichtliche Erwarten' ('optimistic expectation(s)'; see Lexer 1: 772), and this quite adequately describes the attitude expressed by Dietrich towards his Amelungs and also explains his incredible distress when he is deprived of that hope for continuity and a positive future through their decimation in the fighting against the Burgundians.

din varvve ist dir erblîchen.
von Giselhers vvnden.
vvist ich an disen stvnden.
[1735] an vvem ichz rechen solde.
vvi gerne ih dih nv vvolde.
dienen tvgenthafter man.
als dv mir diche hast getan.
desen mag et leider niht gesin.
[1740] aller der trost min.
der lit hi an dem ende.
min langez ellende.
hat vaste sih gemeret.
der tag si gvneret.
[1745] daz ich ie schiet von Berne.
ir vvaret bi mir gerne.
mine mage vnd mine man.
svvaz ich ce tvnne ie gevvan.
des hvlfet ir mir gemeine.
[1750] nv sten ich alterseine.

Do sprach meister Hildebrant.
ovvi vil edel vvigant.
vvan lat ir ivver chlagen stan.
solden vvir des frvmen han.
[1755] so chlagt ich immer mere.
disen degen here.
er vvas miner svvester svn.
herre irn svlt is niht tvn.
von iamer vvendet ivvern mvt.
[1760] chlage div ist niemen gvt.
Den recken man do hin trvch.
er vvart geschovvet genvch.
von den lant livten.
si begonden trivten.
[1765] den helt nah sinem [142/431] ende.
von maneger vvizen hende.
vvart der helt gegriffen han.
ez vvære vvip oder man.
di in e bechanden.
[1770] mit zv gedrvchten handen.
vveinten si sere.
sol des iemen haben ere.
der nach tode vvirt gechleit.
so het er mit der vvarheit.

You have been drained of all your color from the wounds inflicted upon you by Giselher. If I knew at this moment on whom I could vent my revenge, how readily I would serve you, virtuous warrior, as you so often served me. But that, unfortunately, can never be. All of my hopes have been dashed here and my long exile has been made so much worse. May the day be cursed on which I ever left Verona. You willingly went with me, my kin and my vassals. Whatever endeavors I undertook with success, you all helped me to accomplish. But now I stand quite alone."

[1751] Sir Hildebrand said: "Alas, most noble warrior, when will you stop your weeping? If anything were to be gained by it, I myself would lament forever this fine knight. [After all,] he was the son of my sister. My lord, you should not do this. Turn your thoughts away from despair. Lamenting does no one any good." The dead warrior was then carried off. The people of the land had taken a good look at him. They began to embrace him now after his death, and he was grasped by many white hands. Women or men who had known him previously grieved greatly [for him], wringing their hands. If a person should be accorded honor who is lamented after his death, then he, in truth,

[1775]　eren vil er vvorben.
　　　　an im lach ver dorben.
　　　　vil maneger svvinder svvertes svvanch.
　　　　chlagte man tvsent iare lanch.
　　　　so mv̂se mans doh vergezzen.

[1780]　<D>er vvirt vvas gesezzen.
　　　　vnder di tv̂r in daz plvt.
　　　　so sere chlagte der helt gvt.
　　　　daz in nieṁ trôsten chvnde.
　　　　dar nach in chvrcer stvnde.

[1785]　funden si den edeln vvigant.
　　　　Giselhern von Bvrgonden lant.
　　　　da er Vvolfharten slvch.
　　　　bi im lag ir noch genvch.
　　　　di er ovch het erslagen.

[1790]　do begonden si ir vient chlagen.
　　　　her Dietrich vnd Hildebrant.
　　　　Si sprachen ôvve daz din lant.
　　　　von dir nv erblosez lit.
　　　　Ovve daz din golt git.

[1795]　nv niemen sam dv tæte.
　　　　dv vvære so êr stæte.
　　　　daz dich des ni gedvhte vil.
　　　　svvaz dv ce frevden vnt ce spil.
　　　　der vverlde chvndest machen.

[1800]　dv bist von hohen sachen.
　　　　chvmen vnz an din ende.
　　　　vns habent dine hende.
　　　　der leide hi so vil getan.
　　　　daz ni tvmber helt began.

[1805]　sich rechen also sere.
　　　　drizech oder mere.
　　　　slvch mir din ellen mære.
　　　　der chv̂nen Bernære.
　　　　Ovve vvan vvære daz er gan.

[1810]　als im riet der spilman.
　　　　der chv̂ne degen Volker.
　　　　so vvære der ivnger kv̂nech her.
　　　　vvorden der margravinne man.
　　　　mit rate trvgen si daz an.

[1815]　do si ce Bechlarn.
　　　　bi Rvdgere vvarn.
　　　　er lobte si cen vibe.

had acquired much honor. Many a fierce swordblow was lost when he died. Yet, even if one were to lament for a thousand years, one would nevertheless have to get over it [eventually].

[1780] The king had sat down in the blood below the door, and the good man was grieving so much that no one could console him. Shortly thereafter they found noble Giselher of Burgundy where he had cut down Wolfhart. There were many others lying around him whom he had also killed. Lord Dietrich and Hildebrand began to grieve for this adversary. They said: "It is a great pity that your land has now been left without an heir, and that there is no one who can distribute your gold as you would have done. Your sense of honor was always so constant that you never felt the joy and entertainment which you provided for everyone was too much.[59] You were a man of great deeds up to the time of your death. We have sustained so many injuries here at your hands. Never before has a young warrior avenged himself with such vigor. Thirty or more of my brave Veronese have been killed through your remarkable strength. Alas, if only things had turned out as the brave minstrel Volker suggested. Then the noble young prince would have become the husband of the countess.[60] That was a well-considered proposal which was suggested when they were guests of Rüedeger in Pöchlarn. He became betrothed to her

[59] The posthumous praise bestowed upon Giselher of Burgundy by Dietrich and Hildebrand is centered on his generosity, an indispensable attribute of any true ruler in the Middle Ages. The bestowing of gifts was an integral function of anyone of stature. In the thirteenth-century epic *Kudrun*, the royal couple Sigeband and Ute cannot refrain from providing guests who have attended their festival with gifts prior to their departure, even though their only son has just been abducted by a griffin. In Hartmann von Aue's Arthurian romance, *Erec*, the hero is not only remiss in his immoderate behavior when he spends too much time in bed with his wife. His lack of attention to courtly affairs, including the sponsoring of festivals and tournaments, precludes him from having the opportunity to dispense gifts and this is destined to deal a considerable blow to his reputation. In the eyes of Dietrich and Hildebrand, Giselher was a model benefactor to all those who looked to the Burgundian ruling family as their lords. Note also verses 2060-2064 and the effusive praise that Attila has for Rüedeger's generosity ("milde").

[60] Dietrich and Hildebrand are referring here to the proposed marriage in the *Nibelungenlied* between Giselher and Rüedeger's daughter. In strophe 1675 of that epic, Volker intimates that, were he a king, he himself would seek her hand in marriage. It is Hagen, however, not Volker, who suggests the union with Giselher in strophe 1678.

ce liebem lanchlibe.
ze trῦte lobt ovch si den degen.
[1820]   nv ist vil ῦbele gelegen.
ir gedinge vnt div vrevde min.
ich solte vil vnvertriben sin.
von chῦnegen immer mere.
ob lebte der degen here.
[1825]   div margravinne Gôtlint.
div ist miner / basen chint.
da von erbet si mich an.
nv ist div magt vvol getan.
ver vvitvvet leider alce frv.
[1830]   nvne vveiz ich anders vvaz ich tv.
ine bit iz got ver enden.

Mit chra(ch)enden henden.
man hῦp den helt mære.
er vvas ein teil ce svvære.
[1835]   er enpfiel in vvider in daz vval.
vor vῦffe erdoz do aber der sal.
von vviben vnd von mannen.
idoh trῦch man in dannen.
da man Criemhilde vant.
[1840]   div chint von Bvrgonden lant.
hiez man cesamne bringen.
daz geschach vf den gedingen.
daz si vvaren Cristen.
ir engel vil vvol vvisten.
[1845]   vvar ir sele solden chomen.
vvart ê vῦffes iht vernomen.
von hercenlichem leide.
daz taten nv di beide.
di christen vnt di heiden.
[1850]   ir chlage vvas vn bescheiden.

Do vant man Gernoten.
so sere verschroten.
mit einer verchvvnden.
gein der brvsten vnden.
[1855]   vvas si vvol ellen vvit er slagen.
svvi vvol ce scherme chonde tragen.
der recke sinen schildes rant.
in het div Rῦdgeres hant.
ver vvndet also sere.

with the prospect of a happy, long life, and she promised herself as bride to the warrior. But now their hopes and my happiness lie dashed here so miserably. If the noble warrior were still alive, I would never again be cast into exile by kings. The Countess Gotelind is the daughter of my aunt, and will, therefore, become my heir. Now this high-bred maiden has become a widow far too early. I do not know what else to do except to ask God to end it all."

[1832] Straining as they did so, they lifted up the renowned knight, but he was too heavy for them, and fell down out of their arms against the ramparts. The Hall resounded again with the lamentations that emanated from both the women and the men. Nevertheless, he was carried away to where Kriemhild lay. They had the Burgundians brought together. This was done in the hope that, since they were Christians, their angels would know where their souls were to be brought to. If there had been great lamenting earlier on account of their terrible suffering, both Christians and heathens now grieved together and without moderation.

[1851] They found Gernot cut down with a fatal wound that extended about an arm's length across his lower chest. Regardless of how well the warrior had borne his shield, Rüedeger had wounded him so badly

[1860]   daz der helt mere.
           der vvnden mohte niht genesen.
           da von mvser tot vvesen.
           vvand in het bestanden.
           ein helt zv sinen handen.
[1865]   Rv̈dger von Bechlaren.
           da si in stvrme vvaren.
           ovch het er Rv̈dgere erslagen.
           den ma<n> nimmer ver chlagen.
           ce dirre vverlde chvnde.
[1870]   vnz an di lesten stvnde.
           Do sah der alte hildebrant.
           di gabe in Gernotes hant.
           di im het Rv̈dger getan.
           het ez der helt ver lan.
[1875]   vvaz ob er vvære genesen.
           niem̄ dorfte chv̈ner vvesen.
           danne der herre Gernot.
           man sah im noch daz svvert rot.
           von blvte naz an siner hant.
[1880]   do sah meister Hildebrant.
           nach des svvertes ecke.
           scharten noch [143/432] <noch> vlecke.
           man da niender an vant.
           vvant div Rv̈dgers hant.
[1885]   chvnde vvnsliche geben.
           er het allez sin leben.
           gevlizen sich vf ere.
           man chlagt in deste mere.

           Do sprach der kv̈nech r(i)che.
[1890]   zem hern Dietriche.
           solde dirre helt leben.
           so het ich allez min geben.
           an minem svne vvol gevvant.
           nah den von Bvrgonden lant.
[1895]   het daz chint geraten.
           di iê daz beste taten.
           sam het ovch <min> sun getan.
           dem het ich miniv lant lan.
           der vvære vvol so riche.
[1900]   daz si al geliche.
           heten trost an <den> degen.
           Nu ist sin chv̈nne hi gelegen.

that he could never recover from it. He died as a result, for a most courageous knight, Rüedeger of Pöchlarn, had fought against him when they met in combat. But he had also slain Rüedeger, for whom one could never grieve enough even if one lamented until the Day of Judgment. Then old Hildebrand saw in Gernot's hand the gift which he had received from Rüedeger. If the warrior had only refrained from taking it, would he not have survived? No one could have been more courageous than Lord Gernot. His sword, wet with red blood, could still be seen in his hand. Sir Hildebrand looked at the edge of the sword but did not find any nicks or [blood] stains on it. For Rüedeger's hand dispensed good things, and throughout his entire life he had striven for honor. All the more reason for him to be lamented.

[1889] The mighty king said to Lord Dietrich: "Had this warrior [Gernot] lived, I would most assuredly have turned everything over to my son. He would have flourished with the Burgundians as his model, who had always acted in the best way. My son would have followed in their footsteps. I would have left him my lands and he would have been so powerful a warrior that everyone could have turned to him for protection. Now his kinsman,

daz beste daz er ie gevvan.
ovve daz ich niht vvenden chan.
[1905] dinen vvndeⁿ vnt dinen tot.
vil tvgenthafter Gernot.
des mvz mir <min> leben leiden.
ez het vvol gescheiden.
Criemhilt hagenen von in drin.
[1910] nivvan daz lv̂cel vvibes sin.
di lenge fv̂r di spannen gat.
an tvmben hercen rat.
so hant si sinne mere.
danne iemen der vf ere.
[1915] sinne hv̂rten chvnde.
daz ist an dirre stvnde.
an miner trivtinne schin.
daz si so vvise vvolde sin.
daz mit sinne ein lihter man.
[1920] het ein bezzerz getan.

Do hiez er Gernoten.
den shvldehaften toten.
vvegen vf mit handen.
der von allen schanden<.>
[1925] het gevvendet sinen mvt.
do gebot iz der chv̂nech gvt.
daz man in tragen solde dan.
vvol gevvahsen vvas der man.
an grôze vnd an lenge.
[1930] div tv̂r vvart in ce enge.
da man di toten vz trv̂ch.
ê do vvas er snel genv̂ch.
der edel vnt der mære.
svvi svvære ab er nv vvære.
[1935] do sin brahten vz der tv̂r.
zv zim giengen dar fv̂r.
di ere gernden vrovven.
di in da vvoldn schovven.
ez vvære in ê gezemen baz.
[1940] von schvlden vvil <ich> sprechen / daz.
do er hete noh daz leben.
got der vvoldes in niht (g)eben.
daz in daz lieb geschæhe.
daz in deheiniv sæhe.
[1945] bi gesvndem sinem libe.

the best whom one could ever have found, is lying here dead. What a pity that I cannot reverse your wounds and your death, most virtuous Gernot. It causes me nothing but sorrow. Kriemhild could assuredly have separated Hagen from the three of them, except that a woman is not endowed with much common sense. Yet in their simple minds they believe they have more sense than someone whose heart is bent on acquiring honor. That is evident in [the actions of] my own wife, who thought she was so wise, but [in comparison to whom] a lesser man with some sense would have acted better."

[1921] The good king then ordered that Gernot, that dead warrior who bore such responsibility [i.e, for the death of Rüedeger],[61] a man who had turned away from all shameful acts, be picked up and carried away from that place. The man was of such fine stature, both in build and height, that the door through which they were carrying out the dead proved to be too narrow. Although heavy now in death, this noble and renowned warrior had previously been the most agile. Once they had brought him out through the door, women who sought honor approached him and wished to look upon him. I feel obliged to say, however, that it would have been more appropriate for them to have done so earlier when he was still alive. But God did not wish to grant them the good fortune that even one of them might see him while he was alive.

---

[61] The adjective "shvldehaften" in verse 1922 should not be understood in the sense of 'guilty' in a moral sense as it might appear at first glance. I follow here a suggestion by Werner Hoffmann that Gernot's "guilt" (or rather the "responsibility" that he bears) lies in his having brought about the demise of Rüedeger by avenging the deaths of so many of his own men who had been killed by the Margrave. It was, in fact, his responsibility to meet Rüedeger in combat after having lost his liegemen. There is a sense of 'obligation' implicit in the term, I believe, which is also reflected in the adjective "schuldec" as listed by Lexer 2: 811: 'verpflichtet (zu zalen od. zu leisten),' which, to be sure, alludes primarily to the contractural obligations of a liegeman to his lord.

er vvart von manegem vvibe.
gechlagt harte sere.
dane vvas et nv niht mere.
nivvan vveinen vnd chlagen.
[1950]   di tvmben daz vvil ich iv sagen.
chlagten mit den vvisen.
di toren mit den grisen.
chlagt al gemeine.
daz sich di mûvver steine.
[1955]   mohten chlieben her dan.
do braht man den chûnen man.
verrer an di vvite.

Dar nach in chvrcer zite.
do vant man Rûdgere.
[1960]   daz ein helt so sere.
ce vverlde ni mer vvart gechleit.
an dem vvas mit vvarheit.
verlorn der vverlde vûnne.
daz vz einem chûnne.
[1965]   so vil eren ni ver darp.
als do der margrave erstarp.
Nv lazen sin di svvære.
vnd sagen iv div mære.
vvaz nv riete Dietrich.
[1970]   do er den margraven rich.
in sinem schilde ligen vant.
er vnd meister Hildebrant.
do sprach der herre von Berne.
nv môht ich als gerne.
[1975]   sin vor zvvelf iaren tot.
dv hast mich lazen in der not.
daz mir bezer vvære begraben.
zv vvem sol ich nv trost haben.
min aller beste chûnne.
[1980]   min vrevde vnd min vûnne.
ist an dir einem belegen.
ez vvart ni getrivver degen.
vnd vvæn ovch vf der erde.
mer deheiner vvrrde.
[1985]   daz tæte dv mir vil vvol schin.
do ich den vianden min.
mvse rûmen miniv Lant.
di trivve ich nind[er] do vant.

He was greatly lamented by many women. There was nothing left but crying and wailing. I have to tell you that the young and inexperienced lamented along with the old and experienced, fools and old men lamented together to the point where the stones in the wall could have split in two. Then they brought the brave man further out onto open ground.

[1958] Shortly thereafter they found Rüedeger. Never before had a hero been so lamented by the world and, in truth, with his passing the joy of the world was lost. So much so, in fact, that no clan had ever sustained such a loss of honor[62] as was the case when the Margrave died. Now let us take our leave of this sorrowful sight and tell you what Dietrich said when he and Sir Hildebrand saw the mighty earl lying on top of his shield. The Lord of Verona said: "I should rather have died twelve years ago. You have abandoned me in my time of need, so that it would be better were I already in my grave. With whom shall I now find consolation? All of my best kinfolk, as well as my joy and happiness, have died with you. There never was a more loyal warrior and I suspect there never will be again on the face of this earth. You demonstrated that to me clearly enough when I was forced to flee my lands before my enemies. At that time I found no sense of loyalty at all,

---

[62] It is appropriate at this point to recall that the sense of honor ('êre') as 'esteem' was predominant in the High Middle Ages and certainly pertains here. Rüedeger was of such renown that his demise would have caused the family to have lost some of the stature accorded it during his lifetime. It is not an issue of "inner" honor, of the basic integrity of the individual or the clan.

vvan an dir einem Rv̊dger.

[1990] Ecel der chv̊nech her.

vvas mir so vientliche gram.

daz ez ni manne zam.

der mir daz gehieze.

daz er mich leben lieze.

[1995] do reit ich vf den trost din.

zv den vvider vvinnen man.

do lobestv daz Rv̊dger.

daz Ecel der kv̊nech her.

dih ê mv̊se hahen.

[2000] ê dv mich liezest vahen.

Do [144/433] ervv̊rbe dv mir hvlde.

daz Ecel miner schvlde.

also grozer vergaz.

mit trivven tæte dv daz.

[2005] do heten min ovh lovgen.

den di mich mit ir ovgen.

bi dir vil diche sahen.

ich vvaz Ecele nahen.

helt in diner hv̊te.

[2010] vnz frovve Helche div vil gv̊te.

div edele chvneginne.

an dir des vvart inne.

daz dv mich enthielte in der not.

Der vrovven ir tvgent daz gebot.

[2015] daz si sich immer mere.

begonde vlizen sere.

svvi si daz bedahte.

daz si mich ce hvlden brahte.

mit dir vil tvgenthafter man.

[2020] allez trv̊ge dv daz an.

hin Ecele dem richen.

daz er genædechlichen.

in sine hvlde mich enpfie.

dar zv̊ verlieze dv mich nie.

[2025] mit trivve vz den genaden din.

svves mir vnt den mannen min.

gebrast in ellende.

din milte vnt dine hende.

taten mir sin alles bvz.

[2030] Ovve der mir dinen grvz.

so verre nv gefremdet hat.

der hat mir allen minen rat.

except in you alone, Rüedeger. Mighty King Attila was so ill-disposed towards me that it did not appear appropriate for anyone to predict that he would let me live. But then with assurances from you, I rode to my enemies, and you swore, Rüedeger, that mighty King Attila would have to hang you before you would allow me to be taken prisoner. It was you who gained for me Attila's favor so that he forgot the great transgressions [I had committed against him]. You did that out of your sense of loyalty. You could also have denied knowing me to those who often saw me with you. When I was in the vicinity of Attila, I enjoyed your protection, brave warrior, until the good Lady Helche, that noble queen, took note that you were shielding me in my [hour of] need. Her womanly virtue required her to do whatever she could to devise a way to allow me to gain [Attila's] favor with your help, most virtuous knight. You used every argument with mighty Attila to persuade him to receive me with favor. And in truth, you yourself never turned your back on me. Whatever my men and I lacked in our homeless state, your generosity made it all up to me. Alas, the person who has robbed me of your greeting has also deprived me of all good counsel.

                  vz miner chamere genomen.
                  din sterben ist vil ͮbele chomen.
[2035]   mir vil ellendem man.
                  Got der hete vvol getan.
                  het er dich leben lâhen.
                  mit schrien ane mazen.
                  so lͮt er vveinte Dietrich.
[2040]   daz Ecel der kͮnech rich.
                  da von vil sere erschrahte.
                  als er von schvlden mahte.

                  Do sprach der fͮrste riche.
                  ia sol ich <pilliche>.
[2045]   mit iv <Rͮdgere> chlagen.
                  sin trivve hat mich en bor getragen.
                  alsam di vedere tvt der vvint.
                  ezen vvart ni mͮter kint.
                  so rehte gar vntrivvenlos.
[2050]   ich vvæn ovch kvnech ie verlos.
                  deheinen chͮnern man.
                  sit ich sin chͮnde ie gevvan.
                  so misseriet er mir nie.
                  svvenner an mine sprache gie.
[2055]   svves mich der helt denne bat.
                  daz m(ͮ)se ich leisten an der stat.
                  daz ist nv cer gangen.
                  min herce deist bevangen.
                  mit maneg[er] hande svvære.
[2060]   ob er nv lebendech være.
                  so være er vvol so milte.
                  daz in des niht bevilte.
                  svvaz tvsent kͮnege môhten han.
                  daz het er / eine vvol vertan.
[2065]   Ovve daz niem̄ sterben mach.
                  vnz im chomt der leste tach.
                  so være ovch ich nv tot gelegen.
                  sit ich so manegen tivvern degen.
                  hi toten vor mir sihe.
[2070]   si ligent rehte als ein vihe.
                  daz erbizzen hant di levven.
                  si mͮgen nv lihte mir gedrevven.
                  di mir ie vvaren gram.
                  den pin ich allen vvorden zam.

Your death is a terrible thing to me, wretched exile that I am. God would have done well to have let you live." Dietrich wailed so loudly and immoderately that mighty Attila was quite rightly taken aback by it.

[2043] The powerful monarch said: "By rights I should lament Rüedeger along with you, for it was his loyalty that helped me rise to power, just as the wind raises up a feather. No mother's child was ever so free of treachery. I also imagine that no king ever lost a braver man. As long as I knew him, he never provided me with bad counsel. Whenever he came to give me advice, I always had to do whatever he suggested. All of that is gone now, and my heart is burdened by a multitude of sorrows. Were he still alive, he would surely be so generous that he would not have considered it too much to have provided by himself what a thousand kings might have offered. A pity that one cannot die until his appointed day. For otherwise I, too, would be dead since I see so many valiant warriors lying here before me. They are scattered about like ordinary beasts brought down by lions. Those who have always been opposed to me could easily threaten me now, for I have become easy prey."

[2075] Do sprach der herre Dietrich.
edel kŭnech bedenche dich.
nach dem grozzem dienste sin.
vnd an der lieben nifteln min.
vnd an Rŭdgeres chinde.
[2080] di in dinem hove gesinde.
dir cen eren vvaren.
vnt dir lobes vil gebaren.
Do sprach der Botelvnges svn.
daz solt ich pilliche tvn.
[2085] vnd bætet ir des nicht Dietrich.
si svln immer an mich.
gedingen sam ich si vater.
hildebranden do bater.
daz er den helt gŭte.
[2090] hŭbe vz dem plŭte.
Vvnt vvas selbe Hildebrant.
daz tet des grimmen hagenen hant.
do sich neigete der man.
sin vŭnde plvten began.
[2095] daz mŭte den helt mære.
im vvas ein teil ce svvære.
Rŭdger der lobs riche.
er trvch in angestliche.
Do er in brahte zv der tŭr.
[2100] ine chvnde der helt niht derfŭr.
vor vnchreften bringen.
ez môhte noch misselingen.
mit sôlhem dienste einem man.
der kŭnech sah den recken an.
[2105] dem vvas sin chrapft entvvichen.
vnd ovch div varvve erblichen.
er seich nider zv Rŭdegere.
des er chom vil sere.
der edel Bernære.
[2110] ez vvas im harte svvære.
Nach vvazzer man do sande.
daz man Hildebrande.
siner chrepfte hŭlfe vvider.
der chŭnech Ecel do der nider.
[2115] zv zim chniete in daz plŭt.
do vergoz in der helt gvt.
Sich ershamte hildebrant.
sin hovbt vf des kŭneges hant.

[2075] Lord Dietrich said: "Noble King, consider the great service [he provided] to my dear niece and to Rüedeger's child who, among your courtly entourage, were an honor to you and earned you much praise." Attila, Botelung's son, replied: "I will quite rightly do so, even if you had not made the request, Dietrich. They can always place their trust in me, just as though I were their father." He then asked Hildebrand to lift the good warrior out of the blood. Hildebrand himself was wounded (grim Hagen had dealt him the blow) and as the man bent down his wound began to bleed, causing quite a strain on the warrior. The renowned Rüedeger was almost too heavy for Hildebrand, and it was with some anxiety that he carried him off. When he brought him to the door, the warrior was too weak to carry him any further. Such a task was simply too much for one man. The king observed the warrior. His strength had left him and the color had gone out of his face. He sank down upon Rüedeger, which greatly startled the noble Veronese and he was very sorry to witness it. They sent for water to help Hildebrand regain his strength. King Attila knelt down to him in the blood and sprinkled the noble warrior with water. Hildebrand was ashamed of himself, for his head

         vil harte svveizigez lach.

[2120]   dem er da diente manegen tach.

         der diente im ^{nv} von schvlden.

         er het nah sinen hvlden.

         [145/434] vil harte diche vvol geritten.

         ez vvære ꝟbele vermitten.

[2125]   daz Ecel hete getan.

         hildebrant der bat do lan.

         vîter offen den sal.

         sich hꝰp vngefꝰger schal.

         hi vze von dem mære.

[2130]   do man sagete vvaz da vvære.

         Sine sꝰmten sich niht mere.

         do truch man Rꝰdegere.

         vater maneger tvgende.

         daz in alter von der ivgende.

[2135]   getrivver niemen vvas bechomen.

         do vvart svvigen gar benomen.

         vil maneger mꝰt$^{[er]}$ chinde.

         allez daz gesinde.

         mit vngelichem mvnde.

[2140]   schrien do begunde.

         Si rꝰften al geliche.

         beide arme vnd riche.

         gar ane frevdehaften sin.

         daz div erde vnder in.

[2145]   sich môhte haben vf getan.

         meide. vvip. vnd man.

         di chlagten Rꝰdegere.

         so hercenlichen sere.

         daz di tꝰrne vnd palas.

[2150]   vnd svvaz gemꝰvers da vvas.

         antvvrte von dem schalle.

         der ovgen grvnt valle.

         von hercen do den flvz trvch.

         man sah da sinnelos genvch.

[2155]   vil der schonen vvibe.

         div vvat von ir libe.

         vvas in cerizzen sere.

         vil manech magt here.

         von ir hovbte brach daz har.

[2160]   ir het der vngenaden var.

         oberhant gevvnnen.

lay dripping with sweat in the king's hand. The man whom he had served for a long time was now quite appropriately serving him, for Hildebrand had often ridden into battle in the service of Attila. It would have been wrong for Attila to have refrained from doing this. Hildebrand asked that the [doors to the] Hall be opened wider. A terrible cry arose outside once the news spread of what had transpired therein.

[2131] They hesitated no longer. Rüedeger, father of all virtue, was carried away. No one had ever gone from youth to old age demonstrating greater loyalty. Many a mother's child could remain silent no longer, and everyone began to wail. The poor and the rich, devoid of any joy, lamented together, so much so that the earth could have opened up beneath them. Young maidens, older women, and men lamented Rüedeger so intensely that the towers and palace and whatever walls there were resounded from the noise. Tears flooded through the barrier of the eyes, right from the heart.[63] Many lovely women were beside themselves and had rent their garments and many a splendid young maiden had torn her hair. Misfortune's treachery had gained the upper hand.

[63] Or, perhaps: "Wave after wave of tears from their hearts flowed through their eyes."

mit plͦte bervnnen.
man manech antlͦze vant.
da vvart von maneger vvizen hant.
[2165]   gein hercen gesvvngen.
di alten zv den ivngen.
vͦften also sere.
daz iz nimmer mere.
von livten vvirt verno�m.
[2170]   als ob Chraneche vværn chomen.
shriende in daz riche.
Ecele vnt Dietriche <.>
vvart gemeret do ir leit.
mit schædlicher vvarheit.

[2175]   Do hiez man bârn cehant.
svvaz man der besten da vant.
der vvart vz besvndert.
sibenzehen hvndert.
christen von heiden.
[2180]   di lieben zv den leiden.
vvrden gelegt vf den re.
svvaz da vvas gechlagt ê.
daz vvas allez gar ein niht.
da vvider vnd / nv hi geschiht.
[2185]   von manegem edeln chin(de.)
(da)z riche hove gesinde.
mit (ia)mer ane vͦnne.
der hohen (k)ͦnege chͦnne.
der chom dar (mit) leide.
[2190]   vvol sehs vnd ahzech m(eide.)
di vrov Helche het er zogen.
(den ê) vͦffen regenbogen.
mit f(revd)en vvaz gebͦven.
vver moh(te) des getrͦven.
[2195]   daz si so nider solden chomen.
in vvas ir trost gar benomen.

Ein teil ich iv der nenne.
di ich von sage bechenne.
vvande si an geschriben sint.
[2200]   dar gie vrovn helchen svvest[er] chint.
frov Herrat div riche.
do merte sich Dietriche.
sin vngefͦge herce ser.

So many faces were covered with blood and many a white hand beat against the breast. The old and the young wailed so much that people will never again hear such a lament.[64] It was as though cranes had descended screeching upon the land. Attila and Dietrich's sorrow was increased all the more through the truth which brought them such losses.

[2175] Orders were given to prepare biers straightaway for the best to be found there. Seventeen hundred Christians were segregated from the heathens. Friends were placed together with enemies on the bier. However much they may have lamented previously, it was nothing at all compared to what transpired here now on the part of many a noble child. The rich courtiers felt only sorrow and no joy, and from the kinfolk of the mighty kings, there now approached in great sadness eighty-six maidens whom Lady Helche had raised under her tutelage and who, up until now, had been the epitome of happiness.[65] Who could have imagined that their hopes could be dashed so terribly? All of their solace had been taken from them.

[2197] I will name some of them for you, for their names have been written down in the story. There went the child of Lady Helche's sister, noble Lady Herrat. The pain Dietrich felt in his heart grew greater.

[64] Anton Ritter von Spaun has rendered verses 2168-2171 into New High German as:

> Daß es immermehre
> Von Leuten wird vernommen
> Als ob Kraniche wären komen,
> Schreinde in die Reiche.

(Anton Ritter von Spaun, *Die Klage. Ein deutsches Heldengedicht des zwölften Jahrhunderts* [Pesth: Verlag von Gustav Heckenast, 1848] 32.) There do not appear, however, to be any instances of "immer mêre" in the other manuscripts which would help to justify such an emendation. If we remain with the original, then verses 2168-2169 are to be linked more with the preceding two verses than with those following, producing a sense as I have suggested in the translation above. Von Spaun's alteration of "nimmer" to "immer" will bring verses 2168-2169 into closer association with 2170-2171 with a corresponding change in semantics of the participle "vernomen": '... so that people will always imagine that it was just as though cranes had come screeching upon the land.'

[65] The text (verses 2192-2193), with its image of the rainbow (of joy), is much more colorful in its description of the earlier happy demeanor of these maidens.

Noch chom der hohgeborner mer.
[2205] des kŮnech Nîtgers chint.
div minnechliche Sigelint.
dar chom dvrch leide schovve.
Goldrvn div vrovve.
eines ChŮneges tohter her.
[2210] der vvaz geheizen Livdeger.
vnd saz in Vranchriche.
dem hete minnechliche.
helche erᶻhogen sin chint.
mit der ivnchvrovven sint.
[2215] chomen hildebvrch vnd Herlint.
zvveier richen fŮrsten chint.
Hildebvrch div schanden vri.
vvas geborn von Normandi.
herlint vvas von kriechen.
[2220] von chlage man vil der siechen.
vnder den vrovven vant.
Nach den chom do sa cehant.
div hercoginne Adellint.
des chŮnen Sintrams chint.
[2225] den helt man vvol bechande.
er saz bi Osterlande.
ein hus an der Vngermache stat.
PŮten noch den namen hat.
da vŮhs von chinde div magt.
[2230] von der ich hie han gesagt.

Sine sint vns alle niht erchant.
di Helche zoch in hivnen lant.
vnd Criemhilde chomen an.
Ecele man si sande dan.
[2235] vnd Helchen cen eren.
niemen also heren.
man <in> allen landen vant.
dem Helchen tvgende vvas erchant.
ern liez ir gerne dar sin chint.
[2240] vvol ahzech graven toht[er] sint.
chomen zv dem schalle.
di vvitvven chomen alle.
der man vnd mage da lagen tot.
sich hŮp von [146/435] clage div meiste not.
[2245] di man cer vverlde ie bevant.
des vvart daz Eceln lant.

But then more of the high born ladies arrived: the child of King Nitger, the lovely Sigelind. Lady Goldrun also arrived to see the pitiful sight, the noble daughter of a king. His name was Liudeger and he had reigned in France. Helche had raised his daughter for him in loving kindness. Hildeburg and Herlind, the children of two powerful noblemen, came with the young lady. Hildeburg, free of blemish, had been born in Normandy, while Herlind was from Greece. Many of the women were weak from their grieving. Duchess Adelind, daughter of brave Sintram, arrived shortly thereafter. Her father was a well-known warrior who resided in Osterland. There is a house which is located in the Marches of Hungary and also has the name Püten, and this was where the maiden of whom I have been speaking spent her childhood.

[2231] We do not know the names of all [the women] who were under Helche's tutelage in the land of the Huns and who had subsequently joined Kriemhild's entourage. They had been sent to honor Attila and Helche. There was not a nobleman throughout all the lands who, being aware of Helche's virtues, would not have been happy to send his child to her. About eighty daughters of counts had come to the scene of the calamity. All of the widows had come whose husbands and kinfolk were lying there dead. With all this grieving there arose the greatest despair which had ever been known in the world, and for that reason, Attila's realm

allez vrevden lære.
von disem grimmem mære.
hůp sich dar zv div lantschapft.
[2250] mit vil chlagelicher chrapft.
beide spate vnd frů.
daz livt seich allenthalben zů.
si giengen sůchen ir frivnde zv der stvnde
di in dem plůte lagen vvnde.
[2255] allenthalben vffem vval.
vor dem hůse vnd in dem sal.
sam ce marchte dvrch di chrâmen.
der tot hete sinen sâmen.
gesæt vil vviten in div lant.
[2260] do ieslicher der sinen vant.
svva er nider vvas geslagen.
genůge sah man dannen tragen.
ir frivnde vz dem plůte.
do hvben vrovven gůte.
[2265] ir chlage zv den stvnden.
sam sis ê ni begvndn.

Ir trivve man bi iamer vant.
man sach von Ivnch vrovven hant.
vnd manegem edeln vvibe.
[2270] gebrochen von ir libe.
manech vvol gezieret chleit.
sine vvolden niht daz ir leit.
dem golde gezæme.
svvi rehte vngenæme.
[2275] di toten sin den livten.
chůssen vnd trivten.
sach man da manegen toten.
ce verhe verschroten.
Er læret vvas der palas.
[2280] der ê so vol der veigen vvas.
done chvnde niemen trôsten.
di besten vnde di bôsten.
svvaz ê iemen hat gechleit.
oder von chlage her geseit.
[2285] oder noch gechlagen chůnde.
der chlagt daz vrgrůnde.
vvas allez vf ein ander chomen.
do het her Dietrich ver nomen.
der schônen Herraten mvnt.

was devoid of all joy. When they heard this grim tale, the people from the countryside began to arrive in terrible despair from all sides, day and night. Just as though they were wandering through traders' booths in the marketplace, they went about searching for their friends who were lying wounded in the blood, on the battleground, in front of the palace and in the Great Hall. Death had sown his seed widely throughout the land. One by one they found their kinsmen lying where they had been killed, and many folk could be seen removing their friends from the blood. Good women once again raised their voices in lament in a way they had never done in the past.

[2267] Their loyalty was expressed through their sorrow. Maidens along with numerous noblewomen ripped the well-fashioned clothes from their bodies. They felt that their misery did not accord well with the gold. However unpleasant the dead may be for people, they kissed and embraced there many a dead warrior who had been cut to pieces. The palace,[66] which had previously been filled with corpses, was cleared. No one could offer any solace to either the high-bred or the commoners.[67] However much one may have grieved previously, or had related of [great] lamenting, or however capable of grieving one might still be, the origins of all lamentations had congregated here. Lord Dietrich heard the voice of lovely Herrat.

---

[66] Zeune begins the fourth part of his translation with verse 2279: "Begräbniss" ('Burial,' 375).

[67] Zeune translates verse 2282 simply as 'die Guten und die Bösen' (375). I suspect, however, that the poet is referring to the mixed group of people who have gathered at the place of slaughter, i.e., the noblemen as well as the country folk or commoners, all of whom are searching for relatives and friends.

[2290] svvi vil im leides vvære chvnt.
idoch erbarmte im ir leit.
si vnd ander manech meit.
mvsen tvn daz er gebot.
ein teil schiet er si von der not.
[2295] Er bat si leiten von dan.
vvi grozze vmmv̊ze do gevvan.
her Dietrich vnd her Hildebrant.
si hiezen sarchen sa ce hant.
di drie Chv̊nege riche.
[2300] got lone Dieteriche.
daz er di trivve ie gevvan.
daz man si svnderte dan.
di edeln vnt di richen.
daz tet man pillichen.

[2305] Der Chvnech gie sa cehant.
da er sin vvip ligen vant.
vnd sin chint an dem re.
vor iamer vvart im also vve.
daz er viel in vnmaht. /
[2310] in het der iamer dar zv (bra)ht.
daz im zv d(er) stvnde.
vz(en) orᵉn vnd vz dem mvnde.
b(egond)e bresten daz plv̊t.
so (sere) chlagte der helt g(v̊t).
[2315] daz ez (ein gr)ozer vvnder vv(as).
daz er (der) chlage ie genas.
vver chv(n)de chlage da gedagen.
si begunden alle mit im chlagen.
di den iamer mvsen schovven.
[2320] ritter vnde vrovven.
in iamer chlageliche.
baten den Chv̊nech riche.
daz er den lip iht so verlv̊r.
vnt daz er bezzern trost chv̊r.
[2325] daz vvære in beidenthalben gv̊t.
do getrosten si dem helde den mv̊t.
do vvas bereitet in ein sarch.
der vvas vvit vnd starch.
da man sie in legen solde.
[2330] ein pfellel von golde.
tivver vnd riche.
gevvorht vil spæheliche.

Regardless of how much sorrow he might have felt, he nevertheless took great pity on her in her despair. She and many other maidens had to follow his directions. He managed to alleviate their distress somewhat and had them led away from this place. Dietrich and Hildebrand had much to do. They immediately had the three mighty kings put into coffins. May God reward Dietrich for demonstrating his loyalty, for he separated out the rich and powerful lords. This was only fitting.

[2305] The king then went over to where he found his wife and his child lying on the bier. He was in such a terrible state from his sorrow that he collapsed in a faint. The grief that he felt caused the blood to flow out of his ears and his mouth. The good warrior lamented so much that it was truly a miracle that he ever managed to survive. Yet who could refrain from lamenting there? All those who were forced to view this miserable scene began to weep along with him. Knights and ladies alike, in terrible distress, begged the mighty king not to torment himself so much[68] and to find a better means of consolation. That would be to everyone's advantage. In this way, they attempted to console the warrior. A wide and sturdy coffin was made ready into which they [Kriemhild and Ortlieb] were to be placed. Both his child and his wife were wrapped in a beautiful and rare sheet lined with gold

---

[68] The original text of verse 2323 is actually much more graphic. Zeune translates: '... daß er den Leib nicht so verderbe ... ' ('that he not do such injury to his body,' 375).

verre braht vz heiden lant.
da man si beide in vvant.
[2335]   sin chint vnd sin vvip.
do bestate man ir beider lip.
nach Chꝰnechlichen eren.
dvrch ir heil ce meren.
si baten got der sele pflegen.
[2340]   Sam tet man Blodelin den degen.
des vverden Botelvnges svn.
vvaz moht her Dietrich nv tvn.
vvan als iz trivven tohte.
svvaz man der vinden mohte.
[2345]   di messe solden singen.
di hiez er balde bringen.
also chonder iz da schaffen.
den Cristen ir pfaffen.
den heiden der ovch den gezam.
[2350]   dar nach man do zehant nam.
den gꝰten Rꝰdegere.
mit dem vil michel ere.
vvart geleit in sin grap.
do sach man manegen chrivz stap.
[2355]   da den pfaffen an der hant.
svvaz man ir vnder stole vant.
di baten al geliche.
got von himelriche.
vnde sande Michehele.
[2360]   ce genaden ir aller sele.
di da fꝰrsten hiezen.
niht langer si di liezen.
sine bræhten si cer erde.
di chꝰnege vvrden vverde.
[2365]   bestatet in manegem sarche.
Hagen der starche.
vnd sin geselle Volker.
vnt Danchvvart der recke her.
di vvrden do alle dri.
[2370]   ir herren gelegt nahen bi.
Havvart der starche.
der kꝰnech [147/436] von Tenemarche.
Irinch vnd Irinfrit.
di dri vvrden ovch da mit.
[2375]   bestatet herlichen.
di dar vz andern richen.

which had been brought from a heathen land far away. Then their bodies were interred with all honors befitting royalty. To enhance their chances of salvation, they asked God to watch over their souls. The same was done for the warrior Blödelin, son of worthy Botelung. What else could Lord Dietrich do now other than to follow the dictates of loyalty? He had brought to him right away however many [people] could be found to sing a mass. He arranged it in such a way that the Christians and heathens alike had their respective priests. After this they immediately carried off good Rüedeger, who was accompanied into his grave by great honor. Many crosses could be seen there, which were carried by the priests. Every single one of the vested priests begged God in heaven, as well as Saint Michael, to have mercy on their souls. Those who were noblemen were not left [lying there] any longer, but were rather buried. Many coffins were used to give the kings a worthy burial. Mighty Hagen and his companion Volker, along with Dancwart, that noble hero, were laid to rest near their lords. Hawart the Strong, King of Denmark, as well as Iring and Irnfrid — these three were also given a magnificent burial. Those warriors from other countries

zv der hohzit vvaren chomen.
der vvart ovh da vvar genomen.
mit g#tlichen dingen.
[2380]   man iltes alle bringen.
di chvnden vnt di geste.
zir langen bette reste.

Daz volch do r#vens niht enpflach.
diz vværte vnz an den dritten tach.
[2385]   ê man begr#b di hêren.
ir m#de mvsen meren.
ê di andern vvrden begraben.
di mvsen ovch ir recht haben.
Ecel vnt Dietrich.
[2390]   di berieten do sich.
ezen chvnde niemen ver enden.
vvolt man di ellenden.
alle svnder begraben.
si m#sen ein grab haben.
[2395]   so tief vnd also vvit.
daz man ce etslicher zit.
vvol ver enden chvnde.
der k#nech shvf da ce stvnde.
daz di lant livte d#.
[2400]   griffen allen samt z#.
vnd grvben eine grvben sit.
siben sper schepfte vvit.
vnd also tief in di erde.
Ich vvæne immer vverde.
[2405]   mit solhem iamer gegraben.
di chnehte vvrden vf erhaben.
daz gesinde von dem Rine.
di G#nthers vnt di sine.
mit in brahten in daz lant.
[2410]   nivn tvsent man da vant.
an den sich erste hvb div not.
den livten iamer daz gebot.
dvrch ir ellende<.>
vvnden si di hende.

[2415]   Man vant da veiger mere.
mit leide vnde ovch mit sere.
als ich iv diche han geseit.
so vvrden si in daz grap geleit.

who had come to the festival were also well attended to. They made haste to commit to eternal repose both their own dead and the guests who had been killed.

[2383] For three days the people had no respite until they had buried the noble warriors. They became even more fatigued by the time all the others were interred, for they, too, had to be accorded their due. Attila and Dietrich conferred with one another, for there was no end in sight if they wished to bury all the foreigners in separate graves. For the latter, a grave had to be dug that was deep and wide enough to allow them to complete the burials within a reasonable amount of time. The king then ordered the country folk to pitch in and shovel out a grave in the earth that was seven spear shafts wide and just as deep. I'm sure that no grave was ever dug in greater sorrow. The [bodies of the] squires were also removed, the company from the Rhine whom Gunther and his brothers had brought along with them into this land. They found nine thousand of them, and they had been the first victims of the catastrophe. Sorrow compelled the people to wring their hands in misery.

[2415] But more dead warriors were found there. As I have often told you already, they were also placed into the grave amidst great despair and sorrow.

Do si alle ce stete vvarn chomen.
[2420]   do vvart al rest do vernomen.
von den di giengen vome grabe.
div aller meiste vngehabᵉ.
der si ceheinen stvnden.
da vor noch ie begunden.
[2425]   Ez vvas ein grimmegez scheiden.
von Cristen vnd von heiden.
di chlagten also sere.
daz man immer mere. /
da von sagen mach.
[2430]   vnz an den ivngesten tach.
Sit in vrevde niht gezam.
niemen des andern vvar nam.
der di noch lebende vvaren.
Eceln man gebaren.
[2435]   vil vngv̓tliche vant.
do er ze vveder siner hant.
der gvten recken niht ensach.
vvider Dietrich er do sprach.
den fv̓rsten von Berne.
[2440]   Ia het ich noch vil gerne.
manegen des ich mich anen mvz.
mir hat min vngelv̓cke bvz.
aller vrevden getan.
Dietrich sprach ia svlt ir lan.
[2445]   ivver groze vngehaben.
sine sint niht alle noch begraben.
di iv ce dienste sint gevvant.
her kv̓nech ia mv̓gt ir ivver lant.
mit helden noch besetzen.
[2450]   got mach ivch ergetzen.
genædlechlich der leide.
ir habt doch noch vns beide.
mich vnd Hildebrande.
bi iv in dem lande.

[2455]   Waz hilfet daz sprach er do.
ine chvnde nimmer vverden vro.
vnd sold ich tvsent iar leben.
vver chvnde mir den mvt gegeben.
oder vver mȯhte mirz geraten.
[2460]   di daz mit vvillen taten.
di sint leider gelegen tot.

Once they had all been brought to their resting place, those who left the grave site realized for the first time just how great their misery was, a feeling the like of which they had never had before nor would ever have again. It was a bitter leave-taking by both Christians and heathens and they all were given so much to their lamentations that people could talk about it until the Day of Judgment. Since it would have been inappropriate for them to have felt joy, no one paid any particular attention to those who were still alive. They found Attila behaving in a most unfriendly manner. Since he no longer had the good warriors serving at his side, he said to Dietrich, the Earl of Verona: "How I would like to have [the service of] many a man whom I now have to do without. My misfortune has robbed me of all joy." Lord Dietrich replied: "You ought to put aside your great despair. Not everyone who wishes to serve you has been laid in his grave. Noble King, you still have warriors enough to maintain your lands. God will most assuredly make good your sorrows in a merciful way. After all, you still have the two of us, Hildebrand and myself, here in your land."

[2455] "What good is that?" he asked. "I could never be happy again even if I were to live for a thousand years. Who could make me have a change of heart or prompt me to be joyful? Those people who would have willingly done so are now unfortunately dead.

vvaz sol mir nv min golt rot.
oder deheiner slahte richtvm.
gevvalt. vverltlicher rvm.
[2465] daz ist an mir verdorben.
mine man sint erstorben.
dar zv chint vnd vvip.
vvar zv sol mir der lip.
ceptrvm <o>der chrone.
[2470] div mir ᵉ vil schone.
stvnt in allen minen tagen.
dane vvil ich nimmer mer getragen.
vrevde. ere. vnd vverdez leben.
daz vvil ⁱʰ allez vf geben.
[2475] vnd vvilz allez nider legen.
des ich cer vverlde solde pflegen.
sît ez mir allez missez(im)t.
ine rͮche vvenne mich der tot nimt.

Si vvolden trôsten im den mvt.
[2480] daz en vvas dehein gvt.
vvand er hete ce vil verlorn.
vͮber in hete gesvvorn.
sines libes vnheil.
im vvas der aller meiste teil.
[2485] siner vngenade chomen.
vvand ez im allez vvas benomen.
daz er [148/437] des besten ie gevvan.
der kͮnech vveinen began.
sam do ers aller erst pflach.
[2490] ein teil ovch nider gelach.
hern dietriches vester mvt.
vor mͮde der helt gvt.
sich in ein venster leinte nider.
Hildebrant der sprach sider.
[2495] dem herren Dietrichen zv.
herre vves beit ir nv.

Da rat ich sprach der vvigant.
sit ver vͮhstet ist daz lant.
vvaz svln vvir nv dar inne.
[2500] daz helche div chͮneginne.
iv gab vil edel Dietrich.
daz dvnchet mich rætlich.
da mit rvme vvir daz lant.

What good are my gold or any of my treasures to me now? Power, worldly fame, all of that is lost to me. My men are dead, as well as my child and my wife. Of what use to me now are my life, the scepter or the crown, which I always wore with such splendor throughout my reign? I never want to wear it again; moreover, I will renounce joy, honor, and a worthy life — I will lay it all aside, everything which I ought to cultivate in the world, since it all seems inappropriate to me now. It would be all the same to me were death to carry me off."

[2479] They tried to console him, but it was all to no avail, for he had lost too much. The misfortunes of his life had conspired against him and the worst of all possible fates had been visited upon him, for he had lost the best of everything he had ever won in his life. The king began to weep, just as he had done the first time. Even Lord Dietrich's staunch spirit was somewhat dejected and the good warrior leaned back from exhaustion against a window. Hildebrand then said to Lord Dietrich: "My Lord, what are you waiting for?

[2497] I would advise you," the warrior continued, "since this country has become a wasteland, what is the point of our staying here? Most noble Dietrich, it seems advisable to me to take what Queen Helche gave you and for us to leave this land."[69]

[69] Zeune has interpreted this section quite differently: "Da das Land verwüstet ist, was Helke die Königin euch, edler Dietrich, gab, was sollen wir noch darin?" 'Since, noble Dietrich, the land which Queen Helche gave you has been devastated, why should we remain here?' (378). I am not at all sure, however, that it is the land which Helche turned over to Dietrich. His plans were, after all, to found a new empire in northern Italy, not to settle in Hungary. It seems more likely to me that Hildebrand is referring to the gifts that Dietrich, as an exile, had received from Helche and that he is suggesting they quit this land and take them along (note verse 2503).

ivver ellen vnd min hant.
[2505]   div bede svln beraten.
mine vrovn Herraten.
vvand vvir sin svŷren beide.
vvir sŷln dvrch vnser leide.
der trivve niht ver gezzen.
[2510]   svvi nider si gesezzen.
ivver frevde vnt div min.
doch sŷln vvir immer di sin.
di stæter trivve chŷnnen pflegen.
daz tvn ich gerne so sprach der degen.

[2515]   Wie sol ich von disen leiden.
mit eren min gescheiden.
sit ich den schaden han genomen.
ovve vvaz leider mære chomen.
mvz hin vvider vf den vvegen.
[2520]   von dannen ein ieslicher degen.
reit zu dirre hohzit.
âch vve vvaz gvter svverte lit.
herrelos in disem sal.
prŷnne. vnd helme ane zal.
[2525]   dine vvizze vvir vvem nv geben.
sît daz di niht solden leben.
di si da ê hant getragen.
Gote vvil ich ez immer chlagen.
daz ich so manegen vverden man.
[2530]   mvz toten hi beliben lan.
Vvir sŷln do sprach Hildebrant.
der gvten recken gevvant.
heizen vvasshen vz dem plŷt.
vnt div zieren vvaffen gŷt.
[2535]   heizen vvol behalten.
vvil Ecele vvitze vvalten.
ez mach im lihte noch gefrvmen.
vnd ce grozzen staten chomen.

Do der kŷnech daz ver nam.
[2540]   den rat er fŷr gŷt nam.
vnd ensŷmte sich niht mere.
nach ir beider lere.
hiez er behalten daz gevvant.
vnt div besten svvert div man vant.
[2545]   hiez er do behalten tragen.

Your strength and my hand should both be placed at the disposal of Lady Herrat, for we are obliged by oath to serve her. We should not forget our sense of loyalty as a result of our sorrow. However little joy you and I may now feel, we should always remain men who observe unequivocal loyalty." "I am happy to do so," the warrior replied.

[2515] "Yet, how can I, with honor, free myself from this misery, given the losses I have suffered? Alas, what terrible news must now be carried back along the path taken by many a warrior as he rode here to this festival! And how many good swords now lie without their masters in this Hall! There are also countless hauberks and helmets and we have no idea to whom we should give them, since those who previously wore them are no longer alive. I will forever lament to God that I had to leave so many worthy men lying here dead." Hildebrand said: "We should have the blood washed out of the clothes of the good warriors, and their finely decorated weapons gathered up for safekeeping. If Attila acts with prudence, this may still be of some use to him and gain him honor and esteem."

[2539] When the king heard this, he considered it to be good counsel and waited no longer. In accordance with the advice offered by the two of them, he had the clothes [of the slain] gathered up and also ordered that the best swords that could be found there be carried away.

her Dietrich sprach ich vvil iv sagen. /
vil edel Chѵnech riche.
vvelt ir nv lobliche.
tvn nach grozem leide.
[2550]　　so raten vvir iv beide.
ich vnd meister Hildebrant.
daz ir in igelichez lant.
svlt vvider den vveisen senden.
des enlat ivch niemen vvenden.
[2555]　　svvaz von ir landen her si chomen.
di der tot hi hat genomen.
des gevvinnet ir noch ere.
di ivngen mvgen iv mere.
gefrvmen danne div sarvvat.
[2560]　　di in der tot erlôset hat.

Do sprach der Botelvnges svn.
daz sol ich pilliche tvn.
vnd volges iv von rehte.
di Rѵdegers knehte.
[2565]　　hiez man aller erste bringen.
den sah man zæhere dringen.
vze den ovgen ce tal.
zv Ecele ir chom͞ fѵr den sal.
siben vnd niht mere.
[2570]　　do sprach der Chѵnech here.
svvi ir nv vvelt her Dietrich.
so enbietet der margravinne rich.
hin ze Bechelarn.
alle di da vvaren.
[2575]　　den besvværet iz den mvt.
idoch tet iz der helt gvt.
Rѵdegers svvert vnd sin gevvant.
vnd sin ros da man daz vant.
hiez man balde bringen.
[2580]　　vvi mohte misselingen.
harter frovven libe.
danne sime vvibe.
do man ir sagte mære.
vvi ez ergangen vvære.

[2585]　　Do sprach meister Hildebrant.
vver sol in Bvrgonden lant.
dirre mære bote vvesen.

Lord Dietrich said: "Let me tell you, most mighty and noble king, that if you desire to act in a way that will bring you much praise after such terrible suffering, then Sir Hildebrand and I would advise you — and let no one deter you from so doing — to send to the orphans in each country those things which have been brought here from their homelands and which death has separated from their owners.[70] In this way you will still gain honor, for the young orphans may prove of more use to you than the armor which death has deprived of a master."

[2561] Botelung's son replied: "I will certainly follow your advice and undertake this." They then had Rüedeger's squires summoned. Their eyes welled tears. Only seven of them appeared before Attila in front of the Hall. The noble king said: "Lord Dietrich, carry[71] whatever you wish back to the mighty countess in Pöchlarn." All of those who were present were sad at heart, but the good warrior nonetheless went through with it. Orders were given to fetch Rüedeger's sword, attire, and his horse. What greater misfortune could have been visited upon any woman than was the case with his wife when they told her what had transpired there.

[2585] Sir Hildebrand said: "Who will be the messenger and carry news of these events to Burgundy,

[70] Verses 2555-2556 could cause some confusion. "Svvaz" would have to refer to *things* that have been brought from the lands of the warriors slain at Attila's camp. If that is indeed the case, one may wonder at the semantics of 2556: 'which death had carried off here,' since it is obviously the warriors themselves who have succumbed to death. I have suggested that the sense is that the weapons (and clothes) have been separated from their previous owners through the death of the latter. It might be suggested that "svvaz" refers to the warriors themselves, which would lend more obvious meaning to 2556. Such an assumption, however, would be predicated upon the idea that Dietrich and Hildebrand are actually suggesting that the corpses of the dead foreign knights be returned to their orphans, something which is both grotesque and illogical, since most of the dead have already been buried.

[71] It should be noted that the verb "enbieten" in verse 2572 could refer to the 'carrying' [back to Pöchlarn] of a message, of news, or to tangible items such as the private possessions of the deceased. There is no way to determine definitively whether the one or the other sense was primarily intended in this case.

sit ir niemen ist genesen.
der ritter noch der knehte.
[2590]   der chꝰnech sol von rehte.
sin selbes boten ꝰber rin.
senden daz si Svvemmelin.
sprach der kꝰnech alcehant.
dem sint di vvege vvol bechant.
[2595]   dar zꝰ shꝰf man zvvelf man.
di daz gevvêfn fvrten dan.
mit dem videlære.
daz di helde mære.
in stvrme heten getragen.
[2600]   vnt daz di boten solden sagen.
da ce ʀine mære.
vvi ez geschehen vvære.
di herren vvrden des en ein.
daz man der boten al dehein.
[2605]   lieze niht beliben.
man sande si ir vviben.
mit den mæren heim ce lande.
vnd ovch mit dem gevvande.
daz di veigen trvgen ê.
[2610]   Ir frivnde̅ vvart dort also vve.
sam disen ê vvas von [149/438] chlage.
ia mohtens immer dem tage.
flꝰchen daz div vvirtschaft.
also maneges heldes chraft.
[2615]   mit tode het geletzet.
si vvrden gar entse'zet.
svvaz si frevden solden han.
den ez chvnt vvart getan.

Di da solden an den ʀin.
[2620]   mit den gie do Svvemmelin.
fꝰr Ecel den kꝰnech stan.
er sprach nv svlt ir niht lan.
irn saget besheidenliche̅.
Prꝰnnhilde der richen.
[2625]   vvi ez allez si ergangen.
vnd vvi mir si befangen.
min lant mit grozem sere.
vnt daz nie geste mere.
getaten vvirte so leide.
[2630]   desen svln si doch beide.

since none of their men — whether knights or squires — have survived? By rights, the king ought to send his own envoy to the Rhine." "That would be Swemmel," the king said immediately. "He is well acquainted with the way there." They assembled twelve men who, together with the minstrel, were to transport the weapons which the renowned warriors had carried into battle. These messengers were also to relate what had happened here once they reached the Rhine. The lords were of one mind that the envoys should be detained no longer.[72] They were sent off to the widows [of the slain warriors] with the news of what had transpired. They also took with them the clothes which had previously been worn by the dead warriors. Their friends were overcome with grief just as had been the case with these folk earlier. They could well curse the day on which the festival had robbed many a warrior of his strength through death. They were deprived of any joy they might have had once they learned what had happened.

[2619] Swemmel, along with the others who were to ride to the Rhine, approached the king. Attila told him: "Do not neglect to tell noble Brünhild in an appropriate way how everything has come to pass here, how my land has been inflicted with great misery, and that no guests have ever caused their host such suffering.[73] Brünhild and Lady Ute should

---

[72] Emulating Christian Heinrich Myller and Friedrich Heinrich von der Hagen (see bibliography), Zeune has inserted "weapons" for "messengers" in translating verse 2604. There are difficulties whether one picks "Waffen" or "Boten," however. Zeune can easily associate "Waffen" with "gevvande" ('attire') in 2608, but conveniently leaves out the reference to the "mæren" (verse 2607) that were also sent back to the homelands of the slain. 'Messengers' would be the likely bearers of "mæren," but what one does then make of the possessive pronoun "ir" in verse 2606? Perhaps the answer is a simple one: 'The messengers were then sent off to their women [i.e., the widows of the slain warriors] with the news of what had happened...,' and this is the solution for which I have opted.

[73] In the case of verse 2629, I have followed the reading to be found in the Berlin manuscripts J and h: "ir wirt." This rendering makes the most sense to me within the current context. Attila is lamenting the fact that his realm has been turned into a wasteland and that his Burgundian guests could hardly be outdone in the suffering they have caused their host. This accords with the verses which immediately follow, namely, that Brünhild and Ute should not feel that they owe Attila compensation. He is, however, intent on underscoring his innocence in the whole matter, as is clear from verse 2634.

niht engelten sprach der gvte.
Prꝷnnhilt vnd frov Vte.
Er sprah irn svlt ovch niht verdagen.
min vnschvlt svlt ir in sagen.
[2635]　di besten da ce ʀine.
daz ich noch di mine.
nie verdienten sôlhe not.
vvand ichz in gꝷtliche erbot.
vnt tet vil vvillechliche daz.
[2640]　da vvider zeigeten si mir haz.
svvaz ich des schaden han genomen.
daz ist ovch in ce schaden chomen.

Do sprach der videlære.
als vnvverdiv mære.
[2645]　div gefvrt ich noh nie mere.
der lande vrevde vnd ere.
div ist nv gar versvnden.
di ê mit vꝷnne chvnden.
vvol leben vnd schone.
[2650]　di diche vnder chrone.
mit vrevden sin gegangen.
von den vvirt mir enpfangen.
so svvinde disiv botschapft.
daz ich in miner sinne chrapft.
[2655]　han michel sorge dar zꝷ.
vvi ih den mæren so getꝷ.
daz ich den lip mꝷge bevvarn.
Der kꝷnech sprach ia svlt ir varn.
mit den von Bechlaren.
[2660]　bereit si schiere vvaren.

Do sprach her Dietrich.
mære als vnfrivntlich.
div mvz ich leider senden.
ovve môht ichz ervvenden.
[2665]　mit min selbes libe.
daz ich dem edeln vvibe.
ir herce leit enbieten sol.
da mit envvirt mir nimmer vvol.
Ir svlt heln sprach Dietrich.
[2670]　disiv mære iæmerlich.
allenthalben vf den strazzen.
ir svlt daz livt niht lazzen.

not feel, however, that they have to make it up to me," the good man said.
He continued: "Do not fail to mention my innocence to those most worthy
folk on the Rhine. Tell them that neither I nor my men ever deserved to
experience such a catastrophe. For I received them with kindness and did
so willingly. They, on the other hand, displayed hatred towards me. They
were paid in kind for whatever losses I have suffered."

[2643] The minstrel replied: "Never before have I been the bearer of
such terrible news. The joy and honor of [our] lands have now completely
disappeared. People who previously have lived in joy and splendor, who
have long worn their crowns in happiness, will react with outrage to the
message I bring them. Quite frankly, I am very concerned how I might
impart this news to them and manage to stay alive." The king replied:
"Well, you shall ride along with the men of Pöchlarn." They made ready
straightaway for the trip.

[2661] Lord Dietrich said: "How unfortunate that I must send such
unhappy tidings. Alas, if only I could avoid doing so by putting my own life
on the line. That I should have to be the one to bring such sorrow to the
noble woman is something I will never be able to reconcile." Dietrich
continued: "See to it that this dreadful news is not spread along the roads.
You are not to let the [country] folk

des schaden / vverden innen.
so ir nv sheidet hinnen.
[2675]   so mᵛten si ivch ce sere.
ir svlt von Rᵛdegere.
niemen sagen sinen tot.
ez vvirt doch ein lange vverndiv not.
svvenne iz in rehte vvirt geseit.
[2680]   so mᵛzen si mit arbeit.
dar nach vveinen manegen tach.
div min ê gᵛtliche pflach.
der svlt ir sagen den dienest min.
vnt daz ich immer vvelle sin.
[2685]   svvi mir gebivtet Gôtelint.
vnd ovch des margraven chint.
min niftel div here.
vragen si von Rᵛdgere.
vvenne er ce hvse vvelle chomen.
[2690]   so sagt ir habt von im vernomen.
der kᵛnech vvelle in niht chomen lan.
vnt daz si ᵈᵃ von getan.
daz er da mᵛze bîten.
vnz daz di geste riten.
[2695]   mit ir gezoge an den ʀin.
der geleite mᵛz er sin.
daz ist in minem sinne.
so vvil ich di margravinne.
mit samt Rᵛdegere sehen.
[2700]   ir svlt ovch Dietelinde iehen.
vnd ob des niht mᵛge sin.
so vvelle ich doch di nifteln min.
gesehen in vil chvrcen tagen.
In ir hercen vvas begraben.
[2705]   den boten manech svvære.
do lie der Bernære.
mit manegen herce leiden.
di boten von im scheiden.

Ovch liezen si da hinder in.
[2710]   des svlt ir vil gevvis sin.
cer gangene vᵛnne.
vil iamerhaftez chᵛnne.
frivnde vnd mage.
in des todes lage.
[2715]   sᵛmeliche di noch lebten.

get wind of the losses they have sustained when you take your leave of us and ride off. Otherwise, they will never stop pestering you with their questions. Tell no one of Rüedeger's death. Once the facts have been told to them at the appropriate time, they will have to suffer long enough and will spend many a day thereafter crying bitterly. Tell my Lady Gotelind, who was always kind to me, that I stand ready to serve her and will do whatever she might ask of me. That also applies to the margrave's child, my dear niece. Should they ask about Rüedeger and inquire when he will be coming home, tell them that he informed you that the king does not want him to leave, and that the way things stand he will have to remain there until the guests depart with their entourage for the Rhine because he has to accompany them. [Tell her that] it is my intention to visit the countess and Rüedeger. You should also tell Dietlinde[74] — even if it is not possible[75] — that I hope to see my niece in just a few days." The messengers had terribly heavy hearts. In great sorrow the warrior of Verona then allowed them to take their leave of him.

[2709][76] You can be sure that they also left behind lost happiness, as well as kinfolk in a miserable state. Friends and relatives were left in the grip of death, some of whom were still alive

[74] Dietlinde is the daughter of Rüedeger and Gotelind, although she is never referred to by name in the *Nibelungenlied*, as Zeune correctly points out (382, fn.).

[75] This might also be understood in the sense that, even though it is impossible for Dietrich to see Rüedeger in Pöchlarn, the message to Dietlinde should be that he intends to visit both Gotelind *and* Rüedeger in the coming days. Zeune (382) elects to disregard the information of verse 2701, which is also included in Manuscript A. There are numerous instances in his translation when verses of the original have not been rendered into New High German, but the majority of these omissions are of little consequence for the semantics of the sections in question. In this case, however, Dietrich's words indicate the extent to which he is aware of the deception he is practicing with Gotelind and Dietlinde and ought to be included in the translation.

[76] At this point, Zeune begins the fifth and final section of his translation: "Heimsendung der Waffen": 'The weapons are returned to their homelands' (382).

vnd mit dem tode strebten.
mit triefenden baren.
di noch niht tot vvaren.
di andern vvaren nv begraben.
[2720]   des mͮs ir herce iamer haben.
da liezens ovch den march man.
man zoch schriende dan.
vil lvt ane mazze.
sin ross vf der strazze.
[2725]   da si da ritten ͮber lant.
mit vrage ez niemen ervant.
rehte vvaz in vvære.
ia heten si div mære.
gesagt vil ofte gerne.
[2730]   do het iz der von Berne.
verboten ieslichem knehte.
do liezen siz von rehte.
Niemene vvart iz noh geseit.
vnz in Osterriche reit.
[2735]   daz Rͮdgeres gesinde.
von maneger mvter chinde.
vvart gahen dvrh gevvonheit.
da der videlære reit.
si vvanden der mære.
[2740]   daz ez der [150/439] kͮnech vvære.
oder Rͮdger der riche.
daz volch gemeinliche.
vragete do den spilman.
vva habt ir den chvnech lan.

[2745]   Do sprach der videlære.
daz der herre vvære.
noch in sinem lande.
mit manegem vvigande.
daz gelovbten di da vvolden.
[2750]   di mære vragen solden.
der vvas so vil noh bi dem vvege.
daz beidiv brvcke vnd stege.
al(lez) vvas bestanden.
von Hivnissc(he)n landen.
[2755]   si ce Vviene chomen in di stat.
mit zͮhten si ce hvse bat.
ein vrovve saz dar inne.
div riche herzoginne.

and, although they had not yet expired, were nonetheless wrestling with death on blood-drenched biers. The others had been buried and that was cause enough for them to feel grief in their hearts. They now took their leave of the margrave.[77] With loud cries of unrestrained despair, they led his horse onto the road and rode out across the countryside. No one was able to get the truth out of them by asking questions. Actually, they would have been quite willing on a number of occasions to have told the tale, but Dietrich of Verona had forbidden each one of the squires [to relate it]. They quite rightly refrained from saying a thing to anybody until Rüedeger's own entourage had ridden into Austria. As was the custom, many a mother's child rushed off to meet the minstrel as he rode up. They thought it must be the king or noble Rüedeger. From all sides the people asked the minstrel: "Where did you leave the king?"

[2745] The minstrel replied that the monarch was still in his homeland with many of his warriors. Those who wanted to believe what he said did just that. There were so many people along the way who wished to ask what had happened that the bridges and roadways were completely filled. They journeyed from the lands of the Huns and arrived in the city of Vienna. They were asked with great courtesy to enter the home of a wealthy Duchess,

[77] A reference to the dead Rüedeger, left behind in the land of the Huns.

Isalde ein vil schoniv magt.
[2760]   dine chvnd iz niht vverden verdagt.
an den boten siz ervant.
si vvart iamerch ce hant.
vnd so trvrech gemvt.
daz ir von her<c>en daz plꝟt.
[2765]   dræte vz ir mvnde.
âch vve vvi ꝟbele gvnde.
si den boten dirre sage.
von der ivnchvrovven chlage.
er schal ez sît vil vvîten.
[2770]   man begonde an allen sîten.
in der stat ꝟber al.
ꝟben also grozzen schal.
di armen mit den richen.
daz sich div chlagelichen.
[2775]   vvol mohte so si iahen.
di dort di chlage sahen.
vnde ovch mit chlage schieden dan.
div chlage ir helfe da gevvan.
daz si nv fꝟr mit breiten scharn.
[2780]   di boten chvndens niht bevvarn.
do er schal diz mære.
vnder di bvrgære.
vnde vnder chovflivte chint.
div gꝟte stat div vvart sint.
[2785]   elliv vngemꝟtes vol.

Do liezen in di boten vvol.
von Vviene zogen vz der stete.
hern Dietriches bete.
vnsanpfte leisten si dar an.
[2790]   vvande in do vil manech man.
vvider reit vf der strazze.
der in gelicher mazze.
mꝟse helfen tragen ir leit.
svs fꝟrens in der arbeit.
[2795]   vnze hin ce Treisenmꝟre.
ritter noch gebꝟre.
ni bevant div mære.
vnz daz der videlære.
ze Bechelaren zꝟ reit.
[2800]   Niht nach ir gevvonheit.
noch nach ir altem rehte.

Isalde by name. She was a lovely woman and the news could not be kept from her. She found out from the messengers what had really happened. This distressed her so much and made her so terribly unhappy that her heart's blood flowed from her mouth. Alas, how much she took it amiss that the messengers brought such news. The wailing of the young woman could be heard far and wide. A great cry went up from all sides, from rich and poor alike, throughout the city. Their lament was comparable to the lament of those who had witnessed the tragedy and who had left that place with heavy hearts. Their lament[78] found its ally there and was transmitted by large crowds. The messengers could not prevent the news from being passed on to the townspeople and also the families[79] of the merchants. The good city was subsequently filled with the aura of despair.[80]

[2786] The envoys then took their leave and left the city of Vienna. They did not honor Dietrich's request, for many a man met them on the road who then had to share their sorrow. And so they proceeded with heavy hearts until they reached Traismauer. Neither knights nor peasants learned the news until the minstrel rode up to Pöchlarn. The manner in which

---

[78] The threefold occurrence of "lament" is intentional and intended to imitate the threefold use of "chlage" in the original text.

[79] The original clearly has the word "chint" here, but it seems unlikely that the poet had the small children of merchants in mind when he composed this verse. Brian Murdoch has suggested that it is possibly a reference to the "families" of the merchants, with "chint" being used for the sake of rhyme. Lexer (1: 1575-1576) presents a diverse spectrum of meanings for the word which includes the possibility that 'young men and women' could be referred to as "chint" in a state of matrimony. Professor Murdoch's rendering strikes me as quite appropriate.

[80] It is intriguing to note how the different manuscripts have portrayed the atmosphere in Vienna once the news becomes known of the catastrophe in the land of the Huns. Manuscripts C, a, and d have "eines tôdes" ('[the aura] of death'), A simply contains "diser mere" ('[all the city became full] with this news'), and D and b contain "vil gar traurens" ('[all the city was filled] with great sadness'). See Bartsch 143, note to verse 2785.

di Rv́degers knehte.
ritten / in di marche.
ia mv́te si vil starche.
[2805]   daz siz versvvigen solden.
daz si doch sagen vvolden.

Vf bi Tvnovve <.>
hete Gôtelint div vrovve.
di straze lange vvol bechant.
[2810]   di boten fv́ren in ir lant.
da si da vor vil diche ir man.
sah riten vrôliche dan.
mit der margravinne.
gestanden an di zinne.
[2815]   vvas vil manech schôniv meit.
riten in grozzer arbeit.
si do di boten sah<ah>en.
dem hv́se also nahen.
daz si einen stovb erchanden.
[2820]   in Rv́degers landen.
nach alter gevvonheit.
do sprach vil manech schône meit.
Lop si dir herre træhtin.
nv schovvet vrovve margravin.
[2825]   vvir sehen livte rîten.
von den hohgezîten.
da chv́mt vnser herre.
der trost vvas in vverre.
da zen hivnen bestanden.
[2830]   von Gernotes handen.
vnd vil ir hercen vv́nne.
der lant livte chv́nne.
chomen nivvan siben man.
von dem margraven dan.
[2835]   di fv́rten sin gezovve.
Gôtelint div vrovve.
het ovch div mære nv vernom̄.
si vvas zv ir tohter chomen.
vnd vvanden beide.
[2840]   liebe ane leide.
enpfahen als ê diche.
von lieben ovgen bliche.
do enpfiengen si nivvan herce leit.
vnde lange vvernde arbeit.

Rüedeger's squires rode into the Marches was not in keeping with their usual custom. It dismayed them greatly that they had to keep silent about things which they wished to relate.

[2807] Lady Gotelind had long been familiar with the road along the Danube. The envoys came into her land [using the same route] as she had previously so often observed her husband riding happily along. Many a lovely maiden stood at the window along with the countess. They saw the envoys approaching at quite a gallop,[81] and they could tell by the dust that they were getting close to the palace in Rüedeger's land, just as they had been accustomed to doing before. Many of the lovely maidens said: "Praise be to God. Now observe, my Lady, we can see people riding up [who are returning] from the festival. Here comes our Lord!" But their protector had been cut down by Gernot's hand in the land of the Huns, and with him much of the joy of their hearts. Only seven of their countrymen returned from service with the margrave; they brought his armor and weapons back with them. Lady Gotelind had also learned the news by now [i.e., that the messengers had arrived], and she had sought out her daughter. They had both anticipated that they would experience joy without sorrow, as they had often done before from such a happy sight. But they were greeted by nothing but grief and distress that would last for a very long time.

[81] I have taken some liberty here with the translation of verse 2816. "In grozzer arbeit" does not literally mean 'at a gallop,' but this phrase seems to me to impart the overall sense of urgency with which the envoys approach Pöchlarn.

[2845]   Di knappen vvarn in den siten.
           so si ce Bechlaren riten.
           daz si fѵren alle.
           mit vrevden vnde mit schalle.
           dem vvas iz nv vil vngelich.
[2850]   ez hete si ir ietslich.
           nider gedrvchet vf daz march.
           vvand ir iamer vvas so starch.
           daz si niht singen chvnden.
           sam ê ze manegen stvnden.
[2855]   Rѵdgers ors Boymvnt.
           vvider sehende an der stvnt.
           gien iz dem knehte an der hant.
           der site vvas an im bechant.
           so ez sines herren niht ensach.
[2860]   daz ez vil opften zovm brach.
           vnd lief vvider vf den vvegen.
           Nu vvas er leider gelegen.
           [151/440] der ez hete dar geritten.
           vnd diche drѵfe gestritten.
[2865]   also von reht ein edel man.
           Sin tohter govmen began.
           der knappen gabare.
           do er sѵfte si zevvare.

           Do sprach daz Rѵdgeres chint.
[2870]   vil liebiv mѵter Gotelint.
           diz ist doh selten geshehen.
           daz ich so vvenich habe gesehen.
           her bi minen ziten.
           mines vater boten riten.
[2875]   svvenne ab si her quamen.
           vvi vvol vvir daz ver namen.
           da si vvaren vvol gemѵt.
           vver et div hohzit gvt.
           gevvesen miner vrovven.
[2880]   des mach ich ѵbele getrivven.
           do sprach div alte margravin.
           rѵchet es got so sol si sin.
           in alln vnschedlich er gan.
           nivvan daz ich in trovme han.
[2885]   erlitten vil der sere.
           dinen vater Rѵdgere.
           sah ich hinte gar gra.

[2845] It was the custom among the pages when they returned to Pöchlarn to ride up making a joyous clamor. Nothing of the sort was done now, however. Each one of them was crouched down over his horse, for their despair was so great that they could not sing as they had done so many times before. Rüedeger's horse Bohemond then trotted in sadly as a page held it [by the reins]. When it did not see its master, this horse tended to break free of its bridle and run off down the road. But now, unfortunately, the man who had ridden this horse and often fought from its back, as one would expect of a noble knight, had fallen in combat. His daughter began to observe the behavior of the pages and, in truth, she sighed deeply.

[2869] Rüedeger's daughter said: "My dear mother Gotelind, never before in all my years have I seen so few of my father's envoys riding [here]. Whenever they returned, how clearly we could see that they were in good spirits! If only this festival has turned out well for my lady! But I am not at all convinced that this is the case." The old countess replied: "If it is God's will, then it will have passed with no injury to anyone. Yet, I have been deeply troubled by my dreams. Last night I saw your father Rüedeger and he was so gray,

sin gesinde bi im da.
daz het bevallen gar ein sne.
[2890]   von einem regene vvart in vve.
da von vvrden se alle naz.
dv̋ solt toht[er] gelovben daz.
min hovbt vvas von hare bloz.
daz ich eines hares groz.
[2895]   mines vahses niht entrv̋ch.
ein gadem vinster genv̋ch.
da hiez er mich in gan.
ich vant in innerthalben stan.
zv sloz er do di tv̋r.
[2900]   nie mer chomen vvir dar fv̋r.
vngerne vvas ich drinne.
sprach div margravinne.

Do sprach Rv̋dgeres chint.
liebiv mv̋ter trevme sint.
[2905]   sv̋meliche senpfte di andern starch.
ich sach mines vater march.
in dem trovme sere springen.
vnd lv̋te an im erchliengen.
sine chovertivvre silberin.
[2910]   nv merche liebiv mv̋ter min.
eines vvazers ez getranch.
sa ce stete ez da ver sanch.
Ein ander si niht mere.
sagten vvan mit sere.
[2915]   si giengen beide ensamt / dan.
do vvarn als ich gesaget han.
di boten chomen so nahen.
daz si al di livte sahen.
zv ir marstalle si do ritten.
[2920]   ninder nach ir alten siten.
gebarten do di knehte.
Aber nach des hoves rehte.
di ritter giengen gegen in.
vnd baten vvillechomen sin.
[2925]   den Eceln videlære.
vvol grv̋zten helde mere.
di boten von der Hivnen lant.
(da)r nach enpfiengen si ce ha(nt).
ir herren ingesinde.
[2930]   mit gedrvchten vvorten svvinde.

and the men who accompanied him were covered with snow. They were suffering from a rain which made all of them wet. My dear daughter, you must believe this: my own head was so bald that it did not have as much as a strand of hair. He [Rüedeger] beckoned me to enter a room that was extremely dark. I found him standing inside, then he closed the door. Never again would we emerge. I did not like being inside." So spoke the countess.

[2903] Rüedeger's daughter replied: "My dear mother, some dreams are to be taken lightly while others are of grave import.[82] In a dream I saw my father's warhorse making mighty leaps and its silver harness resounding loudly. Now note this, my dear mother: it drank some water and then sank below it." They said no more to each other, but rather went off together with heavy hearts. As I have told you, the envoys had now approached [the castle] and they could see all the people. They rode [over] to their stables. The squires did not act at all in accordance with their old customs; but in keeping with the decorum of the court, the knights went over to them and greeted Attila's minstrel. Renowned warriors then welcomed the messengers from the land of the Huns. Afterwards they received their lord's men. With moving, passionate words,

---

[82] Verse 2905 could be literally translated as 'some soft, the others strong/heavy.' I have opted to paraphrase the original in a manner which, I believe, is stylistically more appropriate.

horte man si antvvrte pflegen.
ia vvas ez allez gelegen.
da von si heten hohen můt.
iane chvnden si dehein gůt.
[2935] von der vvirtschapft gesagen.
harnasch sach man si tragen.
di knehte von den rossen dan.

Gotelint erblichte san.
der knappen gebare.
[2940] sine vvart in manegem iare.
ni so trvrech gemůt.
si sprach ich næme dehein gůt.
niht fůr div mære.
daz ich vveste vvi in vvære.
[2945] do sprach der beste vnder in.
iv enbivtet trivve vvernden sin.
genade vnd michel ere.
Ecel der kůnech here.
vnde holden vvillen stæte.
[2950] der vverche vnd ovch der ræte.
si er iv immer bereit.
daz vvizzet mit der vvarheit.
Ovch enbivtet iv min herre.
ern chôme iv nie so verre.
[2955] ern vvære iv doch mit trivven bi.
ir svlt vvizzen daz er si.
iv holt vor allen vviben.
vnd vvil also beliben.
an sinen ivngesten tach.
[2960] Eren vveiz niht ob er chomen mach.
vvider heim in langer zit.
der kůnech im allez an lit.
er leitet im eine hervart.
div lange ê gesprochen vvart.
[2965] di ist min herre nv gevarn.
Si sprah nv můze in got bevvarn.
vnde allez himelissche her.
er var lant oder mer.
svvelhen ende er chere.
[2970] dvrch sins gevvaltes ere.
můze in Christ behůten.
daz Eceln [152/441] viende vůten.
mir niht enbůnne mins man.

the latter answered their questions. After all, everything was gone which might have caused them to be in high spirits. They could not report the slightest good thing about the festival. The squires then removed the harnesses from the horses.

[2938] Gotelind paid close attention to the squires' bearing. In many a year she had never been so despondent. She said: "I would never accept anything [the world might offer] as a substitute for the report which informs how they are faring." The best among them spoke up: "Noble King Attila offers you his loyalty, favor, as well as much honor and eternal good will. He stands ready to assist you always in both deed and word. Rest assured that this is the case. My Lord [Rüedeger] also swears to you that he will never be so far away from you that he would not stand by you loyally. You are to know that he is more devoted to you than to all other women, and that he will remain so until his dying day. He does not know whether he will be able to return home for a long time. The king is constantly making urgent appeals to him. He is undertaking for him a military campaign that was planned a long time ago. My Lord has now set off on that enterprise." She responded: "May God and the entire heavenly host protect him. Whether he travels over land or by sea, to whatever end of the world he may venture, may Christ in all his power and glory watch over him so that the fury of Attila's enemies do not rob me of my husband."

div magt do vragen began.

[2975] Sagt mir boten gûte.

vvi ist nv so zemûte.

minem Vater Rûdegere.

daz mût mich harte sere.

vvande mir ce vorderst sprach div meit.

[2980] div mære ie vvrden geseit.

svvenne er sande in sin lant.

so zornech ich in nie bevant.

mir enchômen siniv mære.

von schvlden ist mir svvære.

[2985] div magt do vveinen began.

do sach si ir mûter an.

vnd ervveinten do beide.

ich vvæne si der leide.

ermante do ir herce.

[2990] in nahete grozzer smerce.

Der bote sprach lat ivver chlagen.

ich sol iv mere mære sagen.

di iv frivntliche.

von dem herren Dietriche.

[2995] sint en boten in daz lant.

vns gebot der vvigant.

di den sinen hvlden.

daz vvir von vvarn schvlden.

iv sagten den dienest sin.

[3000] Er enbivtet iv edel margravin.

liebe vnd allez gvt.

trivve vnde stæten mvt.

Irn dûrfet ovch des niht vragen.

ob iv vnder ivvern magen.

[3005] holder ie vûrde man.

vnd heizzet ivch daz vvizzen lan.

daz svln vvir iv vrovve sagen.

daz er ivch īner zvvelf tagen.

vvil hie ce Bechlaren sehen.

[3010] Daz vvolde got môht ez geschehen.

sprach div margravinne.

von allem minem sinne.

vreûte des harte sich min mvt.

Do sprach div ivnge magt gvt.

[3015] sagt vns der mære mere.

Then the young lady inquired: "Tell me, good messengers, in what state of mind is my father Rüedeger? It worries me greatly," the girl said, "because I was always the first one to whom the envoys he sent back home would come with their reports. I never knew him to be so angry that he would not send me news. I have a right to be very worried." The maiden began to weep. She looked over at her mother and both of them wept. I suspect that their hearts made them aware of their sorrow; great misery was soon to be visited upon them.

[2991] The messenger said: "Do not grieve. I have more news to tell you which Lord Dietrich, in his kindness, has sent into this country. The warrior asked us by his grace to impart to you in all sincerity his readiness to serve you. He offers you, noble Countess, his affection and his generosity,[83] as well as loyalty and steadfastness. You should never ask yourself, therefore, whether there is any man among your kinfolk who is more well disposed towards you. He wanted you to know, my Lady (and we have been charged with informing you), that he wishes to [come and] see you here in Pöchlarn within twelve days." "May God let that come to pass," said the countess. "From the bottom of my heart that gives me a great deal of joy."

[3014] The noble young lady said: "Tell us some more news.

---

[83] The expression "allez gvt" in verse 3001 does not literally mean 'generosity.' It appears that Dietrich has offered Gotelind literally 'all good things,' which is to say that he is willing to serve her and provide her with whatever she needs in the future. This could include the filling of tangible needs as well as moral support in the form of affection and loyalty. 'Generosity' is admittedly a compromise to avoid the stylistically less preferable and semantically ambivalent 'all good things.' The sense may also be expressed as follows: Dietrich is putting himself and all that he has at the disposal of Gotelind.

vvie Criemhilt div here.
enpfienge ir brͧder vnd ovch ir man.
oder vvi vvas der grͧz getan.
den si sprach gein Hagene.

[3020]   vvi gebarte si gegen dem degene.
oder gein Gͧnthere.
ob si noch iht sere.
zvrnde hin zin beiden.
oder vvi ist ez gescheiden.

[3025]   Der bote sprach div Chͧnegin.
gie mit frevden gegen in.
vnd enpfie si minnechliche.
si tet dem vvol geliche.
daz si in / holt vvære.

[3030]   Ecel der Chͧnech mære.
der enpfie di herren alle so.
sam er ir chͧmens vvære vro.
er vnd alle sine man.
niemen ich da gesehen han.

[3035]   der in trͧge deheinen haz.
Si sprach nv sagt mir vmbe vvaz.
lie daz der kͧnech Giselher.
daz mir der ivnge fͧrste her.
her vvider bi iv niht enbot.

[3040]   der vrage mich tvvinget not.
sît er mir niht enboten hat.
ich fͧrhte svvi ez dar vmbe stat.
ich gesæhe in nimmer mer.
ia sagte mir der Chͧnech her.

[3045]   er vvolde mich ce trͧte han.
di rede svlt ir vrovve lan.
vvir liezen in vil vvol gesvnt.
si choment her in chvrcer stvnt.
daz vvizet edel margravin.

[3050]   so si vvider ritent an den Rin.
darvmb ensvlt ir sorgen niht.
der kͧnech ivch vil gerne sihet < . >
svenn er nv ritet in sin lant.
so vvil er ovch vrovve alcehant.

[3055]   mit im fͧren ͧber Rin.
da svlt ir Chvneginne sin.

Dirre lvgelichem mære.
ce scherm in ir svvære.

How did proud Kriemhild receive her brothers and their men? What type of greeting did she extend to Hagen? How did she act towards the warrior or towards Gunther? Was she not still furious at both of them or how was that all resolved?" The messenger replied: "The queen approached them with joy in her heart and received them lovingly. She certainly acted as though she were well disposed towards them. The renowned King Attila greeted all the warriors in such a way as to suggest that he and all of his men were very happy about their coming. I saw no one there who bore them any hatred." She said: "Now tell me why young Giselher, that noble king, has neglected to give you any news to pass on to me. I have to ask the question. Since he has sent me no message, I fear that it could well be that I will never see him again. That noble king told me that he wished to make me his wife." "My Lady, you should speak no more of this. We left him in the best of health. Rest assured, noble Countess, they will be here in a short while, once they set out for the Rhine. Put your cares aside. The king will be happy to see you when he returns to his homeland. My Lady, he also wishes to take you back with him across the Rhine where you will become his queen."

[3057] These mendacious stories [employed] to cover up their distress

daz tet ir einem also vve.

[3060] daz er niht langer mohte me.

verdvlten in sinem hercen.

den schaden vnt den smercen.

im ervveinten div ovgen.

svvi gern ers hete lovgen.

[3065] dar nach ervveinte ir mere.

div margravinne here.

ir træhene nider vliezend sah.

Ir tohter do ze hant sprach.

Âch vve vil liebiv mθter min.

[3070] ich vvæne vvir gar gescheiden sin.

von frevde vnd ovch von vθnne.

min vrovve hat ir chθnne.

leider svvache enpfangen.

ez ist vns θbel ergangen.

[3075] vvir mθgen vvol vveinen von rehter not.

si vnd min vater sint vvætliche tot.

Ir einem do si daz gesprach.

ein vθf vz sinem halse brach.

mit zv getanem mvnde.

[3080] er vvand iz da ce stvnde.

da mit ver heln mohte.

[153/442] neheinem hercen ez tohte.

daz iz versvvigen chvnde.

do brast vz seinem mvnde.

[3085] daz schrien mit dem plθte.

do der knappe gθte.

ane danch so lθt er schre.

do vvart den andern so vve.

daz si ervveinten al geliche.

[3090] Div margravinne riche.

sprach ovve mir armez vvip.

daz ich ie gevvan den lip.

vvaz ich nv verlorn han.

der vrevden der ich hete vvan.

[3095] div mvz nv mit dem leide min.

gar von mir gescheiden sin.

Ir boten dvrch ivver trivve.

lat mih niht in der rivve.

ine vvizze von schvlden vmbe vvaz.

[3100] sagt mir bescheidenliche daz.

vvi schiedet ir von minem man.

so disconcerted one of their number that he could no longer bear the injury and pain in his heart. His eyes welled tears, as much as he might have wished to hide it. Subsequently, many more of them began to weep. The noble countess saw the tears flowing down [their cheeks]. Her daughter immediately said: "Alas, my dear mother. I believe that we have truly been separated from joy and happiness. My Lady [Kriemhild] has accorded her kinfolk a most unpleasant reception. We have fared terribly and have good reason to weep. [The Burgundians] and my father are surely dead."

[3077] As she spoke these words, one of them [i.e., the envoys], his mouth still closed, uttered a cry of despair from his throat. He thought he had been able to conceal it, but no heart was in any position to keep silent about this. A shriek broke forth from his mouth, along with blood. Once the good page had unintentionally let out such a loud scream, everyone else felt such sorrow that they all began to weep together. The noble countess said: "A pity that I, poor woman, was ever born. How much happiness I have lost which I believed was mine. All of that joy must now take its leave of me because of my sorrow. You messengers, in the name of loyalty, do not leave me in such pain without my knowing why I must suffer so. Tell me in all candor, then, how did you take your leave of my husband?"

do mvse div lv̊ge ein ende han.

Do sprach der videlære.
Svvemmelin der mære.
[3105] Vrovve vvir vvolden ivch verdagen.
daz man iv doch mv̊se sagen.
vvand ez niemen verheln chvnde.
irn geseht nach dir stvnde.
den margraven Rvdegere.
[3110] lebendech nimmer mere.
Vil lvte horte man si do chlagen.
herre vver hat in erslagen.
er sprach. daz tet her Gernot.
si slvgen beide ein an der tot.
[3115] Do schre div mv̊t[er] vnt div meit.
vvart ie nach frivnden me gechleit.
daz enist mir niht bechant.
svvaz man bi in livte vant.
oder sit chom zv dem schalle.
[3120] di ervv̊ften alsam alle.
daz cen Hivnen vmbe der helde tot.
vvart ni grôzzer ê div not.

Von dem iamer also vesten.
der margravinne bresten.
[3125] begonde von dem mvnde daz plv̊t.
vnd ovch ir edeln tohter gvt.
si vieln beide in vnchrapft.
so daz ir zv̊hte meisterschapft.
ver gaz vil gar der sinne.
[3130] di livte vvaren inne.
vvorden vvol der vvarheit.
svvaz in mære ie vvart geseit.
des gesaczte si diz mære.
vz frevde in alle svvære.
[3135] Ir hercen iamer vvart / so groz.
daz man mit prvnnen si vergoz.
vnd naczte si vnder ovgen.
ir lip begonde lovgen.
ob si rehte sinne ie gevvan.
[3140] daz bevveinte vvip vnd man.
vnd alle di da vvaren.
in der stat ce Bechlaren.
Von den andern man si trv̊ch.

An end had to be put to this lie.

[3103] The minstrel, that renowned Swemmel, replied: "My Lady, we hoped to keep from you something which, after all, we must tell you, for no one could really keep it hidden. You will never again see the Margrave Rüedeger alive." Many people could hear her lamenting there. "My Lord, who killed him?" He replied: "It was Lord Gernot. They killed each other." Both the mother and her daughter let out a scream. If ever anyone's kin were more greatly lamented, I certainly have no knowledge of it. All of the people who were present there with them or who subsequently arrived to find out what the commotion was all about lamented so intensely that the despair that had earlier been in evidence in the camp of the Huns over the death of the warriors could not have been greater.

[3123] This terrible anguish caused the blood to shoot from the mouth of the countess, as well as from that of her noble daughter. They both began to swoon and the control that breeding exercises was completely abandoned. People had now become cognizant of the truth. Whatever tales they may have been told in the past, this news replaced all of their joy with great sorrow. The heartache they felt was so great that water had to be poured over them and sprinkled under their eyes. Their bodies created the impression that they had never been conscious. Everyone in Pöchlarn, both men and women alike, lamented this sad state of affairs. They carried them away from the others.

do vvarn nothaft genvch.
[3145] beide di margravinne.
si lagen in vnsinne.
man horte vnrehte lͮte.
haben nach ir trͮte.
Gotelinde der richen.

[3150] Vil erbærmechlichen <.>
sprach div tohter ir beider.
Ách ach vnd leider.
vvirt nv meide nimmer mere.
vva vvil min vrovve ere.
[3155] beliben in dem riche.
sît also iæmerliche.
di ere tragenden sint gelegen.
vver sol si danne vvider vvegen.
svvenne ir gesiget div chrapft.
[3160] des hete gar di meisterschapft.
min lieber vat[er] Rͮdeger.
vrov ere div vvirt nimmer <mer>.
mit solhem vvnssche getragen.
als er si trvch bi sinen tagen.
[3165] der tot der hat di vnzvht.
daz er niemen deheine flvht.
zv sinen frivnden haben lat.
svvenne iz an di rede gat.
daz er entvviche gerne.
[3170] ia het der von Berne.
mir vvol genert den vater min.
mͦhte iemen dem tode vvider sin.

Do sprach der videlære.
elliv vnser mære.
[3175] sint iv von sinnen vvol bechant.
di von Amelunge Lant.
di sint allen samt tot.
ia genas mit grozer not.
ivver neve her Dietrich.
[3180] vnd hete man den Chͮnech rich.
Eceln zv dem strite lan.
den mͮse vvir ovh verlorn han.
Si sprach nv sagt mir her Svvæmmelin.
vvi chom daz der vater min.
[3185] zvrnde vvider Gernoten.

Both countesses were in a terrible state of despair and were lying in a daze. Noble Gotelind mumbled incoherently for her husband.

[3150] Their daughter spoke in great despondency: "Alas, alas, no young noblewoman can ever have been more unfortunate. Where will my Lady Honor find refuge in our land now that those who defend honor have died so miserably? Who shall prop her up when her strength begins to wane? To this end my dear father Rüedeger was in command here. Lady Honor will never again be borne as magnificently as she was by my father when he was alive. Death is of such a discourteous nature that he allows no one to flee to his friends when he might wish to escape him. The Lord of Verona would have kept my father safe for me if it were possible for anyone to resist death."

[3173] The minstrel then spoke up: "You had already sensed [the nature of] all our news. Every one of the Amelungs has met his death, and your kin, Lord Dietrich, survived only after the greatest trials and tribulations. If they had allowed King Attila to join in the battle, we would have lost him as well." She said: "Now tell me, Swemmel, how did it come about that my father could [raise his sword] in anger against Gernot,

so manegen bovch roten.
so vvir in gaben hier enlant.
vnd in dem vvillen er si vant.
ia vvas ez in beiden.
[3190] niht gvt daz iemen scheiden.
si mit rate solde<.>
der trivve haben vvolde.

Er sprach magt vil here.
daz entet niemen mere.
[3195] vvand der kᵛneginne lip.
des hat man vnd vvip.
[154/443] engolten also vviten.
daz von den ersten ziten.
vnz an den ivngesten tach.
[3200] nimmer mere vverden mach.
geraten also svvinder rat.
vil chlein ez si gefrvmt hat.
vvand si lit selbe dar vmbe tot.
von der div lange vverndiv not.
[3205] geschach in Hivnen riche.
si ligent al geliche.
di vns da vrevde solden geben.
doch mᵛgt ir vrovve noch geleben.
vil manegen vrôlichen tach.
[3210] svvaz ivverr vrevden an in lach.
di cen Hivnen sint erslagen.
di mᵛzzet ir alle ver chlagen.
vvand got der vveisen vater ist.
frovve ich rat iv an argen list.
[3215] vnd vf mine trivve.
daz ir ivch ivverr rivve.
mazet vnd solher chlage.
der kᵛnech giht alle di tage.
di in got noch leben lat.
[3220] er vvelle iv schaffen al den rat.
den iv schᵛffe Rᵛdeger.
der edel margrave her.

Mit sivften vol dvrch brach ir chlage.
do vvas er offent gar div sage.
[3225] vvi ez allez vvas er gan.
di knehte vvolden daz niht lan.
sine trᵛgen Rᵛdgers gevvant.

with all of the gold arm-rings that we gave them when they visited us and when he found everyone so willing to serve him? It was not at all right for anyone who wished to preserve his loyalty to cause a rift between them."

[3193] He replied: "Most noble lady, it was no one other than the queen who did it. As a result, men and women alike have paid so dearly that from the beginning of time to the Day of Judgment, a more devastating course [of action] could hardly have been contemplated. Yet the woman who is responsible for this catastrophe, which will long be felt in the land of the Huns, has derived little advantage from it. She herself lies dead as a consequence. All of those men who were to have given us joy are lying there in a similar state. Nonetheless, my Lady, you may still enjoy many a happy day. However much your joy was linked to the men who have been killed in the Hunnish camp, you must cease your grieving for them. For God is the father of orphans. My Lady, I advise you in all candor and in good faith to temper your sorrow and your grieving. The king [Attila] says that he will provide you with the same [good] counsel you received from the noble Margrave[84] Rüedeger for the rest of the days God allows him to live."

[3223] Her lamentations were interrupted by sighs. The true story of how everything had transpired was now fully revealed. The squires did not wish to tarry, but rather took Rüedeger's clothes

---

[84] Bartsch has closing quotation marks following verse 3221 (similar to what one also finds in Lachmann's edition). Yet it is clear from Manuscript B that "der edel margrave her" in verse 3222 stands in apposition to "Rûdeger" in verse 3221 and is part of Swemmel's speech. Verse 3223 begins with a bold capital "M" indicating a new section of the manuscript.

svvaz sin vvas hin heim gesant.
da manz gehalten solde.
[3230] svver daz do shovven vvolde.
der sich da plŷtegen glanz.
da ê di ringe vvaren ganz<.>
daz vvas nv dŷrchel vnde shart.
dar inne ir trost erslagen vvart.
[3235] dem Rŷdgeres vvibe.
vnd ander manegem vvibe.

Nv hŷb sich erste svnder not.
den gesten niemen niht en bot.
vvederz vvazzer noch den vvin.
[3240] vvi lange vvelle vvir hie sin.
sprach der videlære.
ez ist in solher svvære.
div edel margravinne.
daz si vor vnsinne.
[3245] ez niemen vvol erbieten mach.
daz volch da anders niht enpflach.
in der bvrch ŷber al.
daz hvs allenthalben schal.
vnd ovch der stein dar vnder.
[3250] Ovch horte man besvnder.
in der stat ze Bechlarn.
di livte also gebarn.
alse si des not an gie.
div margravinne niht enlie.
[3255] sin endete mit iamer daz ir vvas.
vvnder ist daz si genas.
den tach vol / an daz ende.
ez heten ir selb[er] hende.
den lip der vvat gemachet bloz.
[3260] nie chlage vvart so groz.
so man mohte chiesen da.
div mære ovch fŷgten andersvva.
daz maneges hercen brunnen.
mit træhen vz ovgen rvnnen.

[3265] Div frovve senliche bat.
herbergen in di stat.
Eceln boten gŷtliche.
der margravinne riche.
ir sinne do vil gar gebrast.

and whatever else of his that had been sent home to a place where it could be stored. Whoever wished to take a look at it could not fail to see the glimmer of blood. Where before the rings of armor had been whole, they were now hacked to pieces. The protector of Rüedeger's wife as well as of many others had been slain while wearing it.

[3237] Only now did a particular problem arise. No one had offered the guests anything — neither water nor wine. "How long do we wish to stay here?" the minstrel asked. "The noble countess is so distraught that, being beside herself, she cannot offer anyone anything." Throughout the castle, no one reacted any differently. The entire palace shook [with the cries] as did the very foundation stones. In the city of Pöchlarn as well one could hear people behaving as one would expect in the face of such a catastrophe. The countess could not desist from her grieving and lamenting and it is amazing that she ever managed to survive this day. With her own hands she had ripped the clothes off her body.[85] Nowhere had there ever been greater lamenting than was to be found at that place. Elsewhere the news caused the spring of many a heart to have the eyes overflow in tears.

[3265] In her sorrow, the lady ordered that Attila's messengers be given comfortable quarters in the city. The noble countess was in such complete disarray

---

[85] Zeune refers to Gotelind's stripping of Rüedeger's corpse (390), although it is clear from all the manuscripts that Rüedeger was earlier laid to rest in the land of the Huns. (See verses 2351-2353.) Given Gotelind's state of mind as described in verse 3269, it is most likely that she has rent her own clothes to shreds.

[3270]   daz si den frivnt noch den gast.
noch niemen erchande.
do vvolden von ir lande.
di boten vf an den Rin.
do het div ivnge margravin.
[3275]   ein teil noch ir sinne.
frivventliche minne.
en bot si Prṽnnhilden.
der edeln vnt der milden.
Si enbot ovch daz frṽn Voten.
[3280]   vmbe Giselher den gvten.
vvie si im gevestent vvære.
vnde mit vveʰher svvære.
daz allez ende hat genomen.
ez mȏht in nimmer vvirs sin chomen.
[3285]   si en bot ovch ir daz Gernot.
ir vat[er] het er slagen tot.

Vrlovp di boten namen dan.
Svvæmmel riten do began.
da er sine V(ve)ge vant.
[3290]   vf in der Beyer Lant.
vvant da gie sin strazze hin.
zvvisschen Tvnovve vnt dem In.
noch ein altiv bvrch stat.
Pazzovve si den namen hat.
[3295]   da saz ein riche bisschoff.
sin lop. sin ere. vnde sin hoff.
vvaren vviten bechant.
der vvas Pilgrim genant.
dem chomen disiv mære.
[3300]   di stolzen Bvrgondenære.
vvaren siner svvester chint.
vil vvol erfṽr er daz sint.
vvi ez den vviganden.
er gie in Hivnen landen.

[3305]   Di boten ritten ṽber daz In.
di livte lieffen vor in hin.
vnd vvolden sagen in den hoff.
daz der gṽte bisschoff.
sine neven solde enpfahen.
[3310]   dine vvaren niht so nahen.
als er des hete gedanch.

that she recognized no one, whether kin or guest. The messengers wished to depart her land and ride on to the Rhine. The young countess still had some control over her faculties. She sent her love to the noble and generous Brünhild. She also sent a message to Lady Ute regarding the good Giselher and how she had been betrothed to him and with what misery it had all come to an end. But there was even worse to come: she informed her as well that Gernot had killed her father.

[3287] The messengers then took their leave. Swemmel began to ride off to find the proper route that would take him into Bavaria, for that is where the road led. There is an old city which still stands between the Danube and the River Inn and which is called Passau. A mighty bishop resided there, whose reputation, honor, and court were known far and wide. His name was Pilgrim. The news was now brought to him. The proud Burgundians were the children of his sister. He was soon to know how the warriors had fared in the land of the Huns.

[3305] The messengers crossed over the Inn. People ran on ahead of them with the intention of announcing to the court that the good bishop was to receive his nephews. They were not yet as close as he imagined, however.

ez vvart vil maneges tages lanch.
daz er sie sit nie gesach.
zv den rittern er do sprach.

[3315]   Nŭ svlt ir alle gahen.
[155/444] vnde mine frivvende enpfahen.
ein ietslich min ambet man.
der mir deheines gŭtes gan.
der enpfahe miner svvester chint.

[3320]   vnt di mit ⁱⁿ chomen sint.
den lat niht gebresten.
Ia moht er sinen gesten.
sanfte naht sedel geben.
er vvesse niht daz ir leben.

[3325]   zen hivnen het ende genomen.
Vvære im doch ir einer chomen.
im vvære immer deste baz.
schiere sagete man im daz.
daz si vværen alle er slagen.

[3330]   daz mære chonde im niht behagen.
ez dvhte in gar vngelovplich.
Idoch bedaht er sich.
daz erz gelovben vvolde.
do schŭf er daz man solde.

[3335]   den boten schaffen ir gemach.

Mit grozem iamer er do sprach.
nv lit cen Hivnen er slagen.
di vrevde di ich vvande haben.
an den verch magen min.

[3340]   des mŭz ich immer trurech sin.
di vvile ich nv geleben mach.
vnz an minen endes tach.
Ich gedahtes vil vvol sît.
ver vlŭchet si div hohzit.

[3345]   daz ir Ecel ie began.
da von so manech (v)verder man.
so iæmerlich (ist) tot gelegen.
Er sprach hime(li)ssher degen.
vvi hastv also zv mir getan.

[3350]   do chom dar zv zim gegan.
Svvæmmel der videlære.
nach grŭzze er in der mære.
vragen do begonde.
er sagte im als er chonde.

Many days had passed since he had last seen them. He said to his knights: "You are all to go now and greet my friends. Each one of my delegates who wishes me well is to welcome the children of my sister and those who have ridden along with them. See to all of their needs." In fact, he wished to provide his guests with comfortable accommodations for the night. He could not know that they had met their deaths in the land of the Huns. If only one of them had returned here to him, he would have felt somewhat better. He was told immediately that they had all been killed. This news could hardly be pleasing to him and he just found it inconceivable. Yet he realized that he had to believe it. He ordered that the accommodations be prepared for the envoys.

[3336] Then he spoke in the greatest distress. "The joy that I had hoped to have through my blood relatives lies slain in the land of the Huns. As a result, I will be sad for the rest of my life, up to the day I die. I had often thought to myself: cursed be the festival and [the fact] that King Attila ever sponsored it, which led to the miserable deaths of so many worthy men." He continued: "Heavenly Lord,[86] why have you done this to me?" Swemmel the minstrel approached him. After extending his greetings to him, he asked him to tell him what had happened. To the extent that he was able,

---

[86] The expression "hime[li]ssher degen" in verse 3348 is a somewhat unexpected designation for God. "Degen," an old word associated with the world of Germanic warrior society, would normally be translated as 'fighter, warrior,' but also perhaps as 'thane, lord,' although the former are clearly not appropriate in the current context, unless we are dealing with a situation analogous to that in the *Heliand*, in which Christ appears in the garb of a Germanic warrior. Lexer also lists the meaning 'male child, young boy' (1: 414), but this also is not suited to the present context. My translation, 'heavenly Lord,' is clearly a compromise.

[3355]   vvi ez allez vvas geshehen.
              vvand er ^{het} ez vvol gesehen.

              Do ervveinte der Bisschoff.
              ꝟber allen sinen hoff.
              vvas vil grozziv vngehabe.
[3360]   di pfaffen mꝩsen lazzen ab.
              dvrch chlage vil ir tagezit.
              vvant da vveinten vviderstrit.
              di leigen mit den pfaffen.
              dar nach begonde shaffen.
[3365]   der gvte pisschoff Pilgrin.
              daz si ir chlagen liezen sin.
              Ich chan mich des versinnen.
              môhte ich si vvider gevvinnen.
              beide mit vveinen vnde mit chlagen.
[3370]   ich en vvolde nimmer gedagen.
              vnze mir miner svester chint.
              di mir so iæmerliche sint. /
              in Eceln lande.
              mit manegem vvigande.
[3375]   in gꝩten trivven erslagen.
              di ich nimmer chan ver chlagen.
              hey vværn si gesvnt chomen her vvid^[er].
              do sande er allenthalben sider.
              nach mꝩnechen vnd nach pfafffen.
[3380]   der herre ez begvnde schaffen.
              nach Cristenlichem orden.
              den di da vvarn fꝩr vvorden.
              di pri^ester ir messe singen.
              di glocken horte man chlingen.
[3385]   allenthalben in der stat.
              ce den mꝩnstern als der Bisschoff bat.
              Ze dem opfer vvas do groz gedranch.
              der bisschoff ovh do selbe sanch.
              gote von himele ce eren.
[3390]   der Cristen heil ze meren.
              vnt ze helffe ir sele. di da vvarn tot.
              der bisschoff leit vor iamer not.

              Do da gote gedienet vvart.
              di boten vvolden vf ir vart.
[3395]   alda ce hant rîten.
              Ir svlt noh lenger pîten.

Swemmel told him how everything had come about, for he, after all, had witnessed it himself.

[3357] The bishop began to weep and there was great dismay throughout all of his court. The priests could not help but lose much of their time at prayer with all their lamenting for they competed with laymen in shedding tears. Afterwards, however, Bishop Pilgrim urged them to stop their lamenting: "I can imagine that, were I able to bring them back by crying and grieving, I would not be silent until I again had regained my sister's children. In their unbending loyalty, they have been wretchedly slain in the land of the Huns along with many [of their] warriors, and I can never stop mourning them." He then sent out everywhere for the monks and priests. This lord arranged things according to Christian custom. The priests sang mass for those who had been killed, and, in accordance with the bishop's instructions, the bells rang in the cathedrals throughout the city. There was a great push of people to [attend] the requiem mass.[87] The bishop himself sang mass to the honor of God to enhance the salvation of the Christians and to aid the souls of those who had died. In his great sorrow, the bishop was in terrible distress.

[3393] After the divine service, the envoys immediately wished to ride off on their journey. "You should stay here a while longer,"

---

[87] The reference in verse 3387 to the "opfer" is probably the idea of an offering made by the people of Passau in the name of those who had died. We note Lexer's definition in 2: 157: "opfer bei der seelmesse zum gedächtnis eines verstorbenen," 'offering made at a requiem mass in memory of someone who has died.'

sprach zv zim ein kappelan.
ir svlt zv minem herren gan.
der bat mich iv sagen daz.
[3400] er vvil vvæne ich ettevvaz.
bi iv enbieten an den Rin.
frovn Voten der svvester sin.
vmbe ir grozze svvære.
do gie der videlære.
[3405] fûr den gûten Bisschoff.
Er sprach nv ist der Eceln hoff.
mit sôlher not cer gangen.
so hat vil ûbele enpfangen.
Criemhilt div niftel min.
[3410] ir brûder vnt di recken sin.
si môhte haben baz getan.
vnde hete doch genesen lan.
Giselher vnd Gernot.
die ir Sifriden slûgen tot.
[3415] vnde hetens di engolten.
so vvær si vnbescholten.
vvande in slûch doh Hagene.
des habe vvir ce chlagene.
nach frivvenden immer mer genvch.
[3420] daz in sin mût[er] ie getrûch.
daz mûze gote sin gechleit.
daz svs lange vverndiv leit.
vnd also grimmiv mære.
vnd ovch so vil der svvære.
[3425] von im ist erstanden.
so vvîten in den landen.

Svvæmmel sagt der svvester min.
daz si ir chlagen lazze sin.
si vværn doch da heime tot.
[3430] der Nibelvnge golt rot.
heten si daz ver mitten.
so môhten si vvol sin geritten.
zir svvester mit ir [156/445] hvlden.
von ir selber schvlden.
[3435] vnd von ir starchen vbermût.
so habe vvir di recken gût.
verlorn al geliche.
in Eceln riche.
vnd sagt der Chûneginne.

a chaplain said to them. "You are to approach my lord, who asked me to tell you this. I believe he has a message for you to take to the Rhine, to Lady Ute, his sister, regarding her terrible plight." The minstrel then went before the good bishop who said: "Attila's court has sustained such a catastrophe because Kriemhild, my niece, has provided such a wretched reception for her brother and his men. She would have done better had she allowed Giselher and Gernot to live. If those who had killed her Siegfried had paid for it, she would have remained without reproach. After all, Hagen was the one who killed him. As a consequence, we will always have good reason to lament our friends. We should complain to God that his mother ever gave birth to him. He is the one who is responsible for these grim reports, as well as this terrible, never-ending sorrow and so much of this tragedy that has spread throughout the lands.

[3427] Swemmel, tell my sister that she should refrain from lamenting. Even [had they stayed] at home they would have died. If they had simply turned their backs on the gold of the Nibelungen, they could have journeyed to see their sister with her blessing. It is their own fault and a consequence of their arrogance that we have lost all of these good warriors in Attila's land. Tell the queen as well

[3440] daz ich von minem sinne.
ir niht bezzers raten chan.
vvand ich ir vvol gꝩtes gan.
daz si chlage ze mazzen.
man mꝩz di varn lazzen.
[3445] di vns tægelich der tot nimt.
vvande im anders niht en zimt.
vvan scheiden liep mit sere.
ez enist niht anders mere.
Vnd saget ovch Gꝩntheres man.
[3450] daz si vvol gedenchen dar an.
vvie ir der kꝩnech ie pflach.
mit ganzen eren manegen tach.
vnt daz si tvn ir trivve schin.
vnde in bevolhen lazzen sin.
[3455] daz sin vil vvenigez chint.
des doh nꝩ div erbe sint.
vnt den ziehen ce einem man.
des mꝩzzens immer ere han.

Svvæmmel lobt an mine hant.
[3460] so ir vvider rîtet dvrch div lant.
des pitte ich frivvent daz ir.
dann chert her ce mir.
ezen sol niht also beliben.
ich vvilz he(iz)zen shriben.
[3465] di stꝩrme vnt di grozzen not.
oder vvi si sin gelegen tot.
vvi ez sich hꝩp vnde vvi ez quam.
vnd vvi ez allen ende nam.
Svvaz ir des vvaren habt gesehen.
[3470] des sꝩlt ir danne mir ver iehen.
dar zv vvil ich vragen.
von ieslichen magen.
ez si vvip oder man.
svver iht der von gesagen chan.
[3475] dar vmbe sende ich nv ce hant.
mine boten in Hivnen lant.
da vinde ich vvol div mære.
vvande iz vil ꝩbel vvære.
ob ez behalden vꝩrde niht.
[3480] ez ist div grôzeste geshiht.
div cer vverld ie geschach.
Svvæmmel ze hant sprach.

that I cannot give her better advice — for I wish her well — than to keep her lamenting within moderation. We simply have to let go of those who daily are taken from us by death. For it is death's way, after all, to replace joy with sorrow. There is nothing more to it. In addition, tell Gunther's men that they should give some thought to the manner in which the king, with all due honor, looked out for them for many years. They should act in accordance with the dictates of loyalty and allow his small child, who is now the heir, to be given into their charge, and raise him up to be a man. For if they do that, they will always enjoy honor.

[3459] Swemmel, swear on my hand that when you again ride through these lands — this I request of you, my friend — you will return here to me. Things should not simply remain as they are. I will have a written account made of the battles and the great catastrophe, how they [the Burgundians] met their deaths, how it all came about and also how it came to an end for everyone. You should tell me, then, about everything you have actually witnessed. I will also make inquiries of everyone's kin, be they woman or man, whoever might be able to relate something about this. To this end, I will immediately send my envoys into the land of the Huns. I will obtain information [regarding what has happened] there, for it would be very bad if it were not to be recorded. This is the most momentous event that has ever occurred on the face of the earth." Swemmel said immediately:

svves ir herre an mich gert.
des svlt ir vverden gevvert.

[3485]   Di boten ritten balde dan.
do hiez der Bisschoff sine man.
si beleiten ᐁf den vvegen.
so verre vnd er ir mohte pflegen.
mit spise vnde mit gevvarheit.
[3490]   svver in in Beyern vvider reit.
von den vvart in niht getan.
daz mᐁse man dvrh ir herren la^n.
vvan daz si in ir geb gaben.
do cherten si dvrh Svvaben. /
[3495]   mit disen mæren an den Rin.
Svvæmmel vnt die gesellen sin.
do Svvæmmel vf dvrch Beyern reit.
do vvrden ovch von im geseit.
div mære bi den strazzen.
[3500]   vvi chvnd er daz gelazzen.
ern sagte di iamerbærn not.
vnde vvi si vværen beliben tot.
alle da cer hohgezit.
do vvrden disiv mære sît.
[3505]   dem herren Elsen geseit.
der sprach mir solde vvesen leit.
desen chan ez aber niht gesin.
daz sie ie chomen ᐁber Rin.
daz vvil ich immer gote chlagen.
[3510]   min brvder vvart mir erslagen.
von ir hove reise hie.
daz ich doh verdiente nie.
des si mir selbe mᐁse iehen.
nv ist min rache an in geshæhen.
[3515]   alse daz alte sprichvvort sprichet.
svven der vvolf richet.
der ist errochen also vvol.
daz manz niht fᐁrbaz rechen sol.
sprach der margrave riche.
[3520]   do sprachen sᐁmeliche.
got von himel der sis gelobt.
daz et Hagen hat ver tobt.
der chonde ni strites vverden sat.
er ist nv chomen an di stat.
[3525]   da vns sin ᐁbermvt.

"My Lord, whatever you may wish of me, I shall be happy to carry out for you."

[3485] The messengers rode off soon thereafter. The bishop ordered his men to accompany them as far as he was able to provide them with food and with a guarantee of safe conduct.[88] The men they encountered in Bavaria did nothing to [injure] them — they refrained from doing so on account of their lord.[89] All they did was present them with gifts. Swemmel and his companions then travelled on through Swabia, carrying this news with them to the Rhine. When Swemmel rode through Bavaria, he passed on the news along the way. How could he refrain from telling the truth about the terrible tragedy and how all of them had been left dead at the festival? Eventually the news was told to Lord Else.[90] He said: "I ought to be very sorry about all this, but that is impossible. I will always complain to God that they [the Burgundians] ever crossed the Rhine. My brother was killed as a result of their journey here. That is something I never deserved, which they themselves would have to admit. Now I have had my revenge on them, just as the old saying goes: Whoever the wolf avenges has certainly been well avenged, so much so that one ought not to seek vengeance further," the mighty Margrave said. Some of them [his men] responded: "God in heaven be praised that Hagen's rage has come to an end. He could never get enough fighting. He has now reached a point where his arrogance

[88] At this point, Zeune deviates from the order of the following nineteen verses in an attempt to reconcile the discrepancy of the route taken by Swemmel and the other Hunnish envoys, namely, through Bavaria, Swabia, and then again through Bavaria.

[89] Who is (or who are) the lord(s) referred to in verse 3492? Moreover, does "ir" refer to the Bavarians or to the Huns themselves? If the pronoun refers to the Bavarians, then "herren" may be an allusion to local lords who have given the order to let the envoys pass unmolested. If "ir" represents the latter, on the other hand, then "herren" can only mean Attila and the sense is that the Bavarians have not dared to do anything to Swemmel and his men out of fear of the Hunnish leader, a suggestion that has been made by Werner Hoffmann. It is difficult to determine precisely who is meant.

[90] Else was the brother of Gelphrat who was killed by Dancwart as the Burgundians passed through Bavaria on their way to the land of the Huns. See the *Nibelungenlied*, strophe 1614 (*Aventiure* 26).

nv vil chleinen schaden tvt.

Di rede lazzen vvir nv sin.
do di boten ꝟber Rin.
ze Vvormez vvaren chomen.
[3530]   do vvart ir vaste vvar genomen.
ein teil man si bechande.
bi dem ir gevvande.
daz vvas spæhe gesniten.
nach den Hivnisschen siten.
[3535]   Do vvnderte die Bvrgære.
dirre vremden mære.
von vvannen si vværen chomen.
oder vva si heten genomen.
Gꝟnthers ross daz gꝟte.
[3540]   do vvas in dem mvte.
ein teil den livten svvære.
ê daz si div mære.
rehte da ver namen.
ꝟf den hoff do quamen.
[3545]   di verre vvarn dar gesant.
dem gesinde vvas vvol bechant.
ross vnde gereite.
niht langer man do beite.
man sagte ce hove mære.
[3550]   daz da chomen vvære.
der fꝟrsten vvaffen vnd ir march.
do vvart div vrevde also starch.
vor Prꝟnnhilde [157/446] der richen.
Si sprach vil minnechlichen.
[3555]   der mir div mære rehte seit.
dem ist min miete vil bereit.
vva di boten haben lazzen.
di herren vf den strazzen.

Also daz geschehen vvas.
[3560]   fꝟr der Chꝟneginne palas.
di boten vvaren chomen nider.
daz gesinde gahte sider.
dvrch vragen der mære.
vva der Chꝟnech vvære.
[3565]   Gꝟnther der fꝟrste riche.
ein teil blꝟvechliche<.>
antvorte der videlære.

can scarcely cause us any more injury."

[3527] But enough of this. Once the messengers had crossed the Rhine and arrived in Worms, they quickly aroused considerable attention. To some degree they were recognizable by their clothes, for they had been cut according to the peculiar fashion of the Huns. The citizens were puzzled at the strangeness of it all, where they had come from and where they had obtained Gunther's good steed. Some of the people there were heavy of heart even before they had heard what had actually happened. The envoys who had been sent from so far away then approached the court. The horses and their gear were well known to the assembled company. They did not wait any longer, and the court was told that the weapons and the war horses of the noblemen had arrived. Incredible happiness manifested itself there before noble Queen Brünhild. In a friendly tone she said: "I am prepared to reward well the person who will give me a reliable account of what has happened and where the envoys have left the noblemen along the way."

[3559] After that had occurred, the envoys dismounted before the queen's palace. The assembled company hastily asked for news of where their mighty King Gunther might be. The minstrel replied somewhat hesitatingly:

iane sol ich der mære.
svnderlingen niht sagen.
[3570]   ich solse pilliche verdagen.
nivvan da ich si sagen sol.
bringet mich so tvt ir vvol.
da ich si sol von rehte sagen.
dane vvil ich ir niht verdagen.
[3575]   Do gi ein Gvntheres man.
fvr di Chvneginne san.
vnd vragete si der mære.
ob ir daz liep vvære.
daz di boten fvr si giengen.
[3580]   di vvir da vor enpfiengen.
der ist vns einer niht bechant.
idoch bringen's in daz lant.
vnserr herren sarvvat.
Svvæmmel da bi in stat.
[3585]   der Eceln spilman.
si sprach nv heizze si her gan.
ich hete nv gerne ver nomen.
vvenne di herren solden chomen.

Svvæmmel der gvte.
[3590]   ein teil in svværem mvte.
mit den reise gesellen sin.
si giengen fvr di Chvnegin.
do sie si fvr si chomen sach.
div frovve gvtliche sprach.
[3595]   Ir herren sit vvillechomen.
ich het gerne von iv vernomen.
vva habt ir lazzen minen man.
vvi vvol ich iv der miete gan.
di ich dar vmbe geben sol.
[3600]   min herce deist mir sorgen vol.
daz ir mir ringet des ein teil.
daz ist ivver frvm vnde min heil.
ob ir^z chvrzlichen tvt.
gerne gib ich iv min gvt.
[3605]   Des vvnders vvird ich nimmer vri.
di vvile vvi daz chomen si.
daz er mir niemen hat gesant.
der sinen den ich het erchant.
daz getet er mir ni mere.
[3610]   daz mvt mich harte sere.

"Now listen, I will not tell all of you individually what has occurred, but rather I should properly say nothing until I am supposed to. If you will take me — and you would do well to do so — to where I should make my report, I will keep nothing from you." One of Gunther's men went right over to the queen and asked whether she wanted the envoys to approach her. "We do not know a single man among those whom we have just greeted and yet they have brought home our lord's armor. Attila's minstrel, Swemmel, is standing among them." She [Brünhild] replied: "Have them come in, for I am eager to hear when our lords are to arrive."

[3589] With a somewhat heavy heart, the good Swemmel, together with his travelling companions, went before the queen. When she saw them approaching, the lady said in a courteous manner: "Welcome, my lords. I would like to hear from you where you have left my husband, and will quite willingly reward you for the information. My heart is filled with anxiety and if you can assuage my fears somewhat, it will be to your advantage and to my peace of mind. I will be happy to give you my possessions if you will do this right away for me. I cannot help but be amazed that he has not sent one of his men to me whom I would have recognized. He has never done that to me before and it causes me to worry a great deal."

Do sprach der videlære.
erlovbt ir mir div mære.
kv̊neginne riche. /
so sage ich baltliche.
[3615]   svvaz mir der mære ist bechant.
ich dinge hie an ivch ce hant.
daz ez mir ane schaden si.
Si sprach des sol tv̊ vvesen vri.
daz dir hi iemen iht tv̊.
[3620]   da hat ovch niemen reht zv̊.
daz er di boten leide.
si sprach min ovgenvveide.
di vvæne ce verre ist mir enpfarn.
sin chvnde daz niht bevvarn.
[3625]   sine vveinete ê der mære.
do sprach der videlære.

Iv enbivtet lieb vnde gv̊t.
der vil hohegemv̊t.
v̊ze hivnisschem riche.
[3630]   von dem herren Dietriche.
ist iv dienest her bechomen.
vvir haben daz vil vvol vernomen.
daz in allez ivver leit.
ist sorge vnde ovch arbeit.
[3635]   Iv en bivtet ovch den dienest sin.
der gv̊te Bisschoff Pilgrin.
vnd heizzet iv daz frovve sagen.
daz man mæzliche chlagen.
sv̊l ein ieslichez leit.
[3640]   er ist iv alles des bereit.
mit vverchen vnde mit lere.
daz iv an frv̊me vnd ere.
ze dirre vverlde mv̊ge chomen.
Ovch han ich daz von im vernomen.
[3645]   er bittet alle skv̊neges man.
di iht trivve vvellen han.
daz si ivch vnd ivver kindelin.
in vvol bevolhen lazzen sin.
vvand ivver man der ist tot.
[3650]   Gv̊nther vnd Gernot.
mv̊gen chrone niht hie getragen.
si sint alle dri erslagen.
Hagen vnde Volker.

[3611] The minstrel replied: "Mighty Queen, permit me to tell you what has transpired. I shall soon inform you what I know, but I would like to have your assurance that I may do so without fear of injury." She answered: "You need not worry that somebody will do anything to you here. No one has the right to take offense at the envoys." She continued: "I sense that my true love has strayed too far from my presence." She could not restrain herself from crying [even] before hearing the report. Then the minstrel spoke:

[3627] "The high-spirited king of the Huns extends to you both his affection and material assistance. Lord Dietrich also offers you his service. We have certainly noticed that all of your sorrow has given them cause for worry and concern. The good Bishop Pilgrim also offers you his service and would have us tell you, my Lady, that every form of sorrow should be lamented in moderation. To this end he is prepared to assist you in word and deed so that it may be to your advantage and bring you honor in this world. I also have this message from him. He asks all of the king's men who wish to show their loyalty to take you and your child willingly into their care. For your husband is dead. Neither Gunther[91] nor Gernot can wear the crown here. All three of them have been killed. Hagen and Volker,

[91] While I have followed the text of Manuscript B here, it should be noted that other manuscripts refer in verse 3650 to Giselher and Gernot which does accord better with the reference in verse 3652 to "all three" of the kings.

vnt danchvvart der degen her.
[3655] di sint mit in bestanden.
tot in Hivnisschen landen.
(d)a si mit vrevden vvanden vvesen.
ir ist einer niht genesen.
ir gesindes ꝩber al.

[3660] Sich hꝩp der aller meiste schal.
der zen Hivnen ie gesach.
so gahes von hercen nie gebrach.
plꝩt vz deheinem mvnde.
als ir da ce stvnde.
[3665] tet von grozem leide.
di margravinne beide.
di da ce Bechlaren.
ovch mit chlage vvaren.
dine gechlagten ni so sere.
[3670] Prꝩnnhilt div here.
chlagte vvol in ir mazen.
div vrage vvas nv lazzen.
daz zꝩ den boten niemen sprach.
Svvæmmel anders niht ensach.
[3675] vvande mit vvintenden handen.
ir iamer vnd [158/447] ir anden.
chlagtens algemeine.
iane vvaz ez niht eine.
des kꝩnech Gꝩnthers vvip.
[3680] div da quelte den lip.
der chlagenden der vvas mere.

Vte div gar vnhere.
ze Lorse in ir hvse vvas.
da si veniete vnde las.
[3685] an ir salter alle tagezit.
in einem mꝩnster daz vvas vvit.
des si von erste began.
do si des chꝩnde gevvan.
vvaz ze Vvormez vvas geseit.
[3690] von sorgen so vvart ir bereit.
vil manech angestlicher mꝩt.
div mære envvaren ir niht gvt.
von ir vil lieben chinden.
ni frovven vꝩff so svvinden.
[3695] het man mer vernomen.

as well as the noble warrior, Dancwart, have also died alongside them in the land of the Huns, where they thought they would enjoy some happiness. Of all their company, not a single one has survived."

[3660] There resounded then the loudest scream that the Huns had ever heard. Never before had blood from the heart burst forth so quickly from anyone's mouth, as happened now with Brünhild in her incredible grief. The two countesses in Pöchlarn, who were also lamenting, did not, however, grieve as much as she, for noble Brünhild's lamentations knew no bounds. No more questions were put to the envoys and no one spoke to them. Swemmel could only see people wringing their hands as they commiserated together in their suffering and pain. In fact, King Gunther's wife was not the only one who went through agony, for there were others who lamented along with her.

[3682] The most unfortunate Lady Ute[92] was at her home in Lorsch where, in a large cathedral she had built, she followed the canonical hours in her Psalter. Once she had received word of what had been told at Worms, the anxiety she felt gave rise to many fears. To her [mind] the reports concerning her beloved children were not at all good. Never [before] had women been heard to cry out with more passion.

---

[92] Manuscript B and Manuscript d are the only two which contain this description of Ute. All of the others refer to her in positive terms. I have interpreted "vnhere" as an allusion to the queen's plight. She is not portrayed in splendor, but rather in a withdrawn, anxious state. It should be recalled here that Ute had had a particularly frightful dream prior to the departure of her sons for the land of the Huns, one that made it fairly clear that they would not be returning.

gahes vvolde si do chomen.
svvi so daz geschæhe.
daz si Prῦnnhilde sæhe.
Schiere braht man si dar.
[3700] do vvas ein vvage vnd ovch ein var.
daz volch mit lῦten rῦffe.
ir vnt der andern vῦffe.
chonde niht gelichen.
di armen zv den richen.
[3705] gevrieschen ovch div mære.
vvaz div chlage vvære.

In vil chvrcen zîten.
In Vvormez der vvîten.
chlageten vvip vnd chint.
[3710] si hvlffen Prῦnnhilde sint.
vvol bechlagen ir leit.
vil manech frovve gemeit.
vnd ovch der Bvrgære vvip.
di senten also den lip.
[3715] daz man mit frevden niemen vant.
in schonem hare manech hant.
erchrachete offte sere.
vvaz mag ih sagen mere.
vvan daz ir chlage ni gelach.
[3720] sine vverte vnz an den dritten tach.
di besten noch di bôstent.
chonde niemen getrôsten.
Do chom dar div lantschapft.
der gvten helde ein michel chrapft.
[3725] der drier edeln Chῦnege man.
der vvise ez senften began.
der tvmbe machtes ie mere.
ia vvas des landes ere.
bi stvle nider gesezzen.
[3730] da von vvas vnvergezzen.
daz si da chlagen solden.
di besten dine vvolden.
vergezzen niht ir trivve.
si senften vil ir rivve.
[3735] Prῦnnhilde der richen.
vnd schieden vvîslichen. /
vil manech vvip von leide.
idoch vvas vil freide.

She wished to rush off as quickly as possible to see Brünhild and so she was brought to her straightaway. People were milling around lamenting loudly and nothing could compare to the way she and the others wailed. Both the lower and upper classes learned why people were grieving.

[3707] Before long, women and children throughout the length and breadth of Worms joined in the grieving and helped Brünhild to lament her loss. Many a noble lady and also the wives of the townsmen were in such a distressed state that not a single happy person could be found. In many instances [women] tore out their beautiful hair with their hands. What more can I say other than [to tell you] that their lament did not desist, but rather continued through until the third day. No one could offer consolation to either the highest or the lowest. A large number of good warriors, followers of the three noble kings, arrived from the country. The wise man began to temper his grief, while the less experienced fellow allowed it to swell. The [men who represented the] honor of the land sat at the foot of the throne and did not neglect their duty to lament.[93] The best among them were determined not to forget their sense of loyalty. They tempered greatly the pain and suffering of mighty Brünhild, and, in their wisdom, separated many a woman from her sorrow. Nonetheless,

---

[93] The reference here is to the powerful liegemen of Gunther, Gernot, and Giselher who have come to Worms not only to participate in a national grieving ritual, but also to offer some consolation to Brünhild and the other women who had lost their husbands in the land of the Huns.

Prῡnnhilde hoher mῦt.

[3740] vvande si dvhte lῦcel gῦt.

des man ir raten chvnde.

Do chom ovch sa ce stvnde.

des chῦneges schenche Sindolt.

der diente diche trivven solt.

[3745] als ovch da von im geschach.

zῦ der Chῦneginne er do sprach.

frovve nῦ mazet ivver chlagen.

iane chan niemen entsagen.

vvol dem andern den tot.

[3750] vvêrt nῦ immer disiv not.

sine vvrden doh niht lebhaft.

der chlage div vngefῦge chrapft.

mῦse doh ein ende han.

irn sît so eine niht bestan.

[3755] ir mῦgt noh vil vvol chrone tragen.

frovve ez sol in chvrcen tagen.

ivver svn bi iv gechrȏnet sin.

so ergetzet ivch daz chindelin.

vnd vns der grozzen leide.

[3760] vil liebe ovgenvveide.

mῦgt ir noh hie vinden.

iv vnd ivvern chinden.

vvir dienen sam vorhtlichen.

so bi Gῦnthere dem richen.

[3765] Si sprach nῦ mῦze iv lonen crist.

der aller dinge gevvaltech ist.

daz ivver sin vnd ivver rat.

min herce also geringet hat.

vvan sol ih immer genesen.

[3770] daz mvz von disem rate vvesen.

Alrerst hiez man do fῦr gan.

di boten zantvvrte stan.

daz si sageten div mære < . >

vvi ez ergangen vvære.

[3775] Den ivngen chvnech man ᵇʳᵃʰᵗᵉ dar.

Svvæmmel stvnt vor der schar.

er begonde in div mære sagen.

daz Sifrit vvilen vvart erslagen.

da von si alle nv ligent tot.

[3780] Genῦge sprachen ane not.

Brünhild's heightened spirits were short lived, for she did not consider the advice that people could give her of any real help.

[3742] Sindolt, the king's cupbearer, also appeared on the scene. He had always served in the most loyal fashion, and this was the case here as well. He said to the queen: "My Lady, temper your grieving now; after all, no one can keep another person from death. Were this lamenting to continue forever, they would still not come back to life. The immoderate intensity of this grieving must come to an end. You are not alone and you may certainly continue to wear the crown. My Lady, your son should soon wear the crown next to you. In this way the child will help us as well as you to overcome our great sorrow. You may yet find here many other things that will delight you.[94] We will serve you and your children[95] as respectfully as we did mighty Gunther."

[3765] She said: "May Christ, who has power over all things, now reward you because your advice and your intentions have helped to sooth my heart. For if I survive this at all, it will be because of your words." Only now did they let the envoys approach to provide answers and to tell the story of how things had transpired. They brought in the young king. Swemmel stood before the crowd and began to relate the tale. "The reason that they are all dead now is because Siegfried was killed." (There were many who needlessly asked:

[94] This is a somewhat liberal translation of "vil liebe ovgenvveide" (verse 3760), which has the literal meaning 'many a delight for the eye.' The sense, in this particular context, seems to be that Brünhild should take consolation in what the future may still bring in the form of renewed joy, new generations, continuity of the line.

[95] Although the text clearly refers to "children" and not simply to "child," it should be recalled that Gunther and Brünhild in the *Nibelungenlied* appear to have had only one child, a son named Siegfried (see strophe 718,4b).

ist mir min vater da belegen.
den slv̂ch Hagen der degen.
ze leide sinem vvibe.
des sint von dem libe.

[3785]   dvrh ir rache dort gescheiden.
ine gevriesch ni haz so leiden.
als in div frovve geleit hat.
min sin der chreffte niht enhat.
daz ich ez iv vvol chv̂nne sagen.

[3790]   Des kv̂neges brv̂der vvart erslagen.
daz vvas min her Blôdelin.
[159/448] der vvas der erste vnd[er] in.
ce tode slv̂ch in Danchvvart.
da der helt bestanden vvart.

[3795]   an der herberge bi den knehten.
si mv̂sen alle vehten.
beide ivnge vnd alte.
vvande si mit gevvalte.
in daz hv̂s gevvnnen an.

[3800]   vvand ez vvas verre her dan.
da ir herberge vvas.
der knehte einer niht genas.
vveder groz noh chleine.
vvan danchvvart alterseine.

[3805]   vil bald er vzzem hv̂se spranch.
do gie ane ir aller danch.
hinze hove der chv̂ne helt mære.
vnd sagte vvi im gelvngen vvære.
sin̄ herren da si sazzen.

[3810]   zer hohzit vnd azzen.
do slv̂ch Hagen des vvirtes chint.
ze siner angesihte sint.
daz ez fv̂r den tissch shoz.
vnd im daz plv̂t sin hant begoz.

[3815]   Da mit sprvngen in den strit.
ivver drie kv̂nege sit.
des mv̂sez gen v̂ber al.
da vvart vil michel der schal.
von der svverte chlingen.

[3820]   vil vngefvge dringen.
sah man di recken zv̂ der not.
des lagens allen samt tot.

"Was my father killed there?")[96] "He [Siegfried] was killed by the warrior Hagen, much to the sorrow of his wife, and as a result of the revenge she sought, they lost their lives there. I have never heard of a greater hatred than that which the lady entertained. I do not have the power within me to be able to describe it [adequately] to you.

[3790] The king's brother, my Lord Blödelin, was killed. He was the first among them (i.e., the Huns). Dancwart struck him down and killed him, as the warrior had been attacked in the sleeping quarters with the squires. All of them were forced to fight, the young [less experienced] and the old [more experienced], because the Huns forced their way into the building and their quarters were far removed [from the Great Hall]. Not one of the squires, whether big or small, survived, other than Dancwart alone. He quickly jumped out of the house and, much to their [i.e., the Huns'] dismay, the renowned warrior made his way to the court. He told his lords, who were sitting there eating at this festival, what had happened. Then Hagen killed his host's son before his very eyes so that he fell down in front of the table and the blood splashed on his hand.

[3815] Your three kings subsequently rushed into the fight and it spread to encompass everyone. There was a terrible din of clashing swords and much pushing and shoving as the warriors joined the fray, which left them all lying dead,

[96] This is meant as an interjection on the part of the offspring who have gathered to hear what Swemmel has to say. Rather than answer each query of this sort directly, he continues with his explanation of how the slaughter came about in the first place.

iene dort vnt dise hie.
ezen vvart so herter stvrm nie.
[3825] zer vverlde gevohten.
di vvile si leben mohten.
Von alzæi Volker.
tet vil micheliv ser.
mit vvilligen handen.
[3830] ivverr mâge anden.
der helt so grivveliche rach.
vil michel vvnder da geschach.
da chonde niemen bi gestan.
der iht eren vvolde han.
[3835] der m✧se gevvert immer sin.
dvrh den k✧nech vnt di k✧negin.
so m✧sens alle strîten.
In vil angestlichen zîten.
vvart gescheiden doh her dan.
[3840] her Dietrich vnt sine man.
der vogt da von Berne.
vvand er sah vil vngerne.
beidenthalp di svvære.

R✧dger der helt mære.
[3845] lie ovch beliben den haz.
dvrh Giselhern tet er daz.
der het gevestent im sin chint.
daz half in doh vvenech sint.
vvand si so vil der vrivnt verl✧rn.
[3850] vnt den grozzen schaden ch✧rn.
do griffens al gemeine z✧.
daz volch allenthalben d✧.
m✧se / striten dvrh di not.
Ecel bat vnd ovh gebot.
[3855] daz man ræche im sin chint.
Ovch vvarp div Ch✧neginne sint.
mit bæte an R✧dgere.
vnz er di degen here.
mit strite ovh m✧se bestan.
[3860] des m✧ser vnt di sinen man.
in dem stvrme ligen tot.
er vnt der herre Gernot.
beide ein ander sl✧gen.
da von in haz do tr✧gen.
[3865] di ch✧nen Bernære.

some there, others here. Never in the world had a harder battle been fought. As long as they were alive, Volker of Alzeye inflicted great suffering with willing hands. The warrior grimly avenged the injuries done your kinfolk. Many remarkable feats were performed there. No one who wished to have any honor could stand on the sidelines, but rather had to defend himself. For the sake of the king and the queen, everyone had to become involved in the fight. In these most anxious times, it came about that Dietrich, the Lord of Verona, was separated from his men. For it was no joy for him to witness the devastation on both sides.

[3844] That renowned warrior Rüedeger also put aside his hatred. He did this on behalf of Giselher, for he had betrothed his daughter to him. Yet it was not to benefit him at all in the course of events. Because they lost so many of their friends and sustained such terrible injuries, everyone joined in and all of the people necessarily became involved in the fight. Attila made entreaties and also ordered that he be avenged for the loss of his child. Moreover, the queen pleaded so much with Rüedeger until he, too, had to take up the fight against the noble warriors, and as a result, he and his men also met their deaths in the struggle. He and Lord Gernot killed one another. Hence the brave Veronese bore malice towards them [i.e., the Burgundians]

do sprachen di helde mære.
si vvolden rechen Rv̊dgere.
do het iz verboten sere.
den sinen doh her Dietrich.
[3870]   do vvas Vvolfhart so grivvelich.
daz er sis vvolde niht erlan.
sine mv̊sen ivver volch bestan.
Ê iz her Dietrich do bevant.
der von Amelvnge lant.
[3875]   der vvas einer niht genesen.
der in schade mohte vvesen.
nivvan der alte Hildebrant.
ivvers volches man ovh vant.
deheinen lebenden mere.
[3880]   nivvan den kv̊nech Gv̊nthere.
vnd hagen den Tronegære.
Hildebrant disiv mære.
mit einer vvnden mv̊se sagen.
di het im hagene geslagen.
[3885]   da von er chvme sit genas.
Do daz also ergangen vvas.
des er chom vil sere her dietrich.
vvan sin schade der vvas vreislich.
an magen vnd an sinen man.
[3890]   Zehant do gie der helt dan.
da er di recken beide vant.
er vnd meister Hildebrant.
mit iamer vnd mit sere.
ia het der degen here.
[3895]   ienoch genert si beide.
done vvolden si vor leide.
nah den andern niht genesen.
done moht ez anders niht vvesen.
sich en ræche doh her Dietrich.
[3900]   Gv̊nther den chv̊nech rich.
bestvnt in mv̊der als ein degen.
sit tvvanch in mit svvert slegen.
also der Bernære.
daz er den helt mære.
[3905]   zeinem gisel gevvan.
dar nah bestvnt in sin man.
Hagen in chvrcen stvnden.
daz hat man vvol erfvnden.
Sin heten in nimmer lan genesen.

and the renowned warriors declared that they wished to avenge Rüedeger. Yet Lord Dietrich gave strict orders to his men forbidding them to do so. But Wolfhart was so incensed that he did not want to drop the matter and so they had to fight against your people. Before Lord Dietrich discovered what had happened, not a single one of the men of Amelungenland had survived who might have done injury to them [i.e., the Burgundians] other than old Hildebrand. Furthermore, not a single man of your own people was found still alive, apart from King Gunther and Hagen of Troneck. Hildebrand recounted all of this after having been dealt a wound by Hagen from which he almost did not recover. Once things had taken their course in this fashion, Lord Dietrich was in quite a state of shock, for he had sustained terrible losses among his kinfolk and his men. He and Sir Hildebrand immediately went over to where they found the two warriors in sorrow and despair. Actually, the good knight would have spared the two of them, but in their sorrow they did not wish to go on living after the deaths of the others. There was thus nothing Lord Dietrich could do but avenge himself. Mighty King Gunther, although exhausted, fought against him like a [true] warrior. However, the Veronese nobleman defeated him with his sword blows, so that he was able to take the renowned warrior prisoner. Shortly thereafter his liegeman Hagen engaged him in combat. They certainly took note of that and would never have let him live

[3910]   solden si gervͦet vvesen.
vvand si heten da vor gevohten.
daz si niht mer en mohten.
di zvvene svmerlange tage.
ez ist vvar daz ich iv sage.
[3915]   di fͥrsten vnd ir recken her.
vierzech tvsent oder [160/449] mer.
hat ir ellen da ver svvant.
svvaz ir ie helm vf gebant.
der besten vvigande.
[3920]   di von manegem lande.
dem chͥnege Ecele vvaren chomen.
di hant ir ende von in genomen.
Vor den Hivnen si vværen vvol genesen.
vværn di kristen niht gevvesen.
[3925]   di brahtens in di arbeit.
als ich iv ê han geseit.
daz si ein ander slͥgen
vvand si in niht vertrͥgen.
des mͥsens alle da bestan.
[3930]   vnz an dise zvvene man.
Hagen vnd ovh Gͥnther.
mohten do niht striten mer.
do tvvanch si Dietrich beide.
In vil grozzem leide.
[3935]   antvvrte er si der Chͥnegin.
div hiez si beide fͥren hin.
vnd rach sich vreislichen.
den recken lobelichen.
hiez si beiden nemen den lip.
[3940]   dar vmbe do daz Edel vvip.
slͥch meister Hildebrant.
niemen da mere vant.
di da sterben solden.
eteliche di vvolden.
[3945]   mit den andern vvesen tot.
alsvs liez ich si in der not.
von den ich her bin gesant.

Ir livte hͥben sa ze hant.
von chlage harte grozzen vͥf.
[3950]   ir iamer iz do also schͥf.
si gedahten schaden vnd not.
Sit chlagete vnz vf den tot.

if they had been rested. But they had just fought so fiercely for two long summer days that they could no longer continue. What I am telling you is the truth. The noblemen and their fine warriors had, through their courage, killed forty thousand or more. The best knights who had ever strapped on helmets and who had come to [visit] King Attila met their deaths at the hands of the Burgundians. They[97] would certainly have survived [among] the Huns had the Christians not been there. As I have told you, these were the ones who brought them into dire straits, so that they ended up killing each other because they could not be reconciled. For that reason all of them had to fight until only these two men were left. Hagen and Gunther were no longer able to continue fighting and so Dietrich subdued the two of them. In great distress he turned them over to the queen. She had both of them led away and exacted a terrible revenge on them. She ordered both of these illustrious warriors to be killed[98] and that is why Sir Hildebrand killed the noble woman. No one else there was to die, although quite a number wished they were dead along with the others. And so I left them in their distress, those very ones who sent me here."

[3948] Her [i.e., Brünhild's] entourage let out a terrible cry of grief. Their misery caused them to reflect on their losses and their plight. Subsequently, noble Ute lamented unto death

[97] Some confusion could arise here with respect to the significance of the pronouns. The "si" in verse 3923 refers, I believe, to the Burgundians, the sense being here that, had they not been forced to face Christian knights at the court of Attila, the Burgundians would not have had any problem dealing with the Huns.

[98] While it is correct that, in the Nibelungenlied, Kriemhild does have her brother, Gunther, killed, she herself decapitates Hagen which precipitates the radical response from Hildebrand.

Vote div vil riche.
nach den helden iamerliche.
[3955] ir vil lieben chinden.
niemen moht er vinden.
daz ^{si} trôsten chvnde ûz chlage.
dar nach ûber siben tage.
div vrovve lach vor leide tot.
[3960] vil chvme vor der selben not.
genas sit div kûnegine.
vvande si lach in vnsinne.
vnz man mit vvazzer si ver goz.
des volches chlage vvart so groz.
[3965] in allem dem lande.
der Criemhilde ande.
vvas errochen sere.
Prûnnhilt div here.
do si sprechen began.
[3970] do gedahte si dar an.
vvi vvol si ez erholte.
daz leit daz si nû dolte.
vvaz Criemhilde iht leit ê.
ir tet diz leit nv alse vve.

[3975] Div frovve iæmerliche sprach.
ovve daz <ich> ie gesach.
der edelen Criemhilde lip.
do daz ere gernde vvip.
mit rede er zvrnde mir den mvt.
[3980] des verlos der helt gvt.
daz leben Sifrit ir man.
da von ich nv den schaden han.
daz ir frevde ir / vvart benomen.
daz ist mir nû her heim chomen.
[3985] vver chvnde frevde da gehaben.
div edel Vote vvart begraben.
ce Lorse bi ir aptey.
ir brach daz leit ir herce enzvvei.
div ê vor helden chrone trûch.
[3990] do vvaz leide genûch.
beide meiden vnd vviben.
da vvas den shônen liben.
von træhen naz ir gevvant.
allez Gûnthers lant.
[3995] mit iamer vvas befangen.

in misery for the warriors, her most beloved children. No one was able to find a way to console her in her grief. Seven days later the lady lay dead from her suffering. The queen herself hardly survived the same agony, for she lay unconscious until water was poured over her. The lament of the people was exceedingly great throughout all the land. Kriemhild's suffering had been terribly avenged. Once noble Brünhild had again come to her senses, she reflected on how she had brought about the sorrow that she was now forced to bear. Whatever Kriemhild had suffered earlier, it was now her turn to bear this pain.

[3975] The lady said in great distress: "Alas, that I ever laid eyes on noble Kriemhild. When that ambitious woman angered me with her words, it led to the death of her husband, the good warrior Siegfried. Now I must suffer the dire consequences. That her joy was taken from her has now come back to haunt me." Who could have enjoyed any happiness there? Noble Ute was laid to rest in Lorsch at her abbey. Sorrow had broken the heart of this woman, who earlier had worn the crown [and reigned] over warriors. There was a great deal of grief among both maidens and ladies alike and the garments of these beautiful women became soaked with their tears. All of Gunther's land was filled with distress.

do chomen ce hove gegangen.
di hôhesten vnt di besten.
svvaz si des gûten vvestten.
der frovven vnd ir kinde.
[4000]   daz riet in daz gesinde.
dar zû des landes ere.
sine vvolden daz niht mere.
so sere chlagte div kûnegin.
ovch vvolden sie niht vnder in.
[4005]   langer ane vogt bestan.
daz voich do raten began.
man machete ritter daz chint.
da von mûse erlesschen sint.
ein teil ir vngefûgen chlage.
[4010]   vvir vvellen daz er chrone trage.
daz vvir iht ane kûnech sin.

Do hiezen si daz chindelin.
vvol breiten dar zû.
der chrone ingesindes dû.
[4015]   vvol hvndert knappen man dar zû vant.
den man des tages svvert vmbe bant.
Do vvas ovch Rvmolt nû chomen.
der het div mære ovch vernomen.
da heime in sinem lande.
[4020]   mit trivven vvas im ande.
daz sin vil lieber herre.
mit schaden also verre.
vvaz vz sinem rate chomen.
vvir haben diche vvol vernomen.
[4025]   daz er in holt vvære.
di stolzen helde mære.
chlagte er senliche.
er sprach herre Got der riche.
daz ich ie vvart geborn.
[4030]   mine herre di han ich verlorn.
nivvan von Hagenen ûbermût.
div diche grozzen schaden tût.
do er Criemhilde nam ir man.
vnd ir ir gût an gevvan.
[4035]   in grozzen vntrivven.
ich sah ez an ir rivven.
svvie siz ane getrûge.
daz man si dar vmbe slûge.

The best and most noble arrived at court. The assembled company offered
the queen and her child the best advice that they could, also in as much as
it pertained to [preserving] the honor of the land. They did not want the
queen to go on grieving so intensely, nor did they wish to continue any
longer without a ruler. The people recommended that the child be
knighted. That would dissipate somewhat her[99] unrelenting grief. "We
want him to wear the crown so that we are no longer without a king."

[4012] They then had the child prepared [for the ceremony]. About a
hundred squires from the royal household were found for the event who
also received their swords on that day. Rumold had also arrived. He had
heard the news at home in his own country. With his sense of loyalty he
was terribly grieved that his beloved lord had suffered such injury so far
away from his council. We have often noted that he was most well-disposed
towards them. With great pain [in his heart] he lamented the proud,
renowned warriors and said: "Almighty God, [a pity] that I was ever born!
I have lost my lords, all as a result of Hagen's arrogance, [a trait] which
often turns out to be very harmful. When, in a display of great treachery,
he killed Kriemhild's husband and also confiscated her treasure, I could see
from the pain she felt that she was forever contemplating how they might
be killed for what they had done,

[99] It might be suggested that the pronoun "ir" in verse 4009 refers to the Burgundians
who are making the recommendation that Brünhild's son be knighted. As the lamenting
among the latter is also incredibly intense, that would fit contextually. I have opted for "her"
because it appears to me more likely that, with the reference immediately preceding to
Brünhild's incredible grieving, the suggestion that her son be knighted is intended to
alleviate her situation somewhat.

svvenne ioh ez geshæhe.

[4040]   Hagen ir manege smæhe.
zir schaden ane schvlt erbot.
zallen ziten an not.
des er niht tⱴn solde.
ob manz merchen [161/450] vvolde.

[4045]   vvande des vvas im gar ce vil.
dar vmbe ich ez ir niht vvizzen (vvil).
Vvaz het Sifrit ir man.
im ce leide getan.
der vvart ane schvlt er mort.

[4050]   daz han ich sider vvol gehort.
Vvaz denne ob dvrch ir zorn.
di frovven beide vvol geborn.
gezvrnden in ir tvmpheit.
daz solde man hin han geleit.

[4055]   vnde solde in han genesen lan.
do aber des niht moht ergan.
vnde si zen Hivnen frovve vvart.
do solden si di hove vart.
haben pilliche haben lan.

[4060]   hete min herre getan.
als ich im mit trivven riet.
do er von disem lande schiet.
sone vvære er niht erstorben.
mit im sint ver dorben.

[4065]   di besten vvigande.
die in deheinem lande.
chⱴnege ie gevvnnen.
oder gevvinnen chvnden.
di dort mit in sint erslagen.

[4070]   sine chvnden niht ver chlagen.
di in disem lande sint.
man. vvip. vnde chint.
di richen zⱴ den <den> armen.
nⱴ mⱴze ez got erbarmen.

[4075]   daz chvnde helfen niht min rat.
da von daz lant nⱴ ane stat.
frevde vnde maneger ere.
vns mach doh leider mere.
niht gehelffen vnser chlage.

[4080]   Nⱴ shaffet et daz chrone trage.
vnser herre der ivnge.
ir gemeiniv zvnge.

whenever it might come to pass. Time and time again, Hagen had quite without grounds added insults to the injury that he had caused her. This was something he ought not to have done, for if one were really to consider the matter, he was clearly going too far. For this reason I am not inclined to blame Kriemhild for what she did. What had her husband Siegfried ever done to hurt Hagen? He was unjustly murdered, as I have heard people subsequently claim. So what if the two noblewomen railed at each other in such a silly, senseless way? Their quarrel should have been put aside and Siegfried allowed to live. But since that was not possible and she became Queen of the Huns, they should by rights have refrained from making the trip to [the Hunnish] court. If my lord had acted on the loyal advice I gave him when he left this country, he would not have met his death. The best warriors that kings in any land ever acquired or could acquire perished along with him. The men, women, and children in this country, both rich and poor, could never lament them enough. May God have mercy [upon them] for my advice was to no avail, and now the land is deprived of both joy and honor. Regrettably, all of our lamenting will be of no help to us. But see to it that our young lord is crowned." They all

gab geliche do den rat.

Niemen vns gesagt hat.

[4085]   des vvir noh vernomen haben.

daz herlich vv̂rde erhaben.

in also chvrcen tagen.

als vvir di livte hôren sagen.

ein also groziv hohzit.

[4090]   Vvormez div stat vvit.

vvart gar vol der geste.

ia heten si daz beste.

mit grozzen trivven getan.

do sah man vnder chrone stan.

[4095]   den ivngen k̂nech riche.

si entpfiengen gemeinliche.

ir lehen von dem chinde.

der hoff vnt daz gesinde.

vvaren ein teil in frevde chomen.

[4100]   Do het ovch Svvæmmelin genomen.

vrlovp heim ce lande.

der in da von im sande.

vnder di B̂rndenære.

dem sagt er disiv mære.

[4105]   Svs chom er vvider in / hivnen lant.

da er noch Eceln vant.

vnt den herren Dietriche.

si vragten al geliche.

vvi er vvider vvære chomen.

[4110]   svvaz er gesehen het vnd vernomen.

daz sagt er als er chvnde.

an Eceln sit der stvnde.

vrevde niemen vant.

do vvolde ovch vvider in sin lant.

[4115]   her Dietrich von Berne.

daz sahen do vil gerne.

frov Herrat vnd Hildebrant.

do der k̂nech daz ervant.

daz si niht vvolden da bestan.

[4120]   svvaz im ê leides vvas getan.

so geschach im nie so leide.

Er mant si trivven beide.

Hildebrande vnt dietrichen.

vvelt ir mir nv entvvichen.

[4125]   sît ich min volch verlorn han.

concurred with this counsel. We can vouch for the validity of the claim that there has never been a more splendid festival arranged over the space of just a few days. The city of Worms was overflowing with guests. In a display of great loyalty they had arranged things as best they could. Then the people saw the young king wearing the crown and together they all received their fiefs from the child. The court and the assembled company were thus able to enjoy some happiness.

[4100] Swemmel had also taken leave to return to his homeland. He made this report to the man who had sent him forth into the land of the Burgundians. Once he had again arrived in the land of the Huns and found Attila and Lord Dietrich, they immediately asked how he had fared and what he had seen or learned [on his trip]. He informed them as well as he could. From this time on, no one ever again saw Attila happy. Lord Dietrich of Verona also wished to return home, something which Lady Herrat and Hildebrand were happy to hear. Once the king learned that they no longer wished to remain there, whatever sorrow he had felt up until then could not compare to that which he felt now. He reminded both Dietrich and Hildebrand of the loyalty [they owed him].[100] "Do you really wish to leave me, now that I have lost my people?

[100] Verse 4122 may seem on the surface to be straightforward, with Attila reminding Dietrich and Hildebrand of the loyalty they owe him. Yet this could hardly be understood in terms of a binding, legal commitment that the two warriors have to the Hunnish king. They had been granted asylum by Attila, but had not, to our knowledge, ever sworn an oath of loyalty to become his liegemen. Attila is probably thinking more in terms of reciprocity. Since he has shown them good will and allowed these exiles to remain at his court, they, in turn, should not abandon him in his present plight, but should remain and console him in his grief.

vvi sol ich eine nꝰ bestan.

Do sprach der Bernære.
vvi vvoldet ir dach ich vvære.
ane helffe vnd ane ᵈⁱ mine.

[4130] ein ieslich man di sine.
bi im vil pillichen hat.
ir sehet vvol vvi min dinch stat.
ich vnt div trivtinne min.
sꝰln niht mer in ellende sin.

[4135] Svvaz Ecel vlehen chvnde.
oder pitten zꝰ der stvnde.
dar vmbe vvolden siz niht lan.
er mꝰse ane sie bestan.
sie vlizzen sich der reise.

[4140] manech vvitvve vnd vveise.
beliben mꝰse hinder in.
Ecel vvandelte den sin.
von disen starchen leiden.
do si von im vvolden scheiden.

[4145] Als man vns gesagt hat.
do nam div vrovve Herrat.
daz ir div Chꝰneginne helche lie.
doh mꝰses vil beliben hie.
vvande siz ninder bringen chvnden.

[4150] doh fvrten sis an den stvnden.
mit in des hete si gegert.
vvol ahzech tvsent marche vvert.
frov herrat vrlovp do nam.
den vrovven do niht anders zam.

[4155] nivvan vveinen vnd chlagen.
ꝰze der chamere vvart getragen.
ein satel der vvas riche.
den diche vverdechliche.
frꝰ Helche hete geritten.

[4160] vf den satel vvas gesnitten.
der aller beste sigelat.
den iemen in der vverlde hat.
Iane chan ich iv besvnder.
gesagen niht daz vvnder.

[4165] vvi dem vverche vvære.
[162/451] von golde vvas ez svvære.
vnd von edelm gesteine.

How shall I continue on alone?"

[4127] Dietrich of Verona said: "How do you expect me to be without allies and without my men? By rights, everyone wishes to have his men alongside him. You can surely see how things stand with me. My wife and I shall no longer be exiles." Regardless of how much Attila pleaded and begged them [to stay], they could not be moved to change their minds and he had to get along without them. They prepared for the trip and left behind many a widow and orphan. Now, as they took their leave of him, Attila went mad as a result of his terrible suffering.[101]

[4145] We have been told that Lady Herrat took along what Queen Helche had bequeathed to her. Nonetheless, she had to leave a lot behind, for she could never bring all of it along. Still, she wished to take with her at that time goods to the value of eighty thousand marks. Then Lady Herrat prepared to leave. It was only appropriate for the women to cry and grieve. A magnificent saddle was brought out of the storeroom which Lady Helche had often ridden upon in stately fashion. The saddle was embroidered with the finest gold silk that could be found in the world. Well, I cannot tell you all of the marvelous things about this work [or art]. It was heavily laden with gold and precious gems.

[101] The scene in which Dietrich departs from Attila's court is the last time that the Hunnish king actually appears in the *Chlage*, although reference will later be made to his ultimate fate. If one follows the divisions to be found in Manuscript B itself, there is a correlation between the departure of Dietrich and Hildebrand and the radical change of "sin" which Attila experiences and which I have interpreted as a loss of sanity. This would accord with the reaction of Attila over the departure of Dietrich, Hildebrand, and Herrat as described in verses 4185-4189.

kv̊neges vvip deheine.
bezzern satel ni gereit.
[4170] div vil richen pfert chleit.
hiengen nider vf daz gras.
do si nv gar bereittet vvas.
zir verte alsie lv̊ste.
di frovve\<n\> si do chv̊ste.
[4175] alle vil gemeine.
do vvas ir deheine.
sine vveinten also sere.
sam do Helche div here.
mit tode vvas von in bechomen.
[4180] so svvinder vrlv̊p vvart genomen.
nie in dem hove von vrovven.
daz mohte man vil vvol schovven.

Do si cem vvirte vrlovp genamen.
vnd ê si vz dem hove qvamen.
[4185] der kv̊nech vil nider fv̊r tot.
im gap der iamer solhe not.
daz er di sinne niht behielt.
vnd so chrancher vvitzze vvielt.
daz er vnversvnnen lach.
[4190] lebt er sit deheinen tach.
des het er doch vil chleinen frvmen.
vvande im vvas an sin herce chvmen.
div rivve also manechvalt.
daz in daz leit mit gevvalt.
[4195] lie selten sît gesprechen vvort.
ern vvas vveder hie noch dort.
ern vvas tot noh enlebete.
in einem tvvalme er svvebete.
dar nach ine vveiz vvie manegen tach.
[4200] Svvi grozzer herscheffte er ê pflach.
dar zv vvas er nv gedigen.
daz si in eine liezzen ligen.
vnde niemen v̊ffe in niht ahte.
vvi erz sît bedahte.
[4205] daz hat vns niemen noch geseit.
do her Dietrich dan gereit.

Do si nv vvaren v̊ff den vvegen.
do hiez der herliche degen.
Hildebrant den grisen.

No queen had ever ridden upon a finer saddle. A magnificent blanket hung down as far as the grass. Now that she was completely prepared for the journey she desired to take, she kissed all of the ladies [gathered there]. There was not a one of them who did not weep just as much as she had when noble Helche was taken from them in death. Never before had there been such a distressful leave-taking by women at court as the one that could be witnessed there.

[4183] When they had taken leave of their host and before they had departed the court, the king collapsed as though he were dead. His distress brought him into such a quandary that he lost his senses and became so distraught that he lay there unconscious. If he lived a day longer, it was scarcely to his advantage. For such deep sorrow had filled his heart that his terrible suffering prevented him from ever saying another word. He was neither here nor there, he was neither alive nor dead. I do not know for how many days thereafter he moved about as though he were in a trance. However grand his armies may [once] have been, he had now come to a point where people left him to fend for himself and nobody paid any more attention to him. No one has informed us what he might have thought once Lord Dietrich had ridden off.

[4207] When they were riding along their way, that noble warrior ordered the old man Hildebrand

[4210]   sine vrovven vvisen.

gegen Bechlaren.

da sine mâge vvaren.

ir gezoges vvas niht mere.

nivvan div magt here.

[4215]   vnt di einen zvvene man.

vnt daz ein sovmære mit in dan.

der trv̊ch frovven Herraten chleit.

mit grozzem iamer do reit.

dvrh div lant her Dietrich.

[4220]   si gahten allez fv̊r sich.

mit iamer vnd mit sorgen.

an dem sibendem morgen.

dise g(est)e chomen vvarn.

zv der bvrch ce Bechelarn.

[4225]   di livte vriesschen mære.

daz da chomen vvære.

der herre von ₽ne.

daz volch ez horte gerne.

si sagtenz Dietelinde.

[4230]   dem Rv̊dgeres chinde. /

div vvas noch in grozer not.

vvand ir mv̊ter div vvas tot.

da vor inner drien tagen.

si moht ir tovgen niht ver chlagen.

[4235]   vmb ir vil lieben mannes lip.

des starp daz erbære vvip.

von dem vil starchem leide.

Die ivncfrovven beide.

man do zesamne brahte.

[4240]   ieslichiv do gedahte.

vrevde vnd grozer sere.

in zv̊htlicher ere.

si ein ander chvsten.

do tvvanch zv den brusten.

[4245]   Dietlinden frȏ Herrat.

si sprach din mach noh vverden rat.

sol lebn min frivnt her Dietrich.

dv solt vvol gehaben dich.

do sprah si min vvol gehaben.

[4250]   daz ist allez nv begraben.

an vat[er] vnd an mv̊t[er].

vil frivnde so gv̊t[er].

to accompany his lady to Pöchlarn, where his kin were to be found. Their entourage consisted only of the noble lady and the two men, and a packhorse that they brought along which carried Lady Herrat's garments. Lord Dietrich rode through the lands in great distress. They hurried along, each absorbed in his grief and filled with anxiety. On the seventh morning they reached the town of Pöchlarn. The people learned that the Lord of Verona had arrived. They were glad to hear this and they told the news to Dietlinde, Rüedeger's child. She was still in terrible distress for her mother had died just three days earlier. She had not been able to stop lamenting the death of her dear husband, and as a result the honorable woman had died from the terrible grief.

[4238] The two young women were brought together and each of them felt both joy and great sorrow. With all honor and courtesy they kissed one another. Lady Herrat held Dietlinde close to her breast and told her: "You can still be helped. As long as my friend, Lord Dietrich, is alive, you will fare well." She replied: "The joy in my life has been buried with my father and mother.

ih vvæn v[er]l૭r noh ni meit.
In chlagelicher arbeit.
[4255]   vant si h[er] Dietrich.
di ivnge magt loblich.
trost er als ein frivnt sol.
Niftel n૭ gehabe dih vvol.
vnd senffte diner leide.
[4260]   ia rivvent si mih beide.
din vat[er] vnt div m૭t[er] din.
div m૭z ih immer mere sin.
chlagende vnz an minen tot.
૭bervvinde ih imm[er] mine not.
[4265]   vnd chvm ih īmer in min lant.
daz lob ih an dine hant.
daz ih dih gerne scheide.
von iamer vnd von leide.
so ih verreste chan.
[4270]   des vvart ir sicherheit getan.
von dem Pnære.
do sprach d[er] helt mære.
Sol ih deheine vvile lebn.
ih vvil dih einē manne ᵍᵉᵇᵉⁿ.
[4275]   d[er] mit dir b૭vet diniv lant.
hi mit bevalh er da zehant.
di magt ir vat[er] mānen.
do schieden si vō danen.
Lachende ez niht geschach.
[4280]   do von ir rîtende sach.
Herraten div margravīne.
vō allem ir sinne.
erpibente si vil sere.
daz div vil groz ere.
[4285]   an si eine vvas bechom.
doh vvart ir sid[er] vvar genom.
als ez ir eren gezam.
irn vvas niem so gram.
d[er] ir tæte deheiniv leit.
[4290]   alsvs vvarte do div meit.
mit t[ri]vven vnd mit stæte.
als ir gelobt hæte.
d[er] h[er]re da von Berne.
des erbeitte si vil g[er]ne.
[4295]   Von Pazovve d[er] bisscoff Pilgrin.
dvrh liebe d[er] neven sin.

I believe that no noble lady ever lost so many dear kinfolk." Lord Dietrich found her there in terrible grief. He consoled the worthy young woman as a friend might be expected to do. "My dear niece, try to take heart and temper your sorrow. After all, I, too, mourn the loss of your mother and father and I will lament their passing to the day I die. If I ever get over my plight and return to my homeland, I swear to you that I will put an end to your pain and sorrow, to whatever extent I am in a position to do so." The Lord of Verona gave his pledge on this. The renowned warrior continued: "If I live a while longer, I will give you to a man who will help you to take care of your land." He immediately entrusted the young woman to the care of her father's men. They then took their leave of one another, but it was without any laughter. When the countess saw Herrat riding away from her, she shook from head to toe [in the realization] that she alone was now burdened with the great honor [i.e., of ruling her land]. But she subsequently enjoyed the respect that was appropriate to her [position of] honor and there was no one so ill-disposed towards her as to have done her any harm. The young lady was quite happy to wait with loyalty and constancy for that which the Lord of Verona had promised her. Bishop Pilgrim of Passau,[102] out of love for his nephews,

---

[102] In three manuscripts, C, G, and a, verses 4295-4322 have been placed after verse 4360. Bartsch is undoubtedly correct when he states in the introduction to his edition (xxi) that this occurred because 4322 provides a more suitable conclusion to the work.

hiez scriben diz mære.
vvi ez ergangen vvære.
in latinisschen bΰchstaben.
[4300]   daz manz fΰr vvar solde haben.
svverz dar nah erfvnde.
vō d^[er] alresten stvnde.
vvi ez sih hΰb vnd ovh began.
vnd vvi ez ende gevvā.
[4305]   vmbe der gΰten knehte not.
vnd vvi si alle gelagen tot.
daz hiez er allez schriben.
ern liez es niht beliben.
vvand im seit d^[er] videlære.
[4310]   div kvntlichen mære.
vvi ez ergie vnd geschach.
vvand erz horte vnd sach.
er vnde manech ander man.
daz mære priven do began.
[4315]   sin schriber meister CΰnRat.
getihtet man ez sît hat.
diche in Tivsscher zvngen.
di alten mit den ivngen.
erchennent vvol daz mære.
[4320]   von ir frevde noch von ir svvære.
ich iv nΰ niht mere sage.
diz liet heizet div chlage.

Vvi ^{ez} eceln sît ergienge.
vnd vvi er sin dinch ane vienge.
[4325]   do her Dietrich von im reit.
des en chan ich der vvarheit.
iv noh niemen gesagen.
sΰmeliche iehent er vΰrd erslagen.
so sprechent sΰmeliche nein.
[4330]   vnder disen dīgen zvvein.
chan ich der lvge niht gedagen.
noh di vvarheit gesagen.
vvant da hanget zvvifel bi.
des vvnders vvird ich nimmer vri.
[4335]   vveder er sich ver gienge.
oder in der lvft enpfienge.
oder lebende vΰrde begraben.
oder ze himele vf er haben.
oder ob er vz der hΰte trΰffe.

ordered to be put down in Latin how everything had occurred, so that anyone hearing about it afterwards would have an accurate account of how, from the outset, it came about, and how it concluded, about the trials of the good squires and how they all met their end. He had it all committed to writing. He did not just let it rest, for the minstrel told him the tale as it was known to him, precisely how everything had transpired, because he and[103] many another man had been there to see and hear it all. Master Conrad, his clerk, worked on the story, and it has often been written down since then in German. Old and young alike are familiar with it. I shall say nothing more to you about their joy and their sorrow. This lay is called *The Lament*.

[4323] Neither I nor anyone else can truthfully tell you how Attila subsequently fared or how he managed his affairs after Lord Dietrich rode off. Some say that he was killed, but others deny that this was the case. Of these two views, I cannot tell what is the truth and what is a lie, for there is just so much uncertainty surrounding them. I will never cease to wonder whether he simply disappeared or went up into the air, whether he was buried alive or went up to heaven, whether he oozed out of his skin[104]

---

[103] Just prior to the conclusion of verse 4312 in the original, the scribe deviates from the two-column format otherwise adhered to throughout the manuscript. The conclusion of the *Chlage* is presented, still in rhyming couplets, in long lines traversing the bottom of page 451 of the St. Gall manuscript.

[104] This is the literal translation of verse 4339. It may well be, however, as Evelyn Firchow has suggested, that this is the Middle High German equivalent of 'aus der Haut fahren,' 'to become crazy,' a condition that could well describe Attila's state of mind given the intensity of his sorrow.

[4340]   oder sich ver slŭffe.
              in locher der steinvvende.
              oder mit vvelhem ende.
              er von dem libe qvæme.
              oder vvaz in zv zim genæme.
[4345]   ob er fŭre in daz apgrŭnde.
              oder ob in in der tivel verslŭnde.
              oder ob er svs si versvvnden.
              daz enhat niemen noh er fvnden.
              vns seit der tihtære.
[4350]   der vns tihte diz mære.
              ez en vvære von im svs niht beliben.
              er het iz gerne geschriben.
              daz man vviste div mære.
              vvi ez im ergan- <Bartsch: gen wære,
[4355]   wære iz im inder zuo komen,
              oder het erz sus vernomen
              in der werlde von iemen.
              dâ von weiz noch niemen.
              war der künec Etzel ie bequam
[4360]   oder wiez umbe in ende nam. >

or slipped away into holes of the stone walls or how, in fact, he met his end, what might have carried him off, whether he fell into hell, or the devil devoured him or whether he simply vanished — no one has ever yet discovered what really happened. The poet who composed this tale tells us that he would not have simply dropped the matter, but rather would have been happy to record it so that one might know what had happened to him if it had ever been passed on to him or if he had learned it from someone out there in the world. No one, however, knows anything about where King Attila might have gone or how he met his end.

Glossary of Personal Names

Adelind   A countess and daughter of Sintram, a Hungarian nobleman.

Attila   (Etzel) King of the Huns; Kriemhild's second husband. It is at Attila's court that the slaughter in the second half of the *Nibelungenlied* takes place.

Blödelin   Brother of Attila; leads the attack on the Burgundian squires in the *Nibelungenlied* and is subsequently killed by Dancwart.

Botelung   Father of Attila and Blödelin. Deceased at the time the action described in the *Nibelungenlied* and the *Chlage* takes place.

Brünhild   Queen of Iceland in the *Nibelungenlied*; won by Siegfried for Gunther and is brought to Worms as Queen of Burgundy. She has virtually no role to play in the *Nibelungenlied* after the death of Siegfried. In the *Chlage* she is urged to have Gunther jr., her son, crowned so that the continuity of the Burgundian royal line is assured.

Conrad   Clerk in the service of Bishop Pilgrim who wrote down an account of the events of the catastrophe in Latin based on information provided by Swemmel.

Dancrat   King of the Burgundians, father of Kriemhild, Gunther, Gernot, and Giselher. Deceased by the time the action of the *Nibelungenlied* takes place.

Dancwart   Brother of Hagen and renowned as an
                even greater fighter than the latter. He is
                the only Burgundian to survive the initial
                attack by the Huns.

Dietlinde   Daughter of Rüedeger and Gotelind.

Dietrich   Commonly referred to as Dietrich von
                Bern (= Verona in northern Italy). The
                fictional reflection of the fifth-century
                Ostrogothic leader, Theodorich. Probably
                enjoyed an even greater reputation as a
                warrior-hero than Siegfried during the
                Middle Ages. In the *Nibelungenlied*, he is
                living in exile at the court of Attila, to-
                gether with several hundred of his Amel-
                ungs (< Amali), with whom he had hoped
                to found a new kingdom.

Gerbart   A warrior in the service of Dietrich. Killed
                by Giselher in the fighting in the Great
                Hall.

Gernot   Younger brother of Gunther and a Bur-
                gundian King. Slain by Rüedeger.

Giselher   Youngest brother of Gunther and Kriem-
                hild's favorite. Consistently referred to as
                "kint" throughout the *Nibelungenlied*.

Goldrun   Daughter of King Liudeger of France.

Gotelind   Wife of Rüedeger and mother of Diet-
                linde.

Gunther   King of the Burgundians; brother of
                Kriemhild, Gernot, and Giselher.

Hagen   Liegeman to Gunther and murderer of
                Siegfried. Adversary of Kriemhild and
                slain by her. One of the most enigmatic
                figures in German heroic epic.

Hawart	A free nobleman who, along with Irnfrid and Iring, enters Attila's service after falling into debt and dishonor.
Helche	First wife of Attila; deceased, hence Attila's motivation for courting Kriemhild in the *Nibelungenlied*. Among the Huns, Helche was particularly noted for her generosity.
Helpfrich	One of Dietrich's men whom Hildebrand credits with having saved his life by separating him from Volker.
Herlind	A Greek noblewoman, present at the court of Attila. Companion to Goldrun.
Herman	A Polish Duke who puts his troops at the disposal of Kriemhild, with devastating results for himself and his men.
Herrat	Niece of Lady Helche and Dietrich's fiancée.
Hildebrand	Dietrich von Bern's master-at-arms. He kills Kriemhild at the end of the *Nibelungenlied*.
Hildeburg	A Norman noblewoman, present at Attila's court. Companion to Goldrun.
Iring	A nobleman who is described as a native of Lorraine (although he is the Dane Hawart's liegeman!). Together with Irnfrid and Hawart, he enters the service of Attila and is killed by a spear through the head thrown by Hagen in the fighting in the Great Hall.
Irnfrid	A renowned warrior in the service of Attila. Together with Hawart and Iring he had fallen upon bad times and had suffered banishment.

Isalde   An affluent duchess who resides in Vienna
              and who invites the Hunnish envoys bear-
              ing news of the catastrophe to stay in her
              house. The name is derived from Eilhart
              von Oberge's romance *Tristrant und Isalde*
              (ca. 1170).

Kriemhild   Daughter of Dancwart and Ute; wife of
              Siegfried and then Attila. The *Nibelungen-
              lied* is in many ways her story.

Liudeger   A king of France and father of Lady
              Goldrun.

Machazin   One of two pagan gods in whom Attila
              once trusted.

Machmet   A god referred to by Attila and in whom
              he loses faith after the disaster which
              befalls him. Probably a derivative of Mo-
              hammed.

Ner   Father of Wolfwin, one of Dietrich's men
              killed in the fighting.

Nitger   A knight in the service of Dietrich who is
              killed by Giselher.

Pilgrim   Bishop of Passau, brother of Ute and
              uncle to Gunther, Gernot, Giselher, and
              Kriemhild. He is adamant about having
              the events that have transpired at Attila's
              court written down for posterity, based on
              the account provided by the minstrel
              Swemmel.

Rüedeger   A Christian knight who owed homage to
              Attila and Kriemhild; in the *Nibelungen-
              lied* he played host to the Burgundians on
              their journey to Hungary and his daughter
              became engaged to Giselher. Killed in the
              later slaughter while fighting Gernot, who
              also dies by his hand.

Rumold	Master of the Kitchen at the Burgundian royal court in Worms. Originally warned kings about venturing into the land of the Huns. Appears to be much more sympathetically inclined towards Hagen in the *Nibelungenlied* than in the *Chlage*.
Siegfried	Prince of Xanten and husband of Kriemhild. Murdered by Hagen. The *Chlage*-poet attributes his death to the arrogance he displays towards the Burgundians.
Sieglinde	Mother of Siegfried and wife of Siegmund.
Siegmund	Father of Siegfried; King of Xanten
Sigeher	A nobleman from Wallachia who, along with the Polish nobleman, Herman, sides with Kriemhild and, like the latter, suffers total defeat at the hands of the Burgundians. Killed by Gunther.
Sigelind	Daughter of King Nitger
Sigestab	Dietrich's nephew (son of his sister) and Duke of Verona; killed by Volker in the fighting at Attila's court.
Sindolt	Cupbearer of King Gunther, who attempts to console Brünhild.
Sintram	A nobleman residing in the Hungarian March.
Swemmel(in)	An envoy in the service of Attila. In the twenty-fourth *Aventiure* of the *Nibelungenlied*, he and Wärbel carry the fateful invitation to the Burgundians to journey to the land of the Huns. In the *Chlage*, he is entrusted with carrying back the news of the slaughter to Burgundy.
Ute	Wife of Dancrat and mother of Kriemhild, Gunther, Gernot, and Giselher. Survives

her husband but dies when she learns of slaughter of Burgundians.

Volker

A warrior-minstrel from Alzeye in the service of the Burgundians. In the *Nibelungenlied*, he demonstrates a unique cameraderie with Hagen.

Walber

A Turkish warrior who puts 1200 men at the disposal of Kriemhild, thereby forfeiting all of their lives.

Wichart

A knight (in the service of Dietrich?) who is killed by Gunther in the fighting.

Wignant

A knight in the service of Dietrich. Killed by Gunther in the fighting.

Wolfbrant

One of Dietrich's men, killed by Dancwart in the Great Hall.

Wolfhart

Hildebrand's nephew (his sister's son) and a knight in the service of Dietrich. He and Giselher kill each other in the fighting at the Hunnish court.

Wolfwin

One of Dietrich's Amelungs who perishes in the slaughter. Hildebrand's nephew. Killed by Giselher, according to the *Chlage*-poet.

Select Bibliography

Editions (Arranged chronologically in ascending order)

Chriemhilden Rache, und die Klage; zwey Heldengedichte Aus dem schwäbischen Zeitpunckte. Samt Fragmenten aus dem Gedichte von den Nibelungen und aus dem Josaphat.... Ed. Johann Jakob Bodmer. Zyrich: Verlegens Orell und Comp., 1757.

Der Nibelungen Liet. Ein Rittergedicht aus dem XIII. oder XIV. Jahrhundert. Ed. Christoph Heinrich Myller. Berlin: C. S. Spener, 1782.

Der Nibelungen Lied. Ed. Friedrich Heinrich von der Hagen. Berlin: J. F. Unger, 1807.

Die Klage sammt Sigenot und Eggenliet, nach dem Abdruck der ältesten Handschriften des Freiherrn Joseph von Laßberg. 2nd edition. Ed. Ottmar f. H. Schönhuth. Tübingen: C. F Osiander, 1839.

Der Nibelunge Nôt und diu Klage. Ed. A. J. Vollmer. Dichtungen des deutschen Mittelalters 1. Leipzig: G. J. Göschen, 1843.

Die Klage. Schlußgesang des Nibelungenliedes in der alten vollendeten Gestalt. Ed. Friedrich Heinrich von der Hagen. Berlin: Vereins-Buchhandlung, 1852.

Die Klage in der ältesten Gestalt. Ed. Adolf Holtzmann. Stuttgart: J. B. Metzler, 1859.

Diu Klage. Mit den Lesarten sämtlicher Handschriften. Ed. Karl Bartsch. 1875; Darmstadt: Wissenschaftliche Buchgesellschaft, 1964.

Die Klage mit vollständigem kritischen Apparat und ausführlicher Einleitung. Ed. Anton Edzardi. Hannover: Carl Rümpler, 1875.

Der Nibelunge Noth und die Klage nach der ältesten Überlieferung mit Bezeichnung der unechten und mit den Abweichungen der gemeinen Lesart. Ed. Karl Lachmann. 5th ed. Berlin: G. Reimer, 1878.

Die Nibelungen. Ed. Paul Piper. Part One: *Einleitung und Klage.* Kürschners Deutsche National-Litteratur 6. Stuttgart: W. Spemann, 1889.

Das Nibelungenlied und die Klage. Handschrift B (Cod. Sangall. 857). Deutsche Texte in Handschriften 1. Ed. K. Bischoff, H. M. Heinrichs, W. Schröder. Cologne and Graz: Böhlau Verlag, 1962.

Das Nibelungenlied und die Klage. Handschrift C der F. F. Hofbibliothek Donaueschingen. Ed. Heinz Engels. Stuttgart: Müller und Schindler, 1968.

Das Nibelungenlied. A complete transcription in modern German type of the text of manuscript C from the Fürstenberg Court Library Donaueschingen. Ed. Heinz Engels with an essay on the manuscript and its provenance by Erna Huber. New York, Washington, London: Frederick A. Praeger, 1969. The *Chlage* is also included in this edition ("Auenture VON DeR klaGE," [89]-[114v]).

Der Nibelunge Liet und Diu Klage. Die Donaueschinger Handschrift 63 (Laßberg 174). Ed. Werner Schröder. Deutsche Texte in Handschriften 3. Ed. K. Bischoff, H. M. Heinrichs, W. Schröder. Cologne and Vienna: Böhlau Verlag, 1969.

"Div Klage. Kritische Ausgabe der Bearbeitung *C." Ed. Brigitte Ranft. Diss. Marburg/Lahn, 1971.

Translations into New High German (Arranged chronologically in ascending order)

Nibelungennoth und Klage nach ältester Gestalt in ungebundener Rede. Trans. August Zeune. 2nd revised ed. Berlin: Nicolai'sche Buchhandlung, 1836.

Die Klage. Ein deutsches Heldengedicht des zwölften Jahrhunderts. Narrated by Anton Ritter v. Spann. Pesth: Verlag von Gustav Heckenast, 1848. [Only segments of the *Chlage* are translated by von Spann into rhyming couplets with narrative summaries interspersed.]

Der Nibelungen Klage. Zum ersten Male in neuhochdeutschen Reimen. Trans. Friedrich Heinrich von der Hagen. Berlin: Vereins-Buchhandlung, [1852?].

Der Nibelungen Klage. Trans. Franz Ostfeller. Leipzig: In Commission bei Georg Wigand, 1854. [Contains segments of the *Chlage* that are in Middle High German along with New High German translation into rhyming couplets. Narrative summaries are interspersed throughout.]

Secondary Literature

Bartsch, Karl. *Untersuchungen über das Nibelungenlied.* Vienna: Wilhelm Braumüller, 1865. [On the *Chlage* see pp. 325-351.]

Becker, Jörg Peter. *Handschriften und Frühdrucke mittelhochdeutscher Epen.* Wiesbaden: Dr. Ludwig Reichert Verlag, 1977. [*Nibelungenlied* and the *Chlage* on pp. 140-160.]

Bieger, J. "Zur Klage." *ZfdPh* 25 (1893): 145-163.

Bork, Hans. "Nibelungenlied, Klage und Waltharius." *GRM* 15 (1927): 395-415.

Curschmann, Michael. "'Nibelungenlied' und 'Klage.'" *Die deutsche Literatur des Mittelalters. Verfasserlexikon.* 2nd revised ed. Ed. Kurt Ruh. Vol. 6, Lieferung 3/4. Berlin and New York: Walter de Gruyter, 1987. Cols. 926-969.

_____. *"Nibelungenlied* und *Nibelungenklage.* Über Mündlichkeit und Schriftlichkeit im Prozeß der Episierung." *Deutsche Literatur im Mittelalter. Kontakte und Perspektiven. Hugo Kuhn zum Gedenken.* Ed. Christoph Cormeau. Stuttgart: Metzler, 1979. 85-115.

Edzardi, Anton. "Über das Verhältnis der Klage zum Biterolf." *Germania* 20 (1875): 9-30.

Engels, Heinz. "Die Handschrift C des Nibelungenliedes und der Klage." *Das Nibelungenlied und die Klage. Handschrift C der F. F. Hofbibliothek Donaueschingen.* Ed. Heinz Engels. Stuttgart: Müller und Schindler, 1968. 15-48.

Frenzen, Wilhelm. *Klagebilder und Klagegebärde in der deutschen Dichtung des höfischen Mittelalters.* Bonner Beiträge zur Deutschen Philologie 1. Würzburg: Dissertations-Druckerei und Verlag K. Triltisch, 1936.

Getzuhn, Kurt. *Untersuchungen zum Sprachgebrauch und Wortschatz der Klage.* Germanistische Arbeiten 2. Heidelberg: Carl Winters Universitätsbuchhandlung, 1914.

Gillespie, G. T. "'Die Klage' as a commentary on 'Das Nibelungenlied.'" *Probleme mittelhochdeutscher Erzählformen. Marburger Colloquium 1969.* Ed. Peter F. Ganz and Werner Schröder. Berlin: Erich Schmidt, 1972) 153-177.

Günzburger, Angelika. *Studien zur Nibelungenklage. Forschungsbericht — Bauform der Klage — Personendarstellung.* Europäische Hochschulschriften. Reihe 1: Deutsche Sprache und Literatur 685. Frankfurt am Main, Bern, New York: Peter Lang, 1983.

Hoffmann, Werner. *Das Nibelungenlied.* 6th ed. Sammlung Metzler No. 7. Stuttgart: Verlag J. B. Metzler, 1992. [See, in particular, the seventh chapter, "Die Nibelungenklage," pp. 126-140.]

_____. *Mittelhochdeutsche Heldendichtung.* Grundlagen der Germanistik 14. Berlin: Erich Schmidt Verlag, 1974. [See, in particular, pp. 91-95.]

Knapp, Fritz Peter, ed. *Nibelungenlied und Klage. Sage und Geschichte, Struktur und Gattung. Passauer Nibelungengespräche 1985.* Heidelberg: Carl Winter Universitätsverlag, 1987.

Körner, Josef. *Die Klage und das Nibelungenlied.* Leipzig: Reisland, 1920.

Kraus, Carl von. "Die 'latînischen buochstabe' der Klage v. 2145ff." *Paul und Braunes Beiträge* 56 (1932): 60-74.

Krogmann, Willy, and Ulrich Pretzel. *Bibliographie zum Nibelungenlied und zur Klage.* 4th expanded ed. Bibliographien zur deutschen Literatur des Mittelalters 1. Berlin: E. Schmidt, 1966.

Leicher, Richard. *Die Totenklage in der deutschen Epik von der ältesten Zeit bis zur Nibelungen-Klage*. Germanistische Abhandlungen 58. Breslau: M. & H. Marcus, 1927.

Leitzmann, A. "Nibelungenklage und höfische Dichtung." *ZfdA* 61 (1924): 49-56.

Mackensen, Lutz. *Die Nibelungen. Sage, Geschichte, ihr Lied und sein Dichter*. Stuttgart: Dr. Ernst Hauswedell & Co., 1984. [See pp. 180-192 which deal with the *Chlage*.]

McConnell, Winder. "The Problem of Continuity in *The Klage*." *Neophilologus* 70 (1986): 248-255.

Neumann, Friedrich. "Nibelungenlied und Klage." *Die deutsche Literatur des Mittelalters. Verfasserlexikon*. Ed. Karl Langosch. Vol. 3. Berlin: Walter de Gruyter, 1943. Cols. 513-560.

Panzer, Friedrich. *Das Nibelungenlied. Entstehung und Gestalt*. Stuttgart and Cologne: W. Kohlhammer, 1955. [See, in particular, pp. 74-98.]

Schönbach, Anton E. *Das Christentum in der altdeutschen Heldendichtung. Vier Abhandlungen*. Graz: Leuschner & Lubensky's Universitäts-Buchhandlung, 1897. [Section on the *Chlage*, pp. 57-107.]

Scholler, Harald. *A Word Index to the Nibelungenklage*. Ann Arbor: University of Michigan Press, 1966.

Schröder, Edward. "Zur Klage." *ZfdA* 70 (1933): 66-67.

Schröder, Werner. "Das Leid in der *Klage*." In: W. S., *Nibelungenlied-Studien*. Stuttgart: J. B. Metzler, 1968. 182-225.

_____. *Wolfram von Eschenbach, das Nibelungenlied und 'Die Klage.'* Akademie der Wissenschaften und der Literatur. Abhandlungen der Geistes- und Sozialwissenschaftlichen Klasse 5. Mainz: Akademie der Wissenschaften und der Literatur; Stuttgart: Franz Steiner Verlag Wiesbaden GmbH., 1989.

Seitter, Walter. "Zur Gegenwart der Nibelungen-Klage." *manuscripte* 29 (1989) (No. 103): 13-18.

Sommermeier, Hermann Erich. "Die Klage in der Handschrift J des Nibelungenliedes." Diss Marburg/Lahn, 1905.

Störmer, Wilhelm. "Die Herkunft Bischof Pilgrims von Passau (971-991) und die Nibelungen-Überlieferung." *Ostbairische Grenzmarken* 16 (1974): 62-67.

Szklenar, Hans. "Die literarische Gattung der *Nibelungenklage* und das Ende 'alter mære.'" *Poetica* 9 (1977): 41-61.

Ursinus, Alfred. "Die Handschriftenverhältnisse der Klage." Diss. Halle, 1908.

Voorwinden, Norbert. "Nibelungenklage und Nibelungenlied." *Hohenemser Studien zum Nibelungenlied*. Ed. Irmtraud Albrecht and Achim Masser. Dornbirn: Vorarlberger Verlagsanstalt, 1981. 276-287.

Wachinger, Burkhard. "Die »Klage« und das Nibelungenlied." *Hohenemser Studien zum Nibelungenlied*. Ed. Irmtraud Albrecht and Achim Masser. Dornbirn: Vorarlberger Verlagsanstalt, 1981. 264-275.

Weber, Henry W., ed. "Die Klage. The Lament." *Illustrations of Northern Antiquities*. Ed. Henry W. Weber et al. Edinburgh: James Ballantyne and Co., 1814, pp. 211-213, with twenty-eight verses of *Div Chlage* translated into rhyming couplets.

Wehrli, Max. "Die 'Klage' und der Untergang der Nibelungen." *Zeiten und Formen in Sprache und Dichtung. Festschrift Fritz Tschirch*. Cologne and Vienna: Böhlau, 1972. 96-112.

Wilhelm, Friedrich. *Nibelungenstudien I. Über die Fassungen B und C des Nibelungenliedes und der Klage, ihre Verfasser und Abfassungszeit*. Münchener Archiv für Philologie des Mittelalters und der Renaissance 7. Munich: [s.n.], 1916.

Zimmermann, Günter. "Der Krieg, die Schuld und die *Klage*." *Helden und Heldensage. Otto Gschwantler zum 60. Geburtstag*. Ed. H. Reichert and G. Zimmermann. Philologica Germanica 11. Vienna: Fassbaender, 1990. 513-536.